Elias Hicks

Letters of Elias Hicks

Including also Observations on the slavery of the Africans and their descendants,

and on the use of the produce of their labor

Elias Hicks

Letters of Elias Hicks
Including also Observations on the slavery of the Africans and their descendants, and on the use of the produce of their labor

ISBN/EAN: 9783744755238

Printed in Europe, USA, Canada, Australia, Japan

Cover: Foto ©Suzi / pixelio.de

More available books at **www.hansebooks.com**

LETTERS

OF

ELIAS HICKS.

INCLUDING ALSO

OBSERVATIONS ON THE SLAVERY OF THE AFRICANS

AND THEIR DESCENDANTS,

AND ON

THE USE OF THE PRODUCE OF THEIR LABOR

PHILADELPHIA:
PUBLISHED BY T. ELLWOOD CHAPMAN,
No. 5 SOUTH FIFTH STREET.
1861.

ADVERTISEMENT.

In presenting to the public this volume from the pen of Elias Hicks, it is proper to observe, that it might have been much enlarged by the addition of many other letters; but, we believe, that those contained in the present collection, are sufficient to give a pretty full exposition of the views of the writer on the various subjects of which they treat, and which comprehend the most important doctrines of the Christian religion: and though sentiments may, perhaps, be found in it, that may appear new to some, yet, we think, upon an attentive examination, they will be found in accordance with the Scriptures of truth and the doctrines of our most approved and enlightened primitive Friends; and we think, too, that the long life of unsullied integrity and fervent piety of the writer, claims for them a close and impartial examination. Most of these letters were written to his intimate friends, without any expectation, so far as appears, that they would ever be made public; the candid reader will, therefore, readily admit in this fact, a sufficient apology, if the writer has not always been as successful in elucidating some points, as might have been desired. Another circumstance should be noticed. Most of the letters contained in this volume, were answers to letters received, which not being in our possession, we have not been able to state the questions that elicited his replies; and hence some things in the latter may appear to require explanations which, probably, they would not have been thought to want, had those questions been published at the same time. To this we add, that if the reader should discover some things which may *appear* ambiguous, or objectionable, we think he will find the same subjects more fully and satisfactorily explained in other parts of the work.

ADVERTISEMENT.

In giving publicity to the opinions and doctrinal views of Elias Hicks, as exhibited in this work, we believe we shall be doing a public service, and at the same time gratify many of his friends.

The contents of this volume have been carefully transcribed from letters, or papers, in the hand-writing of the author, with the exception of a very few, which have been taken from copies, either written or printed.

The author appears fully to have believed, that the doctrines promulgated in them, were opened to his understanding by that *Divine life which is the light of men;* but, the reader must be left to form his conclusions from the light and evidence in his own mind.

New York, 2d mo. 1834.

OBSERVATIONS

ON THE

SLAVERY OF THE AFRICANS

AND THEIR DESCENDANTS,

AND ON THE USE OF THE PRODUCE OF THEIR LABOUR.

[This Essay was first published in the year 1811, after having been approved by the Meeting for Sufferings.]

PREFACE.

WHEREAS, I some time past published certain observations on the Slavery of the Africans and their descendants, and on the consumption of the produce of their labour, comprehended principally in nineteen Queries and Answers, the design of which was to impress on the minds of my friends and fellow-citizens, and others concerned, as far as might be, by fair reasoning, a full sense of the abhorrent cruelty and unrighteousness of holding our fellow creatures in bondage, and wresting from them, by violence, the produce of their labour; which being well received by many, and affording reason to hope they were profitable to some, I was induced to believe a second edition might be useful.

I have, therefore, revised the original, and endeavoured to compress it as much as the subjects would admit; and have added some quotations from an anonymous pamphlet, published some time since in England, which are so correspondent with the before mentioned observations, as to have a tendency, in my opinion, to elucidate and enforce them.

I shall only add, as a farther apology for the present edition, that the evil still continues: that there are still slave holders, and consumers of the produce of the labour of slaves, wrested from them by violence.

And as the slave holder can have no moral right whatever to the man he styles his slave, nor to the produce of his labour, he cannot possibly convey any to a second person by any transfer he can make: for, having nothing but a criminal possession himself, he can convey nothing to a second person but the same possession: and should this possession be continued through a line of transfer to the twentieth person, still it would be nothing more than the same criminal possession that was vested in the first possessor, and would convey no moral right whatever. And should any other person come forward, and, by the same mode of violence and power that was exercised by the first possessor, in reducing the man he styles his slave to the abject state of slavery, and by which he violently took from him the produce of his labour, forcibly take from such twentieth or more remote possessors, the slave and the produce of his labour, the right of such person, in point of equity, to such slave and the produce of his labour would be just equal to the right of such remote possessor; as neither of them could have had any more than a criminal possession: and whether that possession is obtained by violence or by transfer, (if the person who receives it by transfer is informed of the criminal circumstance,) it can make no possible difference, except that one is protected by the indulgence of a partial law of the country we live in, and the other is not. By which undeniable proposition, it appears, that when any man becomes possessed of a slave, or the produce of his labour, wrested from him without his consent, whether it be by transfer or otherwise, any other person who has power so to do, may, by violence, take from such possessor, such slave and the produce of his labour: and when he has in that way obtained possession thereof, he has as good a right to such slave and to use the produce of his labour as the former; and the former can have no just cause to complain of such usage, as he is only paid in his own coin. For, although the first possessor committed the act of violence, when he took from the man he styles his slave his liberty, and compelled him to work, and by the same cruel force, took from him the produce of his labour; yet, every purchaser of such slave and the produce of his labour, if he is apprized of the criminal circumstance attending it, is as guilty as the first perpetrator: and should such slave and the produce of his labour pass through the hands of twenty persons, all knowing at the time of transfer the criminal circumstances attending, each would be guilty of the entire crime of the first perpetrator. This being assented to, and I conceive it is incontrovertible, I have a hope that this edition may produce a good effect, and tend to raise up many more faithful advocates in the cause of this deeply oppressed people, who may be willing to suffer every necessary privation, rather than be guilty of the least thing that may, in any degree, possibly strengthen the hands of their oppressors. I therefore recommend this little treatise to the candid and impartial consideration of the reader, and subscribe myself his sincere friend,

ELIAS HICKS.

OBSERVATIONS, &c.

The slavery of the Africans and their descendants, has become so established by long continuance, and the force of an unrighteous custom, that many persons consider the practice not only admissible, but consistent with justice and social order.

But I am led to doubt the possibility of any rational, moral person being thus circumstanced, unless he is first greatly blinded by selfishness and partiality; as I consider it a matter of fact, obviously clear to every rational, contemplative mind, that neither custom nor education, nor any law of men or nations, can alter the nature of justice and equity; which will and must, essentially and eternally, rest upon their own proper base, as laid down by the great Christian Lawgiver, viz. "Therefore, all things, whatsoever ye would that men should do to you, do ye even so to them: for this is the law and the prophets." Hence, I conceive, it is a most necessary and important christian duty, for all those who are either directly or indirectly concerned in the slavery of their fellow creatures, seriously and impartially to consider the manner and way in which the slavery of the Africans was first introduced; and by what means it has been so long continued; not doubting, but that every upright, impartial mind, by a full examination into the subject, will readily discover, that it was first introduced by fraud and force, and continued by an unjust and tyrannical power: and will, therefore, be induced to restore to them their just and native rights, as free men, which no law nor power of men or nations ought to deprive them of without their consent.

It is generally acknowledged, by the people of every

enlightened country, and particularly by those who believe in revelation, as testified of in the Scriptures of Truth, that man is a moral agent, (that is, free to act, with the restriction of accountability to his Creator,) agreeably to the declaration of the prophet Ezekiel; through whom, Jehovah, in his benignity and justice, claims the right of sovereignty over the children of men : "All souls are mine; as the soul of the father, so also the soul of the son is mine: the soul that sinneth, it shall die: the son shall not bear the iniquity of the father, neither shall the father bear the iniquity of the son!" This Scripture testimony, perfectly consonant with reason and justice, not only proves, that every man is to bear his own iniquity, but that he also stands fully indemnified thereby, from all the iniquity of his predecessors; and likewise fully establishes man's free agency: and, of course, proves, that every moral agent born into the world, (whatever the conduct and situation of his parents may have been) is born FREE: upon which undeniable truth, I shall found the following Queries and Answers:

Query 1. Were not the people of Africa, at the time when the Europeans first visited their coasts, a free people, possessed of the same natural and unalienable rights, as the people of any other nation?

Answer. They certainly were: for, when the Europeans, whether by fraud or force, or by purchase from those who had stolen or taken them prisoners in war, became possessed of a number of the people of Africa, and by violence reduced them to the wretched and degraded state of Slaves; at the same time it would have been as right and as consistent with equity and moral justice, for the Africans to have done the same by them, had it been in their power: by which undeniable proposition, it is evident, that the slavery of the Africans is the product of mere power, without any possible plea of right: and that the same power of force, fraud, and tyrannical cruelty, that was exercised in reducing the people of Africa at first, to the miserable and wretched state of slaves, has, in like manner, in a continual state of war, been exercised on all the descendants of those unhappy people that are held as slaves, from generation to generation, down to the present day: it being an undeniable truth, that no rational creature can be any longer a slave, than while the force of war is operating upon him: and as before proved from Scripture, and moral justice, that every child of an African, born in America, or elsewhere, is born free: therefore, he suffers the same cruel force of fraud and power while continued under the galling yoke of slavery, as was exercised on his predecessors.

"The lust of power, and the pride of conquest, have doubtless produced instances far too numerous of man enslaved by man. But we, in an enlightened age, have greatly surpassed, in brutality and injustice, the most ignorant and barbarous ages; and while we are pretending to the finest feelings of humanity, are exercising unprecedented cruelty. We have planted slavery in the rank soil of sordid avarice: and the product has been misery in the extreme. We have ascertained, by a course of experiments in cruelty, the least portion of nourishment requisite to enable man to linger a few years in misery; the greatest quantity of labour, which, in such a situation, the extreme of punishment can extort; and the utmost degree of pain, labour and hunger united, that the human frame can endure. In vain have such scenes been developed. The wealth derived from the horrid traffic, has created an influence that secures its continuance; unless the people at large shall refuse to receive the produce of robbery and murder."

Q. 2. Under what name or descriptive mode of property are the slaves to be considered, in relation to the man who holds them as such?

A. The slaves being taken by violence, either directly or indirectly, contrary to their own wills, and in direct opposition to all the power of self-defence, which they are capable of exerting, whether they are taken prisoners of war or stolen, or decoyed on shipboard by the slave merchant, and then forcibly confined and carried off; it must be acknowledged, they are taken in a state of war, and considered by the captor as a prize : therefore, the only true title and description of property they can possibly bear, is prize goods.

Q. 3. Is not the produce of the slave's labour likewise prize goods ?

A. It certainly is ; for the man, who, by mere power and violence, without any just plea of right, not only holds them as slaves, but takes from them, in the same cruel and arbitrary manner, the proceeds of their labour, without their consent, thereby places himself in a state of continual and actual war with his slaves. And, moreover, as the stealing or taking a man by violence, and depriving him of his liberty, and reducing him to the wretched and helpless state of a slave, is the highest grade of felony, and is done purposely to profit by the slave's labour; therefore, the produce of the slave's labour is the highest grade of prize goods, next to his person.

Q. 4. Does the highway robber, that meets his fellow-citizen on the highway, and robs him of all the property he has in his present possession, and then leaves him at liberty, without injuring his person, commit as high an act of felony, as he that steals or buys, or takes a man by violence, and reduces him to the wretched and degraded state of a slave for life ?

A. No ! in no wise. Which answer is founded on the self-evident proposition, that it is more criminal to rob a man of his liberty and property, than only to rob him of his property.

Q. 5. Does it lessen the criminality and wickedness of reducing our fellow creatures to the abject state of slavery, and continuing them therein, because the practice is tolerated by the laws of the country we live in ?

A. No! by no means. Because, every rational creature knows, or ought to know, that, no laws of men or nations, can alter the nature of immutable justice. The criminality remains as great in all cases of slavery, when inflicted without any criminality of the individual made a slave, under the sanction of law, as when it is not ; and in some cases, greater : as in the instance of those governments, where they are not only guilty of the cruelty and oppression of reducing, by mere power, without any possible plea of right, their fellow creatures who have equally a right with themselves to liberty, and the purchase of redemption by a Saviour's blood, to the abject and wretched state of slaves, but are adding sin to sin, by making and continuing cruel laws to hold them still longer under the galling yoke.

Q. 6. Would it be right and consistent with justice and equity, for the legislatures of the several states, and others concerned, to make laws entirely to abolish slavery in their respective states?

A. It would, doubtless, be entirely right, and perfectly consistent with equity and justice to make such laws; and nothing, I apprehend, can exculpate them from the charge of bloodguiltiness short of so doing: as, no doubt, many of the poor victims of slavery suffer daily to the shedding of their blood, under the hands of some of the cruel men who pretend to be their masters, because they do not at all times immediately submit to their cruel and arbitrary wills.

Q. 7. Would it not give just occasion for those who still have slaves in their possession, and especially to such as have lately purchased them, at a dear rate, to complain of wrong in thus taking from them, without their consent, what they esteem as their real property?

A. The making and enforcing such laws cannot possibly give just occasion for any such complaint; as it is impossible for any man to gain any just property in a rational being, as a slave, without his consent; for, neither the slave dealer nor the planter have any moral right to the person of him they style their slave, to his labour, or to the produce of it; so, they can convey no right in such person, nor in the produce of his labour to another; and whatever number of hands they may pass through, (if the criminal circumstances appertaining thereto be known to them at the time of the transfer,) they can only have a criminal possession; and the money paid either for the slave or for the produce of his labour, is paid to obtain that criminal possession, and can confer no moral right whatever; and if the death of the person called a slave, be occasioned by the criminal possession, the criminal possessor is guilty of murder; and we who have knowingly done any act which might occasion his being in that situation, are accessaries to the murder, before the fact; as by receiving the produce of his labour, we are accessaries to the robbery after the fact. Therefore, I conceive, it must appear clear and agreeable to truth and justice, that a man who should dare to be so hardy as to buy a fellow creature, whose liberty is withheld from him by violence and injustice, ought not only to be obliged to set him free, and to forfeit the purchase money, but likewise to make full satisfaction to the person he had injured, by such purchase.

Q. 8. As the Legislature of the State of New York has passed a law, declaring that every child, born in this state of a woman held as a slave, shall be free, the males at twenty-eight years of age, and the females at twenty-five; can such a law be considered as doing full justice to that injured people?

A. Although such might have been the unjust bias, that too generally prevailed on the minds of the inhabitants of this State, at the time of making the law alluded to in the query, that it was the best step the Legislature could then take; nevertheless, in my opinion, it fell very far short of doing them that full justice to which they are entitled; for, as all children born of white women in this state, are free at the age of twenty-one and eighteen years, according to their sex, and as the Africans and their descendants are not here in their own wills, nor agreeable to their own choice, but wholly in consequence of the will and pleasure of the white citizens of this State; therefore, it is impossible, in point of justice, that any disadvantage or penalty should attach to them, as a consequence of their being here: but as free born men and women, they have a right to demand their freedom at the same age as other citizens; and to deny them of it, is depriving them of their just right.

Q. 9. What measures can be adopted by the Legislature and citizens of New York, in order to exculpate themselves from the guilt of that atrocious crime of holding the Africans and their descendants so long in slavery?

A. The least that can be done, in order to effect the salutary end contemplated by the query, would be to declare freedom to every slave in the state, and to make provision by law for the education of all minors that are in a state of slavery; compelling their masters, or those who have the charge of them, to instruct them so as to keep their own accounts, and that they be set at liberty, the males at twenty-one and females at eighteen years of age: and further, that some lawful and reasonable step be taken, to compensate such slaves as have been held in bondage beyond 'that age, for such surplus service.

Q. 10. By what class of the people is the slavery of the Africans and their descendants supported and encouraged?

A. Principally by the purchasers and consumers of the produce of the slaves' labour; as the profits arising from the produce of their labour, is the only stimulus or inducement for making slaves.

" The laws of our country may indeed prohibit us the sweets of the sugar cane," and other articles of the West-Indies and southern states, that are the produce of the slave's labour, " unless we will receive it through the medium of slavery; they may hold it to our lips, steeped in the blood of our fellow creatures, but they cannot compel us to accept the loathsome potion. With us it rests, either to receive it and be partners in the crime, or to exonerate ourselves from guilt, by spurning from us the temptation. For let us not think, that the crime rests alone with those who conduct the traffic, or the Legislature by which it is protected. If we purchase the commodity, we participate in the crime. The slave dealer, the slave holder, and the slave driver, are virtually the agents of the consumer, and may be considered as employed and hired by him, to procure the commodity. For, by holding out the temptation, he is the original cause, the first mover in the horrid process; and every distinction is done away by the moral maxim, *That whatever we do by another, we do ourselves.*

" Nor are we by any means warranted to consider our individual share in producing these evils in a trivial point of view: the consumption of sugar" and other articles of slavery " in this country is so immense, that the quantity commonly used by individuals will have an important effect."

Q. 11. What effect would it have on the slave holders and their slaves, should the people of the United States of America and the inhabitants of Great Britain, refuse to purchase or make use of any goods that are the produce of slavery?

A. It would doubtless have a particular effect on the slave holders, by circumscribing their avarice, and preventing their heaping up riches, and living in a state of luxury and excess on the gain of oppression: and it might have the salutary effect of convincing them of the unrighteousness and cruelty of holding their fellow creatures in bondage; and it would have a blessed and excellent effect on the poor afflicted slaves; as it would immediately meliorate their wretched condition and abate their cruel bondage; for I have been informed, and reason naturally dictates to every one who has made right observations on men and things, that the higher the price of such produce is, the harder they are driven at their work.

And should the people of the United States, and the inhabitants of Great Britain, withdraw from a commerce in, and the use of the produce of slavery, it would greatly lessen the price of those articles, and be a very great and immediate relief to the poor, injured and oppressed slaves, whose blood is continually crying from the ground for justice, as their lives are greatly shortened, and many of them do not live out half their days by reason of their cruel bondage.

"If we as individuals concerned in purchasing and consuming the produce of slavery, should imagine that our share in the transaction is so minute, that it cannot perceptibly increase the injury; let us recollect, that, though numbers partaking of a crime may diminish the shame, they cannot diminish its turpitude; can we suppose, that any injury of an enormous magnitude can take place, and the criminality be destroyed, merely by the criminals becoming so numerous as to render their particular shares indistinguishable? Were a hundred assassins to plunge their daggers into their victim, though each might plead, that without his assistance the crime would have been completed, and that his poniard neither occasioned nor accelerated the murder; yet, every one of them would be guilty of the entire crime. For, into how many parts soever a criminal action may be divided, the crime itself rests entire and complete on every perpetrator.

" But, waiving this latter consideration, and even supposing for a moment, that the evil has an existence from causes totally independent of us, yet it exists; and as we have it in our power jointly with others to remedy it, it is undoubtedly our duty to contribute our share, in hope that others will theirs; and to act that part from conscience, which we should from inclination in similar cases that interested our feelings:" for instance, let us suppose that the way for obtaining slaves from Africa was entirely intercepted, and no other place opened for obtaining any, except in the rivers Delaware and Hudson, in North America; that the slave traders were continually infesting the shores of those rivers, as the only places to be insulted with impunity; that they frequently kidnapped, and sometimes by force carried off numbers of the inhabitants to the West-Indies, and sold them as slaves, among whom were many of our fathers and brothers, with their wives and children. We now view them all hand-cuffed, two and two together, crowded down between the ship's decks, and so closely stowed, as to be almost suffocated; in consequence of which, a number sicken and die, which to them is a very happy release, when compared with the still more cruel sufferings that await the survivors. We next behold them in port, and the day of sale arrives, when they are taken from on ship-board, and driven like a herd of swine to market, but worse treated, being manacled together. They are here herded in a pen or yard, like the beasts of the field, exposed to public sale, and without regard to sex or age examined by those brutal men, who are to be their purchasers, as naked as they were born: and, when one is struck off to any bidder, a red hot iron is ready to brand the poor victim with the name of his tyrant purchaser. This leads to a scene still

3

more grievous, still more deeply afflicting. All nature is forced to yield, when the husband is separated from a beloved wife, and a wife from a beloved husband, who had been for many years the joy of her life, and whom she had expected would have been the strength and comfort of her declining years; but now, alas! they are torn asunder, like bone from bone: a heart-rending separation takes place, without a small indulgence of taking a sympathetic farewell of each other, or the possibility of indulging the most distant hope of seeing each other again.

We behold the fond children, with ghastly look and frighted eyes, cling to their beloved parents, not to be separated from them, but by the lash of their cruel drivers, who make the blood to start at every stroke on their mangled bodies. We next, with heavy hearts and minds overwhelmed with pity, follow them to their destined labour in the plantation field, and by the morning dawn, we hear them summoned to their daily task, by the clashing of cowskin scourges in the hands of their hard-hearted overseers. And should any of them, in consequence of fatigue and loss of strength, fall a little behind their fellow sufferers, they are immediately reminded of it by the lash of their cruel drivers. But here I must stop, as it is too much for nature to pursue farther the dreadfully degrading and cruel theme! And is it not enough to awaken and arouse to sympathy the hardest heart, and lead it to exclaim aloud with abhorrence against such brutal and unrighteous doings? Is it possible that there should be in the United States a man, or would he be worthy to bear the dignified name of man, were he so void of the feelings of humanity, as to purchase and make use of the labour of his fellow citizens, his kindred and his friends, produced in the horrid manner above stated? Would not every sympathetic heart, at the sight of a piece of sugar, or other article, that he believed to be the fruit of their labour, produced with agonizing hearts and trembling limbs, be filled with anguish and his eyes gush with tears? Would it not awaken in the feeling, unbiased mind, a sense of all the cruel sufferings above related? Would it not, instead of pleasing his palate, be deeply wounding to the heart? and, if rightly considered, cause cries to arise from the bottom of his soul, in moving accents of supplication to the righteous Judge of Heaven and earth, that he would be graciously pleased to put a stop to such complicated misery and great distress of his creature man?

But some, who have not given the subject a full and impartial discussion, may object and say, the slaves in the West-Indies and southern states, are not our fellow citizens and friends. But it cannot be objected by the impartial and the just, who know, that although in a limited sense, as applied to a particular town or city, they may not be so, yet upon the general and universal scale of nature, they are our brethren and fellow creatures; all privileged by nature and nature's God, with liberty and free-agency, and with the blessings attendant thereon; of which they are not to be deprived, but by their own consent; and, therefore, have a right to demand of us the same justice and equity, as our fellow citizens and friends, in a more limited sense, as above stated, could have done; and to whom we are accountable for every act of injustice and omission of doing to them as we would they should do unto us, and for which we shall all have to answer ere long, at the dread tribunal bar, that we can neither awe nor bribe, but shall receive a just retribution for all our works, whether good or evil.

The foregoing queries and answers, with the annexed observations, are not intended to criminate such of my friends and fellow citizens whose residence is in the slave-holding states, and necessitated to partake more or less of the produce of slavery; as it is a known principle, that necessity hath no law —but only to persuade those who are not exposed to such necessity, to do all in their power to discourage and put an end to that cruel and abominable sin, of holding our fellow creatures in slavery; as no one living out of the slave-holding States, can plead any necessity for trading in the produce of the labour of slaves, to enrich and aggrandize themselves, on the groans and misery of their fellow creatures; neither can any plead the necessity, who are living in the free States, to indulge themselves in the luxuries raised by the labour of slaves, in the West-Indies and other places; but every one remember, to do unto others as they would that others should do to them, when placed under the like circumstances.

LETTERS.

TO RUFUS CLARK, NEW HAVEN.

Jericho, 17th of 3d month, 1813.

DEAR FRIEND,

After parting with thee at Humphreysville, we passed on pretty comfortably to Woodbury, where we arrived early in the afternoon and procured a meeting the same evening; it was pretty large, and, I hope, a comfortable edifying season to many who attended. The Episcopal minister was present, and passed away quietly without manifesting any dissatisfaction. The following day, we rode to Danbury, and had a meeting there in the evening to good satisfaction: a number who attended, at the close, manifested a desire that we would tarry longer with them and have another meeting, but the way did not appear open in my mind for it at that time; from thence we went directly to Friends in our state, and visited all the meetings in Purchase Quarter, that we had not attended in our way out, except one at Salem. They were generally well attended, and some very large, by the coming in of many of other religious societies. They were generally very solemn opportunities, and I was made glad in believing that the Lord our gracious helper was near, to bless his own work and set home the truth delivered to the several states of the people, and to comfort the hearts of the faithful; to him alone be the praise. I found the work very laborious, having a heavy cold on me, from the time of my leaving thee, until I got home, and it still continues, though some better. I got safe home the 10th instant, and the peace of mind and thankfulness of heart I felt on my return, was more than an ample reward for all my toil. I found my dear wife and children well; for which, with His other mercies vouchsafed, my spirit was bowed in humble gratitude to the Gracious Author of all our blessings, whose faithfulness faileth not, and whose mercies are new every morning.

I have felt much for thy dear wife* since I left you, and the more so, I conclude, as something I expressed in answer to a query of one of thy neighbours, affected, in so serious a manner, her tender feelings. When I expressed what I did on that subject, it was in the simplicity and integrity of my heart, not apprehending that she, in the least, was implicated in the matter. My whole view on the subject was to strengthen the mind of thy neighbour, who I took to be an inquirer after the right way; and, believing as I do, that scarcely any thing more fatal to a right growth in true religion can happen to the sincere inquiring mind, than to be led into a belief, that conversion from sin is effected by a sudden shock on the human frame, which can be effected many ways, by only working on the animal passions. Therefore I have long felt it my duty to endeavour to show every honest inquirer, the danger and inconsistency of such a belief. As, I think, it must necessarily lead those who give way thereto into much exposure, by laying them open to many temptations; for by supposing themselves to be made whole in so sudden a manner, it will be likely to induce a spirit of pride, and lead them to imagine their condition to be much better than it really is. This, I believe, has been the case in many instances, wherein they have manifested a kind of triumph while a fiery zeal has pressed them on, but, after the heat of their spirits has cooled down, they have entirely declined and gone back into as bad, if not worse, state than they were in before; which, I believe, will scarcely ever be the case with a truly converted soul: such a belief, in some, may likewise tend to carelessness,

* At the time this letter was written, she belonged to the Methodists, was afterwards convinced of Friends' principles, and became a member of their society.

in respect to the great and necessary work of true christian mortification, which is to know all the desires of the flesh and of the will of man brought down and reduced into the perfect obedience of Christ, and this can only be effected by many, repeated, and deep baptisms of the Holy Ghost; as it is only by these baptisms and sufferings, that the christian learns true obedience to the will of his Heavenly Father; as is implied in the saying of Christ to those of his disciples who desired an exalted station. "Are ye able to drink of the cup that I shall drink of," which was a cup of suffering and death, and to be baptized with the baptism that I am baptized with?"— and we read, Hebrews v. 8, that even Christ himself "Learned obedience by the things which he suffered," and that not for a day, a month, or a year only, but is sometimes dispensed to man, in his fallen state, for many years, (as it was to Israel of old,) in order to bring him out of his fallen state, and that the old man may be fully crucified and the soul made meet for the kingdom of Heaven, where no unclean thing can enter, which true and real conversion always prepares for.

It is often the fervent prayer of my mind that the many honest seekers, scattered up and down, as sheep without a shepherd, may be strengthened to wait and trust in the Lord, and lean not to their own understandings, nor put confidence in man, "whose breath is in his nostrils; for wherein is he to be accounted of?" but "trust ye in the Lord for ever; for in the Lord Jehovah is everlasting strength;" and he will surely arise in his own time for the help of those who trust in him with the whole heart and patiently wait for his coming.

I must now conclude, and with love to thyself and dear wife, in which my wife joins, I rest thy friend.

ELIAS HICKS.

TO WILLIAM POOLE, WILMINGTON.

BELOVED FRIEND, *Jericho, 5th of 1st month,* 1817.

By these I acknowledge the due and very acceptable reception of thy two letters of last month, the contents whereof tended to revive afresh the cordial friendship and affection witnessed, when I, with my companion, Isaac Hicks, was so kindly entertained under thy roof, by thyself and family, and which was renewed and strengthened by thy kind visit to us last spring.

How precious is the fellowship and affection which arises from the influence of that pure love that binds together, in an inseparable bond, all the children of the Heavenly Father's family; and in which is witnessed the truth of the apostle's testimony, that in this union of spirits, "There is neither Jew nor Greek, there is neither bond nor free, there is neither male nor female; for ye are all one in Christ Jesus, and if ye be Christ's, then are ye Abraham's seed, and heirs according to the promise."—Gal. iii. 28, 29.

It is very pleasant and agreeable, when we are so far separated from our friends whom we love, as not often to have the opportunity of communing with them face to face, to receive from them communications in this epistolary way; and it is likewise comfortable and pleasant, when opportunity and ability offers, thus to communicate in true christian sympathy and affection. But so many and various are the avocations that almost continually engross my attention, that I do not find time and opportunity to visit my friends, in this way, as often as I feel warm desires to do; this I plead as an excuse for not writing to thee ere now, although I have often thought of it. Yet, if thou supposes me still behindhand in that respect, I would have thee remember, that thou art not to do as thou art done by, but in that way that thou desires others should do by thee, then I shall be favoured, I trust, in due time, with more of those agreeable epistolary visits from thee; for it is truly comfortable to me often to hear of the welfare of my friends that I love; and, I trust that I love in an eminent degree, all those who love the Lord Jesus Christ in sincerity.

Thou no doubt remembers the exercise of my mind, as manifested in our last yearly meeting, respecting the superstitious observance of the first day of the week, together with its demoralizing tendency on the morals and manners of a great portion of the inhabitants of our country; and what is extraordinary to me, is, that some in our highly favoured society, who purpose to be leaders and instructers, should appear so blind and ignorant on the subject; as I conceive it is wholly founded on a mixture of Jewish and heathenish superstition; and, therefore, more loudly calls for reformation than if it were altogether of Jewish original. If we should now take up anew the Jewish rite of circumcision, it would not be so inconsistent and hurtful, as the superstitious observance of the first day, as now established by the laws of our country. The first institution for keeping the day was by an edict of the first emperor that professed christianity, and issuing from the unnatural and unchristian union of church and state, it is manifestly nothing but an engine of priestcraft. This emperor's first edict runs as follows, (as appears by the early history of the christian church, about the year 300,) "Let all the judges and town people, and the occupations of all trades, rest on the venerable day of the sun," (the first day of the week being the day on which the heathen worshipped the sun, hence the reason of its being called Sunday,) "but," says his edict, "let those who are situated in the country freely, and at full liberty, attend to the business of agriculture, because it often happens that no other day is so fit for sowing corn and planting vines, lest the critical moment being let slip, men should lose the commodities granted them by the providence of Heaven." These things considered, I conceive there is no heathenish custom, or Jewish rite, that, in the present day, calls more loudly for reformation than the superstitious observance of the day alluded to, and I am fully of the belief, that, had the latter generations of Friends been as faithful to the testimonies we, as a people, are called to bear against all superstitious and heathenish and Jewish rites, as were our predecessors in the morning of the day, this superstition would, long ago, have been done away and lost in oblivion in this enlightened country.

I must now draw to a close, as my paper is not sufficient to contain the fulness of my mind on this, to me, important subject.

Thy affectionate friend,

ELIAS HICKS.

TO J——— N———.

The following Letter was written in answer to one which ELIAS HICKS received from J——— N———, who believed in the doctrine of Universal Salvation:

Baltimore, 10th month, 1817.

FRIEND,

On considering what thou hast attributed to the Infinite Jehovah as comprehending his primary excellences, I should have been greatly surprised, had I not known that man, through the medium of his natural senses, aided by all his earthly or creaturely wisdom, however acquired by the deepest researches in natural things, if unassisted by immediate divine revelation, cannot know God, nor have any just and correct idea of his excellent and glorious attributes; and that therefore all his ideas of the divine character must be vague and uncertain, and founded upon mere supposition, without any certain evidence. And how can it be otherwise, seeing that God is a spirit, invisible and incomprehensible to every thing but spirit, agreeably to the doctrine and conclusive argument of the apostle Paul, "What man knoweth the things of a man, save the spirit of man which is in him? even so the things of God knoweth no man, but the spirit of God;" and again, "The natural man receiveth not the things of the spirit of God, for they are foolishness unto him; neither can he know them, because they are spiritually" and only spiritually "discerned." It therefore necessarily follows, that man with all the wisdom he can acquire, aided by human science, however elaborately studied, and with the further assistance of all the books and writings in the world, if void of immediate divine revelation, never has known, nor ever can know, God, in relation either to his essence or those excellent attributes which are in correspondence and unison with his pure, holy, and unchangeable nature; for that which may be known of God is manifest within man,* and that not by his reasoning powers, but by the immediate impression and unpremeditated sensations which the immortal spirit of man feels and sees by being brought into contact with, and under the certain and self-evident influence of, the spirit of God upon it. And hence man is enabled to attribute to God his due only from sensible and self-evident experience. Just the same as in a natural and outward relation: we see the outward sun, we feel its warmth, and walk in its light, and are thereby enabled to ascribe to it with certainty (and not from blind and ignorant supposition) its real excellences. So also it is as it respects the invisible God; that although as it regards our outward senses or the powers of our reasoning faculties, he is to us an impenetrable secret, yet he is clearly and sensibly manifested to the immortal soul of man, by the light of his spirit, or the radiance of the Heavenly Sun, which is God. By which manifestation the apostle was enabled to declare from self-evident certainty, that "God is light, and in him is no darkness at all;" and that "if we walk in the light, as he is in the light, we have fellowship one with another, and the blood," which means no doubt the spiritual life, "of Jesus Christ his son, cleanseth us from all sin." Hence man in this enlightened state is enabled to ascribe to God his just and righteous due; for as, by an entire submission and faithful obedience to the inspiration and requirings of the spirit of God, man witnesses, by self-evident experience, a redemption from sin, and such an entire mortification of self, as to be brought not only to love his neighbour as himself, but to love even the most cruel of his enemies so as to pray to God for them, he comes to a

---

* Because that which may be known of God is manifest in them; for God hath showed it unto them.—Rom. i. 19.

self-evident knowledge of at least two of the divine attributes, namely, his infinite power and his infinite mercy. For knowing in himself the entire impossibility under which he lies of performing this by any power of his own, he ascribes it all to God, as the sole author thereof. And as by this inward revelation all the secrets of his heart are laid open, without a possibility of hiding any thing from him, so there arises a self-evident sense of his infinite prescience. And so also it is, as it relates to all his other attributes, necessary for man to have any knowledge of in this state of being.

But man cannot rightly and rationally attribute any thing to God but what he has knowledge or experience of, as every thing else must be founded on supposition, as something that may be or may not be; and therefore cannot be a subject of belief, or any part of a Christian's creed. And here let me observe, that the term infinite implies no more, even in relation to the Divine Being, than that there is a great First Cause, not limited or bounded by any other being or cause. But to what extent this unbounded liberty is exercised, at any one time, either as it regards his general or his special providence, or as it regards the attributes of an infinite God, no finite being can have any just idea or conception of; for, no doubt, the infinite Jehovah has ways of seeing, knowing, and acting, which no finite being can comprehend or have any knowledge of. And therefore, how monstrous for any man to assert, that if there be a God, he must from all eternity not only have seen and known, but also have willed and ordained, every event, both small and great, good and bad; yea, every foul action and thought originating in the chambers of wantonness and debauchery; and if he is not such a being, then thou sayst there is no God, or at least thy arguments and reasonings fairly imply such a conclusion and consequence. From which there results, as it relates to the all-wise and infinite Jehovah, the most palpable and daring presumption and absurdity: for what can be more so, than to charge the Almighty with being the author of all the murder, lying, blasphemy, swearing, robbing, and stealing, together with the whole catalogue of sin and iniquity in the world? Would it not have been more prudent to have deferred advancing such erroneous doctrines, until thou hadst become better informed, and hadst a better understanding of the Scriptures? For, although thou hast quoted many passages to give a cover to thy assertions and reasonings, yet they afford no proof. Hadst thou, in thy researches after knowledge, been concerned to know the first step of wisdom—the right knowledge of thyself—such an humbling view of thy own insufficiency and entire ignorance of the Divine Being, and all his glorious attributes, would, I trust, have preserved thee from falling into thy present errors. Errors great indeed, and fatal in their consequences; for if men were capable of believing with confidence thy opinions, either as regards the doctrine of unconditional predestination and election, or the doctrine of universal salvation, both of which certainly and necessarily resolve in one, who could any longer call any thing he has his own? for all would fall a prey to the villains and sturdy rogues of this belief. And, indeed, a belief of these opinions would most assuredly make thousands more of that description, than there already are; as every temptation to evil, to gratify the carnal desires, would be yielded to, as that which was ordained to be; and of course would be considered as something agreeable to God's good pleasure; and therefore not only our goods and chattels would become a prey to every ruffian of this belief, but even our wives and daughters would fall victims to the superior force of the abandoned and profligate, as believing they could do nothing but what God had ordained to be.

But we are thankful in the sentiment, that no rational intelligent being can possibly embrace, in full faith, these inconsistent doctrines; as they are founded on nothing but supposition; and supposition can never produce real belief, or a faith that any rational creature can rely upon. I am fully convinced, that the doctrines thou art endeavouring to disseminate, and which have been professed by thousands in days past, and are held by many in the present day, have their origin in a profound ignorance of God and his righteous attributes, from which source infidelity and unbelief have been produced. For the creature, in his limited and carnal wisdom, undertaking to search out the essence and first cause of all things, without possessing a capacity or power for such investigation, can only proceed therein by guessing and surmising: hence the infidel springs up, who assures us, as his opinion, that all things come by chance; and which, I conceive, fairly embraces thy doctrine of "one eternal now;" which implies, if it implies any thing, that all things have been hurled into existence in an instant, by mere blind chance, and without any intelligent designing First Cause. This difference only excepted; thou guessest or surmisest that there is a First Cause; and thou supposest him to be of such a particular fancied description, and if he is not just what thou hast described him to be, thou assurest us he has no being. And as one supposition or guess is as good and as certain as another, until the one or the other is proved by evidence, therefore the infidel's guess or supposition is not only as rational but even more consistent than thine: for thou supposest a great First Cause, just, pure, holy, and merciful, and at the same time makest him the author of all the injustice, impurity, unholiness, and cruelty which exist; but the infidel believes all things to come by chance, and, therefore, charges no wrong upon any one.

I will now notice thy great struggle to reconcile contradictions, and by which thou art at variance with the doctrine of the apostle, where he says, that "faith without works is dead;" for thou sayst that every individual, who in this life becomes fit for the blessings of paradise, must have been preordained thereto: of course, thou entirely destroys man's free agency, and if that be taken away the work is all done; man can neither fall nor rise; do wickedly nor justly; commit sin nor do good: therefore his actions and thoughts must be all good, and likewise good for nothing, as they can neither make him happy nor miserable. Away then goes all salvation and all reprobation, for by thy doctrine they sink into eternal oblivion.

I will now seriously ask thee, whether the servant in the parable, was condemned to the shades of darkness for having, or not having, a talent to improve? Thou wilt, I trust, most certainly acknowledge, as the scriptures and common sense assure us, that it was for having one. Then certainly he must have had power and ability to improve it: and if he had power to improve it, as the other two did theirs, then certainly it was his master's will that he should have improved it. Hence we are assured, from the tenor of this parable, that a certain act and thing has been done, that the all-righteous and unchangeable Jehovah neither willed nor ordained, unless he willeth contraries; which I conclude neither thou nor any other person would be willing to believe. Hence it further appears, that the act of disobedience originated entirely in the independent will of man; as has every other sin in the world. It is a fact which must be admitted, that every man that has sinned hath self-evident knowledge of it, if any thing can be self-evident to man: and therefore, if thy premises are well founded, that every thing that the Divine Being foreknows he wills and ordains, then the conclusion will follow, according to thy arguments, that he has not foreknown any sin; for I think there is nothing more certain, as above proved, than that the Divine Being never willed nor ordained the commission of any. Sin arises entirely out of the corrupt independent will of man; and which will is not of God's creating, but springs up and has its origin in man's disobedience and transgression, by making a wrong use of his liberty. And as this corrupt will of man is adventitious to him and no part of his original state, but has its origin in the wrong use of his free agency, by which he has fallen from God into a state of darkness and death; so, when through the renewed emanations of the divine light and life, man is again quickened, and brought to see his wretched condition, and in this divine visitation, while lengthened out to him, he makes a new election, in which he chooses God for his portion, and his inward light and law for his guide, and follows it in faithful obedience, then he knows his corrupt will to be slain, and cast out into the ocean of oblivion, and God's will becomes to him all in all. Hence man becomes again reconciled to his Maker, in bonds of filial love and duty, and witnesses the completion of a new birth. But if he still persists in the exercise of his own corrupt will, during the day of his visitation, until his heart is hardened, and he wears out the mercy of a gracious God, then he comes to witness the truth of the apostle's doctrine, "indignation and wrath, tribulation and anguish, upon every soul of man that doeth evil, of the Jew first, and also of the Gentile."

I will now give thee my views of Divine foreknowledge, arising out of my own experience, and not founded on supposition or surmise, but on certainty. I believe that the prescience of the Almighty is infinite, that is, unbounded; but how far he extends it in the unbounded liberty of his own free will, I would not dare to say, because it is beyond all finite comprehension. I also believe, that his all-searching eye "beholdeth the evil and the good" according to his own good pleasure;— but I believe, seeing and knowing a thing, stand entirely distinct from willing and ordaining it. And I have admired from whence that presumptuous idea should have arisen in the minds of men, which obliges the Divine Being to will and ordain every thing he foreknows; seeing, it not only limits his liberty and power, but also makes him the sole author of every sin and evil in the world. Surely, these men would think it very hard and cruel, were their neighbours to accuse them of being the authors of all or any part of the evils that transpire among them, because they had a just sense thereof before they came to pass; for we know, that man by the strength of his reasoning powers, does foresee some events connected with causes and effects, and such as he had no agency in bringing about, but were entirely the product of the will and design of another. And so it is in regard to the Divine Being: for, seeing man was created a rational, intelligent creature, in order that he might be a happy creature, and as no rational creature could be happy without liberty, and this liberty to be useful in procuring happiness, must be an uncontrolled one, Divine Wisdom saw it right and needful to confer this uncontrolled liberty on his creature man, so far as was necessary to render him an accountable and a happy being. And I think there is no truth more plain, than that a rational, intelligent being, can neither be accountable nor happy without being placed in a state of entire independence as it regards the choice of things which constitute his accountability and happiness.

Now if this be the case, many things may and will transpire, originating in this free agency of man, which the Divine Being never willed nor ordained; and in this correct view of things we fairly and fully exonerate the divine Author of all good, from being the author of sin, in any degree, and from willing any thing but good; and justly place the odium where it belongs, on man's independent and corrupt will.

I think every sensible person must see the vast difference there is between these two doctrines. The first, that of preordination or universal salvation, which resolve in one, tending continually to set people at ease in their sins, and to encourage them in the pursuit of their own carnal desires and gratifications; the other, to wit, his free agency, and consequent possible happiness, tending continually to stimulate to every virtuous pursuit, and the necessity of living under the cross to the carnal inclinations: being bound to do justly, love mercy, and to walk humbly with God, as duties, not only required of every man, but as certainly as they are required, so certainly to be attained, if sought after and laboured for through the assistance of divine grace.

The principal cause of the darkness and ignorance which prevail amongst men, in regard to a future state of rewards and punishments, arises, I conceive, from the want of a right knowledge of God, and of those general and immutable laws, by which all things in heaven and in earth are governed, and which result from the united and unchangeable attributes of the infinite Jehovah; to wit, his justice, wisdom, power, mercy, and love, which never act independent of each other, but always in unison. And there is one general and immutable law, that pervades all nature, that is, that like produces its like; viz. the fig-tree will produce figs; the thorn-tree will produce thorns; of course every tree its own fruit. A good tree good fruit, and a corrupt tree corrupt fruit; and at the same time God dispenses to those different kinds alike, in justice, wisdom, power, mercy and love. He causes his rain to descend equally on each, and his sun to shine on all alike. Just so it is in relation to his free-agent creature man, who, through the power conferred upon him in his free-agency, whilst in this probationary state, may be, speaking figuratively, a good tree, or a corrupt tree, agreeably to his own election; yet God dispenses to all alike in justice, wisdom, power, mercy and love. Hence those who make their election to good, and choose to follow the teachings of the inward law of the spirit of God, are of course leavened into the true nature of God, and consequently into the happiness of God. For nothing but that which is of the nature of God, can enjoy the happiness of God. But he who makes his election, or choice, to turn away from God's law and spirit, and governs himself, or is governed by his own will and spirit, becomes a corrupt tree; and although the same justice, wisdom, power, mercy, and love, are dispensed to this man, as to the other, yet by his contrary nature, which has become fleshly, by following his fleshly inclinations, he brings forth corrupt fruit.

Hence each has his own reward according to their different natures, without any change in the Divine Being towards them. For, to the first, his justice, power, wisdom, mercy and love, constitute happiness and heaven; whilst to the latter, they constitute misery and hell, without the least change in their common Creator. Hence all the happiness of the one, and the unhappiness of the other, arises solely from their different natures; and this difference is not of God, but wholly from the effect of their own choice, and the nature and influence of their different leaders. And we have no reason to suppose, that any rational creature, who, in making his election, chooses to follow the lust of the flesh, the lust of the eye, and the pride of life, and becomes so wedded to those carnal pleasures and delights, as to continue in them during the day of his visitation and probation, would, if he had an eternity of probation, either here or hereafter, ever alter his course; as his whole nature would be so interwoven into the very nature of the evils which he had chosen to follow, as not to feel any inducement or power to change. Just in the same manner it is with him who makes his election to God, and faithfully follows the leadings of the spirit of truth, during the day of his probation here; he becomes so wedded to it, interwoven, and swallowed up into its divine nature, as not to have any possible inducement or power to change. And, therefore, had he to pass through an eternity of probation, either here or hereafter, it would have no tendency at all to alter him; which I hold to be according to the doctrine of the beloved apostle John: "Whosoever is born of God doth not commit sin, for his seed remaineth in him, and he cannot sin, because he is born of God."

With real concern, and desire for thy present and future welfare, I conclude with recommending the foregoing remarks and observations to thy candid and unprejudiced consideration, and rest thy assured friend,

ELIAS HICKS.

TO WILLIAM POOLE, WILMINGTON.

Jericho, 15th of 6th month, 1817.

DEAR FRIEND,

Thy favour of third month last came duly to hand, and was very acceptable: the contents whereof have obtained my serious attention, and, notwithstanding I concur with thee, in thy general observations, relative to our cherishing a disposition of forbearance and charity towards one another in things of an indifferent nature, and in those where our views may be diverse, although, at the same time, each may act from right and sincere motives; yet, I do not suppose, to advance doctrines and opinions that we believe are founded in truth, and in the very nature and reason of things, and to enforce them with all the energy and demonstration that we are capable of, is in any respect contradictory to such forbearance and charity, but rather, I conceive, goes to establish such a disposition, as it manifests a desire of improving and advancing others at our own risk, and the endangering the loss of our own reputation, at least with the unthinking multitude, and he that prizes his reputation higher than he does his Christian duty, is seldom found in the practice of it.

Thy arguments in favour of the retention of a Legal Sabbath, in my opinion, carry very strong evidence against it. Thou queries,—is the appropriation of one day, the reason for the abuse of all days, or is it not rather that latent root of evil in the mind that respects no day? To which I may answer, I have no idea of any latent or hidden root of evil in the heart of man, when viewed as the offspring of infinite perfection; but I believe him to be possessed, as the good gifts of his bountiful Creator, with the power of free-agency, or freedom of will, and with propensities, tending to induce him to seek after, and strive to obtain, the means of preserving life, and suitable sustenance to these mortal bodies, together with comfort and joy. But at the same time, liable so to be acted upon, by things without him, as not to make a right use of these blessings, but to abuse them, so as to produce evil to himself and injury to his fellow creatures, and, I apprehend, these evils have been greatly increased by the setting apart, by law, the first day of the week, as a day of idleness or rest, forbidding all the inhabitants, under certain penalties, doing any act of useful business on that day, either small or great, although laudable and praiseworthy if done on any other day. This I assert from experience, and from my observation for more than fifty years past, and I cannot see how it can be otherwise, in the view and observation of any sensible persons, unless their minds have been fettered by the undue force of custom and tradition: for when we consider that in this enlightened country, where the inhabitants are taught to think for themselves, and not receive their faith from their parents or tutors, any farther than as their counsel accords with the dictates of their own consciences; the number that can persuade themselves that there is any thing sacred or holy in that day, more than another, is very small, and many, I believe, acquiesce in the custom of keeping it as a Holyday, more from the popularity of the measure, than from any sincere belief of the rectitude thereof. Therefore, in this view of the subject, it appears to me impossible that any good should come from it; and to consider it as a mere moral Sabbath, or day of rest from our outward avocations and useful labour, is, in my opinion, altogether irrational, as there is not a trace of any practice of the kind recorded in any history, that I have met with, except since the reformation; and it is particularly objectionable as now observed, as some members of our own Society, and some others, seeing the inconsistency of admitting the idea under the Christian dispensation of a seventh day Sabbath, as a day more holy than another, in order to accommodate their conduct to a compliance with a superstitious law of the government they live under, have metamorphosed it to a moral Sabbath, or mere day of rest from their useful vocations, and so, by far-fetched arguments, founded in suppositions, but without evidence as to the truth of them, have quieted their consciences, so as to get along easy in the mixture with the multitude, whereby our usefulness as a peculiar people, called to hold forth to the world pure and peculiar testimonies, has been very much lessened, and the reformation obstructed.

Thy arguments on this head, in my opinion, contradict themselves. Thou sayest, it is a pleasure to reflect that the poor horse, after six days' labour, is entitled to the seventh as a day of rest. But let us query,—is it so? I conceive not; neither will it ever be so; unless we are brought again under the Jewish code, with its severe restrictions. I believe, it is so far from being a day of respite, generally speaking, to the poor horse, that it rather increases his burden; for thou allows, that if all were brought under the influence of a true Christian spirit, such an appropriation would not be needed: therefore the benefit of it, if any, must result from its influence on the covetous and avaricious, which nothing but self-interest will govern. For their business is often so planned as to do, if possible, as much work in six days as would have been done in seven, had there been no such appropriation; hence those animals are driven in the six days, agreeably to this view, as much as they would have been in seven, as the seventh is considered a lost day. Add to this, that those men have many cares, therefore there are many portions of business allotted for the first day, such as money to collect, and men to be seen to converse about some particular business; here the poor horse is called upon, and must go, whip and spur, say ten, twenty, or thirty miles, and back at night, and to make this appear plausible, and as they may more likely meet their friends, who also come with the same views, they attend some place called a place of worship; hence instead of being a day of rest, it is often a day of greater fatigue than any in the week, to both man and horse. But the case thou mentions of the poor slaves, is in favour of my views, as they are generally driven, by their hard-hearted claimants, so as in six days, if possible, to gain the seventh, as their masters consider that as so much lost time to them, unless the slaves work hard on the seventh for themselves, as they term it, which, however, is only nominally so, for their masters reap the principal profit thereof. These considerations prove, that a mere moral Sabbath, or day of rest from labour, as plead for by some, is not necessary, nor consistent, as it not only defeats its supposed use, but impeaches the divine character as not having rightly divided the time for labour, and the time for rest, and that he has acted partially towards the children of men in not having enlightened any of them to see the utility of such an appropriation, nor even, from what appears, suggested the idea to any, until he appointed it to Israel with the rest of their shadows, and then to no other but that people, and he has not even given it to them with a view of moral advantage, or profit, as a mere day of rest from bodily labour; but as pointing and leading to a more excellent state, the subjugation of their wills to the divine will: the same as circumcision, their sacrifices, &c.: and, as certainly to be ended at the close of that dispensation, as any other ritual thereof. And, therefore, I consider the institution of a first day Sabbath, or the setting apart one day in seven as a day of rest, and the sanctioning of the same by a penal law, utterly inconsistent with the Gospel dispensation, and unsupported by revelation and right reason, and altogether the offspring of superstition, and idolatry; which is clearly evinced by its fruits, for it has always been, from its first institution, a source of persecution, and naturally tends, especially in this enlightened age, to lessen the authority and use of magistracy; for some of these, through their own superstition, and many others, by the instigation of their hireling teachers, whose interest lies in involving the people in ceremony, are induced to persecute their innocent neighbours, by enforcing penalties upon them for what they term a breach of the Sabbath, when only doing a small share of useful and commendable labour, and, at the same time, will overlook acts of gross immorality. By which they not only lose their authority as magistrates, but greatly impair their own reputation, and that of the government they act under.

But there is another consideration, that will, I think give conclusive evidence in the case, and which will be found in an answer to this query, viz: Has, or has not, Divine Wisdom established, by an immutable law, as old as the world, a right distribution of time, and so divided it into appropriate seasons, with a time for labour and a time for rest, that the most consummate wisdom of man can never amend? The answer appears to me obvious, and natural—he has. For when I reflect upon the beautiful order displayed by Divine Wisdom in the universe, I am at a loss to conceive how the rational creature man should have conceived the idea of amending it, without great presumption: for when we view the regular succession of day and night, surely no rational creature can ask for more time to rest than is given by this arrangement.

Had the society of Friends persevered consistently with

their first principle, the inward light and law, and their declared sense respecting the first day of the week being instituted as a sabbath, there is little reason to doubt, but that the Society would long before this have been liberated from the superstitious observance thereof, and of being continually liable to persecution for a breach of it. For, as Barclay well observes, "We, not seeing any ground in Scripture for it, cannot be so superstitious as to believe, that either the Jewish Sabbath now continues, or that the first day of the week is the anti-type thereof, or the true Christian Sabbath; which, with Calvin, we believe to have a more spiritual sense, and therefore we know no moral obligation, by the fourth commandment or elsewhere, to keep the first day of the week, more than any other, or any holiness inherent in it."

Could it be proved from Scripture (which nevertheless, I conceive, it cannot) that the apostles and primitive Christians did use the first day of the week, for the purpose of worship, in preference to any other day, yet that is no more than can clearly be proved concerning many other superstitious rites, retained among the greater part of professed Christians, such as water baptism, their bread and wine, &c. Therefore the reasons which some give for our joining with others in setting apart the first day of the week, for the purpose of worship and a day of rest, go as fully to prove the necessity of our compliance with them in those other superstitious rituals: for I do not find any thing in all the New Testament, enforcing the present manner of observing the first day of the week: therefore I think it is altogether unfounded in revelation, scripture, and right reason.

But nevertheless, I agree with thee, and I have had no other sentiment in the case, that the great mass of the people, even in this enlightened country, are not prepared for a sudden change; and it is a subject that will take some time to spread and prevail, but that ought not to hinder those who are prepared, and who clearly see the injury attached to the measure, from spreading their prospects, and giving them all the force they can; as such an improvement of their time and talents is comprehended, both in their duty to their Creator and to man their fellow creature.

As to thy question, relative to the origin of evil, I may take the liberty, as my best present answer, to say I consider it a useless occupancy of our time and talents, and but a vain stretch of our imagination, to seek after that which is rendered incomprehensible by our gracious Creator to our finite understandings. Let us be content with what we experience in ourselves, in accordance with the testimony of the apostle, that what is to be known of God, or the real Good, is manifest within man; so likewise all that we know of the real source of evil, is manifested within; but in both cases, in a limited degree, suited to our present state; yet in sufficient fulness to effect every good purpose to man, as he patiently abides in his proper allotment.

I may just add, and I think with real gratitude to our all-gracious and beneficent benefactor, that our late yearly meeting was one of the most favoured, through the several sittings, of any in my present remembrance, although we had a less number of visiters, from other yearly meetings, than for many years past.

My wife and children join me in love to thee and thine, in which I rest thy affectionate friend,

ELIAS HICKS.

TO WILLIAM POOLE, WILMINGTON.

Jericho, 1st mo. 11th, 1818.

BELOVED FRIEND,

Thy affectionate lines of 11th mo. 27th, came to hand soon after their date, while I was visiting the meetings of Salem quarter, by the attentive care of our mutual friend, Samuel R. Fisher: their contents were truly grateful, and met the fullest accordance of my mind. I unite with thee in feeling a desire, that all who hear sentiments and doctrines delivered, that embrace man's best interest here, and which may effect his happiness hereafter, may be not only convinced of their truth and rectitude, but also be in the practice of what they teach; nevertheless, we have no just reason to hope, that this will in any general way be the case, not even if those doctrines are delivered in the clearest manner, and under the influence of Divine wisdom. This, I conceive, is a truth as fully demonstrated in the Scriptures, as any truth they contain, and some know it in their own experience and observation. I have no doubt but Divine wisdom and impartial goodness, has opened a medium to every intelligent and rational mind, through which, if it willingly improves the means afforded, every truth necessary to be known in the way of its salvation will be manifested; but if they are neglected and turned from, although doctrines may be delivered with all the clearness of evidence that Divine wisdom and goodness may see meet to unfold, yet such will cavil and call for more clear evidence. As they disregard the evidence of Divine truth in their own minds, so neither will they regard any other evidence. This was abundantly evident in regard to the doctrines and miracles of the Saviour when manifested in the figure. For although he preached doctrines and wrought miracles, greater and more excellent than any other ever had done on earth, yet how very few believed on him.

Now I do not conceive that the reason of their unbelief was because the doctrines delivered were not sufficiently elucidated, or clothed with sufficient evidence, but because those who heard them had their minds pre-occupied, with principles and doctrines that were more congenial to self and selfish views, and therefore no doctrine, unless it could be brought to correspond with theirs, would be admitted by such to be clearly unfolded; when, at the same time, had they been willing to have received the doctrine with the elucidation and evidence which accompanied it, it would then have been sufficiently clear.

That this disposition is tenfold more the cause of the unbelief of mankind, than the want of evidence or clear elucidation attending the rightly commissioned servants of the Lord in opening doctrine to the people, in every age of the world, I cannot doubt; and this, I conceive, is fully evinced by the sufferings and persecutions, that the faithful in all ages have had to pass through. For, as man, in his fallen state, is in every age the same, therefore the doctrines of truth are ever opposed to him, and he to them; but as soon as he is brought to see his wretched condition, and, under a sense thereof, sincerely seeks for salvation, the witness for God in his own heart will begin to act; then, a word to the wise, as the saying is, is enough; only to mention a subject, however new, if founded in truth, the witness for truth in his own mind, with very little elucidation, will immediately assent thereto. But if the mind is preoccupied with its own selfish and preconceived principles, strongly enforced by tradition, and in which man, in his natural state, has taken up a rest, such will not be convinced of any doctrines that run counter thereto, until they are first brought to feel their wretched condition, which such very rarely do, without the pressure of some very heavy calamity or sore disappointment, which razes their superstructure to the very foundation.

Multiplied testimonies of Scripture might be brought to prove the truth of this doctrine, but I will mention only one to close these observations: "Go unto this people and say, Hearing, ye shall hear and shall not understand; and seeing, ye shall see and not perceive: for the heart of this people is waxed gross and their ears are dull of hearing, and their eyes have they closed, lest they should see with their eyes and hear with their ears," &c. Acts xxviii. 26, 27. This I conceive to be a clear description of the states and conditions I have before mentioned. But I do not mention these things to prevent, in any degree, a right care, according to thy remarks, but only to show that when that has been all done, there will be cavillers and fault-finders: therefore we ought to be careful not to blame the speaker, when the blame may be altogether with those who find fault; and that not because they do not see, but because, as the prophet declares, they are unwilling to understand or perceive, having hardened their hearts previously against the witness in themselves; therefore they will not receive it from another, but will be making objections merely to ward off the truth, rather choosing to eat their own bread and wear their own apparel, and clothe themselves with the name Christian, only to take away the reproach of men. And, I fear, there are a considerable number under our name of this description, who not only love the world, but also its friendships, manners, maxims, policies, customs, fashions, vanities, pleasures and amusements, yet like to bear the name of Quaker, because it has become honourable among men. Alas! how much better would it be for the Society and the promotion of truth, if it was still a name of reproach.

I got home from my western journey the 19th of last month, found my family in usual health, to our mutual comfort, and with a thankful heart and a peaceful mind, which I attributed to the goodness and mercy of Israel's bountiful Shepherd.

With love to thyself and family, and Friends in thy neighbourhood, I subscribe thy friend,

ELIAS HICKS.

TO PHEBE WILLIS.

DEAR FRIEND, *Jericho, 5th mo. 19th, 1819.*

Thy acceptable epistle I have perused, and believing it to be the product of real friendship, it was gratefully received, and the language it utters would, not many years since, have been my own. But having for a considerable time past found from full conviction, that there is scarcely any thing so baneful to the present and future happiness and welfare of mankind, as a submission to tradition and popular opinion, I have therefore been led to see the necessity of investigating for myself all customs and doctrines, whether of a moral or of a religious nature, either verbally or historically communicated, by the greatest and best of men or angels, and not to sit down satisfied with any thing but the plain, clear, demonstrative testimony of the spirit and word of life and light in my own heart and conscience; and which has led me to see how very far all the professors of Christianity are from the real spirit and substance of the Gospel. And among other subjects, I have been led, I trust, carefully and candidly, to investigate the effects produced by the book called the Scriptures since it has borne that appellation; and it appears, from a comparative view, to have been the cause of four-fold more harm than good to Christendom,* since the apostles' days, and which, I think, must be indubitably plain to every faithful, honest mind, that

---

* Phebe Willis was a near neighbour of Elias Hicks, with whom he was in habits of frequent social intercourse, and with whom he had often conversed on the subjects embraced in this letter, and, on this account, it is probable he was not so particular in explaining his views, as doubtless he would have been, if he had expected it would have fallen into the hands of strangers, or been made public. This will apply to what he says when speaking of the Scriptures, that they "have been the cause of fourfold more harm than good to Christendom." This sentence is explained, and we trust satisfactorily, in his letter to Moses Brown. See page 171.

It was, no doubt, the *improper use of the Scriptures*, and not any objection that E. H. had to the writings themselves, that induced him to believe they had done more harm than good. This is evident from the whole scope of the letter, and more particularly from the paragraph (page 49) beginning, "But my views respecting the Scriptures, are not altered, *although thus abused by others*," &c. And however some may think he has overrated the evil consequences arising from the perversion of them, we find some of our early Friends bearing as strong a testimony against their improper use as E. H. Samuel Fisher, one of the most eminent of George Fox's early contemporaries, in reply to the celebrated John Owen, thus reprehends the idolatry of exalting the Scriptures above their proper place, and thus diminutively speaks of them when brought in competition with "the word of life itself," the only sure rule of faith and practice: " So, then, as to evince it that I am none of those idiots that idolize any mere men's writings, as many do the unskilful scribblings of their scribes for the Scripture, little less than Israel did the golden calves, after which they dotingly ran from God himself, saying of these images in their own imaginations. 'These are thy gods,' &c. Nor yet any mere writings of those holy men that wrote the Holy Scripture itself, as most of our misty ministers and their people do, because they were written by Divine inspiration, little less than Israel did the brazen serpent, because it was hung up by Divine institution: I shall first take occasion to thrust down that enthroned calf of thy anti-scriptural tributary, treatises, thesis, and atheological thoughts upon the Scripture, from that high place it hath in the thoughts of such as fall down before it, as Moses threw down that molten image, (which the high priest made, and ignorant people made a god of,) and stamped it to powder. And secondly, as Hezekiah, not without God's own approbation, took down the brazen serpent, which had its being, (as the Holy Scripture itself had) not without God's own appointment, when once men began to do homage to it, and called it more than Nehushtan, that is, a piece of brass, that they might know it was no God: so shall I take down the dead corpse, and bare carcase, of the best copy of the Scripture, since men begin to go a whoring after it from God and Christ, and the Word of Life itself, out of that high and stately throne wherein thou, J. Owen, statest it."—*Sam'l. Fisher's Works*, pp. 239, 240.

has investigated her history free from the undue bias of education and tradition. Mark the beginning of the apostacy. When the professors of Christianity began to quarrel with and separate from each other, it all sprang from their different views and different interpretations of passages of Scripture, and to such a pitch did their quarrels arise, as that a recurrence to the sword was soon deemed necessary to settle those disputes. And the strongest party in that line, finding that as long as the people were at liberty, and had the privilege of searching the Scriptures and putting their own interpretations upon them, and making them their rule, diversity of opinion and differences would increase, this led the strongest party to that disagreeable and unchristian alternative of wresting them out of their hands and forbidding their being read by the people at large. And this state of things continued for many years, until the beginning of reformation by Martin Luther.

It will be now necessary to consider, whether the Scriptures were in any wise accessary to this infant beginning of reformation? I think it is clear they were not; but as Luther and his adherents gained strength, they began to shake off the yoke of papal oppression, and, among other things, the restriction on the Scriptures was taken off, and every citizen that joined Luther's party, had the privilege of reading the Scriptures at his pleasure. And what was the result? A diversity of sentiment, respecting what they taught, which soon set the reformers one against another, and produced such divisions and animosities among them, that recourse was again had to the sword to settle disputes. In this condition things continued until George Fox was raised up to bear testimony to the light and spirit of truth in the hearts and consciences of men and women, as the only sure rule of faith and practice, both in relation to religious and moral things, and which was complete and sufficient, without the aid of books or men, as his doctrine and example clearly evinces; as his reformation was begun and carried on without the necessary aid of either. But, as the professors of Christianity then held the Scriptures, or their interpretations of them, as their chief idol, and [as] such was their veneration for them, that for any one to hold up any thing else as a rule, he was immediately pronounced a heretic or schismatic, and not fit to company or associate with in any way, this led George and his friends to show, that their doctrines were in nowise derogatory to those written by those who were inspired by the same spirit in former days. And all goes to prove, that every step of reformation from the fall, in every age of the world, has been begun and best carried on when the reformers kept close to the leading and inspiration of the spirit of truth, and suffered nothing, whether books or men, to turn them aside from their ever-present and ever-blessed sure guide; seeing they have the Anointing to be their teacher, and the Spiritual Lamb to be their light.

And, I conceive, every man and woman, who has a right understanding and correct ideas of the Divine character, must have the same views; for otherwise they must contradict their own professions, as every one who believes in the existence of God, attributes to him justice, mercy, and love, and that he is unchangeable in his nature, and incapable of partiality; hence he must, and no doubt has, given to every man and woman, a complete and sufficient rule of faith and practice, without the aid of books or men; and hath so ordered in the course of events, that the more strictly and faithfully every man and woman lives up to the guidance and teaching of this inward anointing, and never turns aside to the right hand or to the left, for the precepts and traditions of men, the more instruction and help they afford one another. And to suppose a written rule to be necessary, or much useful, is to impeach the Divine character, and charge the infinite Jehovah with partiality and injustice, as the greater part of his rational creation have never been furnished with those means. And had they been needful, he certainly would, in order to deal with an even hand of justice, have furnished all his rational creatures with them; as it was equally in his power so to have done from the beginning. But as man's fall principally consists in his turning from his inward spiritual guide, to the direction of his outward senses and animal passions and affections, so [man having so far departed] that he lost almost all right knowledge of this inward guide, the Lord in mercy dispensed to him divers outward manifestations, as a means to lead his attention back to his spiritual guide; and these means have always been suited to the states of those to whom they were dispensed, and therefore often very different to different nations and people. To the family of Abraham he dispensed a very peculiar system of rituals and outward shadows, to which he required obedience, in order to bring them back to a submission to his will, as manifested by his Spirit in their hearts. But he dispensed them to no other people but to Israel, and those that came of their own accord and joined them; and as soon as the effect was produced by bringing them back to their inward guide, all those outward means became obsolete and useless. So likewise he made use of the ministry of Jesus Christ and his apostles for the same end, to turn from darkness to the inward light, and when that was effected, their ministry had done all it could do, and to such, as they continued to walk in the light, their doctrine became obsolete and useless. And so in every age where any real reformation has been produced, it has always been by instruments newly raised up, by the immediate operation of the spirit. And where any people have depended upon what has been written to former generations, such make no advancement, but just sit down in the labours of their forefathers, and soon become dry and formal, and fall behind those they are copying after or propose to follow.

This is very manifestly the case with our Society, although so highly favoured with almost every possible means to gather them from all outwards, to their true inward teacher, who teaches as never man taught—nothing but the truth. And this is the cause why many turn from him, to the teachings of men or books, because they can mostly turn their teachings to suit their own ends; hence plain truth is disagreeable to them, but teachings that they can interpret to suit their own inclinations, as most men do the Scriptures, these they cry up and speak highly of. And such as these cause all the animosities and divisions in Christendom, and from hence most of their quarrels and wars have arisen. And there is great cause to fear, that if those in our Society, who are united with those among others, in very improperly setting up the Scriptures above their true value, are adhered to, they will finally divide and scatter us, as they have all other professors of Christianity. For considerable disputes have already arisen concerning passages of the first importance. I will mention one wherein the very leaders are divided. And surely if it is so wrapt up in mystery that we cannot understand it alike, how much better should we be without it. It is Peter's testimony concerning the more sure word of prophecy, which many of those considered as the most wise and learned amongst us, tell us is the Scriptures. And should I be by these convinced that Peter really meant the Scriptures, it would, to me, render all his writings as unworthy much attention. And I have no kind of doubt if Friends generally, of the foremost ranks, should honestly and plainly speak their sentiments on the Scriptures in general, so great would be their diversity of prospects, that little help or edification, in a society capacity, could be derived from them; and it is altogether reasonable it should be so in the dispensings of a wise Providence, seeing, as we have the Scriptures at our command, that if there was sufficiency in them to point the way to Heaven, we might then by our own strength and labour arrive at that happy place and outstrip the sons of Noah. But the all-wise Jehovah, who hath declared that he will not give his glory to another, nor his praise to graven images, hath also decreed, that should all the various professors of Christianity associate and bind themselves together, by the strongest ties that lie within the reach of human contrivance, to circulate the Scriptures in their own will and wisdom, or pursue any other means or method to promote the spiritual interest of immortal souls, it will all prove abortive, and confusion of language, if not in a natural, yet in a spiritual sense, will be their portion: for, in my view, there has no event transpired since the building of the Babel Tower, on Shinar's plain, that is so fully representative thereof, as the multiplied Bible societies of the present day.

But my views respecting the Scriptures are not altered, although thus abused by others, and trust I shall, as I heretofore have done, as my mind is opened to it, call upon them as evidence to the truth of inspiration ; and to show that the upright and faithful in former ages, were led and instructed by the same spirit as those in the present day; and that the Lord is graciously willing to reveal himself as fully to the children of men in this day as in any day of the world, without respect of persons, as each is attentive to his inward and spiritual manifestations. And how much more reasonable it is to suppose, that an inspired teacher in the present day, should be led to speak more truly and plainly to the states of the people, to whom he is led to communicate, than any doctrines that were delivered one thousand seven hundred years ago to a people very differently circumstanced to those in this day, I leave to every rational mind to judge. And that the doctrines of George Fox and our primitive Friends, should be easier understood, and plainer, being written in our own language, than the doctrines of the primitive Christians, appears very reasonable. But we are all, or have been, so bound down by tradition, being taught from the cradle to venerate the Scriptures, and people generally considering them so sacred as not to be investigated, but bound to receive them as we have been taught ; hence we have all been more or less, dupes to tradition and error. I well remember how oft my conscience has smitten me when I have been endeavouring to support the society's belief of the Scriptures,* that they so very far excelled all other writings, that the fear of man had too great a share in leading me to adopt the sentiment, and custom rendered it more easy, but I never was clear in my own mind as to that point ; and had I carefully attended to my own feelings, I should have been

---

* From what we have heard Elias Hicks say on this subject, as well as from what is to be found in his writings and printed discourses, we think he would have expressed his views more correctly on this point, if, instead of saying, " the Society's belief," he had said, *the belief of some in the Society.* We think however the closing paragraph in his letter is a sufficient apology to every liberal mind for any inaccuracies which may be found in it.

preserved, I believe, in a line of more consistency in that respect. And I may now acknowledge to thee, that I never expressed my own genuine feelings and prospects so clearly, and so much to the peace of my own mind, as in our last quarterly meeting; and indeed such was the view I had, and the clearness of the opening, that I apprehended there could not have been a rational mind present, acquainted with the subjects of my communication, but would have assented thereto. Much more might be said in proof of the foregoing, but my time and leisure will not reasonably admit me to proceed further. *And what I have written has been done in scraps of time, that I have as it were stolen from my other many avocations, without any time to copy it, or give it much examination; therefore, I hope thou will excuse the improprieties that may have escaped my notice, believing that thou will be able to apprehend the main drift of the arguments, and be willing to put the best construction on such parts as may, to thee, appear erroneous.* Thy assured friend.

ELIAS HICKS.

TO WILLIAM POOLE, WILMINGTON.

Jericho, 12th mo. 28, 1819.

DEAR FRIEND,

Thy acceptable letter of the 8th instant was duly received, and its various parts afforded particular satisfaction. I was much pleased with the account from Baltimore, as I had, at different times, taken much interest in the unhappy difficulties between those two monthly meetings; and had made use of my best endeavours for the settlement thereof.

It was pleasing to find, that thou and thy wife contemplated a visit to us, in the course of the ensuing year, if way should open for it. If I should live to see it brought into effect, it would be truly grateful. Thy freedom on some points of doctrine advanced by me, was also pleasing, as I am established in the sentiment, that truth never loses by close investigation, but rises thereby more bright and clear.

I have often thought, that nothing more sullies and degrades the scriptures of truth, than the fears that many of their advocates manifest, in regard to the investigation of them, and insisting upon their being taken and believed *literally* just as they are, whether consonant with reason, yea or nay.

That book that will not bear the test of all the investigation that the human mind is capable of going into, and still rise superior to all the cavils and false insinuations that may be cast upon it, cannot be of much use to mankind.

The letters thou alludes to, that I read at thy house, from St. Domingo, I have put in a friend's hand for printing; but whether they are to be printed in a pamphlet or a newspaper, is yet uncertain, but let it be which it may, I will endeavour to furnish thee with a copy.

Thy affectionate friend,
ELIAS HICKS.

TO WILLIAM B. IRISH.

Jericho, 1st mo. 15th, 1820.

Thine of the 4th inst. came duly to hand and was very acceptable. Thy object in writing as it regards thy religious queries, attracted my attention, and although thou assures me that, from present appearances, thou wilt never become a Quaker or Friend, yet, I apprehend, that which induced thee to drop the sentiment is a favourable omen, and leads me to hope, that if thou attendest faithfully to that which has begun a good work on thy vision, and has enabled thee to "see men as trees walking," and shown thee the baneful effects of the prejudice of education, and how mightily tradition and custom tyrannize over the human mind, and bind it down as with fetters of iron, too strong for reason alone to rend asunder, and set the captive soul free;—I say, if thou willingly and patiently adheres to that which has begun a good work in thee, by showing thee the difference between things that differ, I not only feel a hope (although it will be through deep inward sufferings and the cross, as none can become real Christians, or Quakers, without it,) that thou wilt yet become a Quaker, or Christian, which are one, and, I trust and hope, a good one.* But to come to this happy experience, depends very much on thyself, for if thou willingly surrenders thyself as an offering to God, to do his will, as by the light in thy own heart and conscience he is pleased to manifest it to thee, thy understanding will be more and more opened into those things that concern thy present and everlasting peace.

I do not admire at the difficulties thou hast had to encounter, in regard to the mode of redemption generally held by professing Christians, as being effected by the death, or outward dying of Jesus Christ, on the outward wooden cross. This, as it regards the redemption of the immortal soul from the bondage of sin, I consider a vulgar error, that came in with the apostacy from primitive christianity. The redemption effected by the outward offering could only, according to the true analogy of things, be a redemption of outward bodies. For under that legal dispensation, there were many legal institutes that were binding upon the people of Israel and on no other people, and a breach of these produced legal crimes, to which penalties were annexed, and these were inflicted on the bodies of the Israelites. Now I consider that the offering of the body of Jesus Christ on the outward cross, applied only, as a matter of redemption, to the Israelites, redeeming them from the curse of that covenant, and the penalties attendant on any breach thereof; and this redemption was the top stone of that figurative dispensation, as by it that dispensation, with all its legal rites and ceremonies, was abolished and done away. Hence the Jews could no longer be guilty of any of those legal crimes, as the law that required those rites was dead and done away, by the outward death of their

---

* W. B. I. not long afterwards became a member of the Society.

Messiah: And this outward redemption of the outward bodies of the Israelites, from the penalties of their outward law, is a complete figure of the inward redemption of the soul from sin, by *the life*, or *spiritual blood of Christ*, inwardly sprinkling our consciences, and thereby enabling us to die to sin as he died for sin; by which we are redeemed from dead works, to serve the living God in newness of life, which makes, and alone can make, the true Christian.

Why should thou think it cruel or painful, that God sent his son into the world, and when in the world permitted him to suffer death by the hands of wicked men, when history informs us, that many thousands of righteous men and women have, by the permission of the Almighty, been persecuted to death by wicked men? Yet, nevertheless, we do not believe that God sent any of these into the world *purposely* to suffer death in the cruel way they did, by the power of the wicked; neither do I believe that God sent Jesus Christ into the world *purposely* to suffer death, in the way he did, any more than all these. For I do not believe that God created any rational being and sent him into the world to suffer death for other men, because they were wicked and he was righteous, but that it was the righteousness of all these, that aggravated the wicked, and was the procuring cause of their hatred and vengeance towards them, when they cruelly persecuted them to death. But their suffering was entirely opposite to and inconsistent with the purpose and will of God; for if it was not, the perpetrators of those dreadful crimes and most atrocious deeds, would all stand justified in his sight. Hence we clearly see that all those kinds of doctrines that naturally and necessarily impeach the all-good and all-gracious Jehovah with apparent cruelty and incorrectness in his purposes and designs, concerning his rational creation, are founded on, and have their origin in, that false and inconsistent doctrine of predestination and election, which ought to be exploded by every rational being, as it destroys all the nobility and excellence of God's rational creation, and places them below the poorest animal on earth.

I believe that the Almighty Creator of the universe, had but one sole purpose and design in creating man, and placing him on this terraqueous globe; and that was to do his will, and thereby to continue in a happy state of union and communion with him, through the spirit; and he has so ordered and arranged all things here on earth, in his wisdom and goodness, as to constitute a state of probation to man, during his militant state, or while his immortal spirit continues in connexion with these mortal bodies, which are not to continue any longer in existence, than during the time of this probationary scene, which was necessary to give the rational intelligent creature, man, a fit opportunity to rise above that innocent state in which he was created, to the exalted state of virtue and glory, by a just and righteous improvement of the liberty and power conferred upon him by his gracious Creator for that purpose, and that purpose only, agreeably to the instruction of Divine Wisdom. Hence we conclude that God never sent his son Jesus Christ, nor any of his rational creation, into the world, *purposely* to suffer death by cruel men; but only, in his own free and voluntary choice, to attend to and do his holy will in all things, and thereby glorify and enjoy him; which all agree to be the chief end and design of man's creation.

Therefore, all the persecution and cruel deaths that have transpired in the world among mankind; not only the persecution and crucifixion of Jesus Christ; but also, all the suffering and martyrdom caused by wicked men, have had their rise and spring from man's unjust and unrighteous use of his liberty and power, conferred upon him only to do his Maker's will in all things.

But the sequel, as well as the very reason of things, clearly shows, that man, in his probationary state, was possessed of a power and liberty (uncontrolled by any other power) to do his Maker's will, by his instruction and aid, which was fully offered to his acceptance, or not to do it, if he chose to comply with temptation: as he had communicated to him, by his Maker, a power of entire free choice. For if this was not the case, he could never have been virtuous or wicked, as all virtue consists in his choosing the good, and all sin in his choosing the evil, independent of any other cause but his own choice. And, no doubt, had the Israelites all been faithful to that outward covenant given them through Moses, they would all have been prepared to have received their Messiah in the way of his coming, as did those that believed on him, and by which the end of his coming would have been much more fully answered; as all Israel then, like the disciples of Jesus Christ, would willingly have passed from the old, and cheerfully entered into the new dispensation. Hence no crucifixion, no suffering or death of Jesus Christ would have taken place; but when his ministry on earth was finished, by fulfilling the law and abolishing that outward covenant, and turning the minds of the people to the inward, to the law written in the heart, and when, by a life of perfect righteousness and self-denial, he had introduced his disciples into the Gospel, he would then have been (like Enoch and Elijah) translated, without suffering the pains of death. But as Divine Wisdom foresaw, that his people Israel would revolt from his commandments, and rebel against his law, and become cruel and hard-hearted; so likewise he foresaw, that the wicked among them would cruelly persecute and slay many of the righteous, and his son Jesus Christ among the rest. Therefore he inspired many of his servants to testify of these things amongst them, before they came to pass, as warning and caution, that so those who were seeking after the right way, might be preserved from taking any part therein, while those who wilfully hardened their hearts against reproof, might suffer the penalties resulting from their crimes, which they had committed in their own free choice, contrary to the counsel and will of their Creator.

The doctrine of the Trinity, as held by many professing Christians, I also consider a weak and vulgar error: that of three *distinct persons* in one God, and that each of these persons is whole God, as, I think, is inserted in some of the confessions of faith. As I believe there cannot be a greater absurdity, than to apply *personality* to God, in any right sense of the word, as personality implies locality, which signifies limited to place, which would be very impious to say of the infinite Jehovah. It is also a doctrine unwarranted by Scripture, as the word trinity is not to be found in the Bible: for although the apostle is made to say, agreeably to our present translation, that there are three that bear record in Heaven, yet he assures us, that *these three are but one.* We have no certainty, however, that they have given us the apostle's sense clearly, as we have no reason to believe the translators were inspired men, for they tell us that inspiration has ceased. But admitting the translation to be correct, yet it carries in it no clear evidence of any such doctrine, as we ought to receive all written testimonials according to their most easy, natural, and rational sense, and especially so, when they in any degree contradict other and more plain and clear testimonies of as high, or higher origin. There was nothing more plainly, nor more fully impressed upon the Israelites by their great lawgiver, than to acknowledge but one God; and although they often asserted that the spirit of the Lord came to them, or was upon them, yet they manifest no idea of any *divisibility,* or *distinction of persons,* between God and his spirit; but wherever the holy spirit of God is, there is God, and where God is, there is the Holy Spirit, or Holy Ghost, which are one, as the terms are synonymous: for God is a spirit, and nothing but spirit. And when this Spirit, or God, acts or operates on the spirit of man, in his first operations, he quickens and enlightens man's spirit, and in this operation he bears record of his own life in the soul of man, as the Holy Spirit or Holy Ghost, and as the spirit of man yields and submits to his operation, there is a birth of God brought forth in the soul or spirit of man, and by which he now bears record of his own life in the soul as *father,* and this birth of God in the soul, being begotten by God, unites in record or witness, in unity with God as *son,* and still it is only God, working all in all in the soul, agreeably to his own will and pleasure. And which agrees with the doctrine of the apostle, where he says, that it is God that worketh in us, both to will and to do, of his own good pleasure. And again: "For as many as are ed by the spirit of God, they are the sons of God."

As to John's revelations, they are some of that apostle's ast writings, written at a time when he was far advanced in deep experience; and we find that the most deep and mysterious writings of the prophets and apostles, are often couched in allegorical similies: therefore, it requires our coming to the same experience, rightly to comprehend or understand them; and hence, when I meet with parts or passages of scripture that I do not understand, I leave them until I may arrive at a state of deeper experience, by which means I have come clearly to comprehend and understand some things, that, at a previous time, seemed mysterious to me; and this, I have no doubt, will be thy case, in respect to what Paul says of women keeping silence in the churches, as also in some other respects; for I apprehend, if Paul hath said what we find recorded in 1st Corinthians, xiv. 34, 35, and 1st Timothy, ii. 11, 12, that he had no allusion at all to their preaching or prophesying in the churches: and if he had, we have no right, nor reason, at all to admit it as sound doctrine, as it contradicts a number more of his own declarations on that point, (as also the general testimony of scripture,) which are much more rational, clear, and plain, as may be seen in his epistle to the Romans, xiv.; Philippians, iv. 3; 1st Corinthians, xi. 5—13; and Paul assures us, that male and female are one in Christ, that is, when they become real Christians, of whom Christ is the head. Also, under the law there were prophetesses as well as prophets, and the effusion of the spirit in the latter day, as prophesied by Joel, was to be equally on sons and daughters, servants and handmaids; and, to believe otherwise, is irrational and inconsistent with the Divine attributes, and would charge the Almighty with partiality and injustice to one-half of his rational creation. Therefore, in my belief, it would be wrong to admit it, although asserted in the most plain and positive manner by men or angels.

ELIAS HICKS.

TO WILLIAM POOLE, WILMINGTON.

Jericho, 3d mo. 22d, 1820.

BELOVED FRIEND,

Thine, of the 28th of 1st month, did not come to hand until the 20th instant, and although long on the way, yet when it arrived was very satisfactory, except the account of thy rheumatic complaint and lameness in thy right arm, which excites my sympathy, having latterly had a very severe turn of my old complaint; but I am again restored to pretty good health, which is the state of my family at present.

Our valued friend and neighbour, Fry Willis, departed this life this morning about five o'clock. He was in apparent good health the evening before last. About nine o'clock, he went down into the cellar on some occasion, and fell whilst there, and wounded his head; and when found was incapable of giving any account how it happened; but by searching the wound, it was not thought sufficient to affect him in the manner he was, that it has become the opinion he had a stroke of the apoplexy. He continued to decline until his dissolution took place. We are of late very frequently notified of our mortality, and the uncertainty of time.

Thou seems to desire my opinion on the trinity, and should I add to that, my views on the atonement by Jesus Christ, thou may possibly consider me very officious: however, as I have lately, in answer to a request from an acquaintance, given partly, if not altogether, my views on those two subjects, I will give thee an abstract from my letter; take it as follows:

[Here follows an abstract from the letter to W. B. Irish. See page 44.]

* * * * * * * * * * * * * *

First day afternoon, 2d of 4th month, a snowy stormy day; it began snowing about 11 this morning, and has been snowing till now—at present it falls quite fast, and is near 5 o'clock.

We have had quite cold weather for several days past, and it is not only cold without, but I thought, at meeting to-day, it was pretty generally cold within, as we had, I think, a pretty hard and silent meeting; but I do not murmur, as I am often comforted in believing, that we are much more favourably dealt with than we deserve; and thou knowest that this will keep the honest above repining or finding fault, hence we cannot be very miserable if we are not altogether as happy as we could wish.

My wife and daughter join me in love to thee and thine, in which I rest thy affectionate friend.

ELIAS HICKS.

TO WILLIAM POOLE, WILMINGTON.

Jericho, 7th mo. 23d, 1820.

BELOVED FRIEND,

Thy acceptable letter of 4th month last came duly to hand, and although the answering of it has been thus long procrastinated, yet, I may assure thee, it has not been occasioned by forgetfulness, or a lack of warm desires about me at times to do it; but my avocations, since receiving it, have been so many and various, that no time previous to the present seemed to open; and, I may add, the incapacity I have generally felt to write any thing that would be in any degree edifying, has led me thus to put off: And now I have begun, I see but little more than just to acknowledge the reception of thy letter, and the satisfaction I had in the perusal of it, as corroborating my sentiments fully.

Thy views in regard to many professing Christians, considering Heaven as a located place, are undoubtedly correct; for surely they are the most absurd and inconsistent: and I should rejoice, could I believe that the members of our Society were all redeemed from that false and vulgar idea. But until mankind come rightly to believe in the inward light, and receive it as a redeeming principle, sufficient for their complete salvation, as they obey it in all its manifestations, they cannot have any just and correct ideas of God, or of the right way of salvation, and, of course, must remain in ignorance as to those things:

For what was declared by Jesus Christ will remain an infallible and unchangeable truth; that "no man knoweth who the Son is, but the Father; and who the Father is, but the Son, and he to whom the Son will reveal him;" and this Son, according to John's testimony, which testimony is truth, is "the true light that lighteth every man that cometh into the world"—and this light was the divine nature that dwelt in the man Jesus Christ, and in which he was one with his Father: so that he could say in truth, "I and my Father are one," for "he that is joined to the Lord, is one spirit."

I may also add, that the anticipation of a visit from you, as noted in some of thy past favours, tended somewhat to the procrastination before alluded to, as hoping to speak with thee face to face; and I still flatter myself with the hope, that I shall not be wholly disappointed.

With love to thee and thine, I conclude, thy affectionate friend. ELIAS HICKS.

TO WILLIAM POOLE, WILMINGTON.

Jericho, 8th mo. 6th, 1820.

BELOVED FRIEND,

Thine, of the 25th ultimo, came duly to hand, and was very acceptable. By it I learn, that mine of last month had not reached thee. This induces me to take my pen, and, with this duplicate, acknowledge not only the reception of thy last, as above, but also the one previous. I was glad to find by its contents, that my views on the two subjects, viz., the Atonement, and what is called the Trinity, were consonant with thine.

Thy views respecting Heaven, or a state of happiness, likewise perfectly agree with mine. Great, and fatal, I fear, are the errors of many, on this important point. For if Heaven is a *place*, it must of course be *local*, and, if this is admitted, it will imply locality in the infinite Jehovah, as Heaven is his place of abode. But the idea appears, to me, too gross for any enlightened, intelligent mind to admit. But when we consider Heaven a state, in which the mind, or rational spirit, must be brought to enjoy complete felicity, then, of course, Heaven is every where to such a soul or spirit ; and so it must be of course to the infinite Jehovah, who fills all the regions of unlimited space ; for where God is, there is Heaven, and no place can be found without him. But none can enjoy this heaven of bliss, but such as are partakers of his Divine nature, which none experience, but such as are born of his spirit.

I have likewise long believed, that the doctrine of election and predestination, is not only false and inconsistent, as standing in eternal contrariety with the divine attributes, but is likewise injurious in its effects to a very considerable portion of Christian professors, and, as such, I have found it my duty to oppose and reprobate it, as being very inimical to man's present and future good. And, although, as thou very justly observes, it has been often combated, and its inconsistency manifested, yet it seems to maintain its ground with many : one cause of which, I have believed, is the cowardice of some, who have been better taught and instructed, some of whom are within our own pale, even ministers and elders, who are ready to criminate their brethren, for publicly opposing and exposing those false doctrines, and such like opinions and tenets of others, although they themselves believe them to be erroneous; but they love to keep up a fair side to all, lest, as they say, they should give offence ; and so balk their testimony, rather than lose the friendship, and, what is still more with them, I fear, the praise of men.

The doctrine of Predestination and Election, with many other erroneous opinions, have their source in mistaken ideas and views, that many people have formed, of the Divine character ; especially as it regards his agency and power, for as he is acknowledged to be Almighty, and all things possible with God, most people, in this unlimited view, think he can do any and every thing, and therefore as whatever is done by this unlimited and Almighty power is right, they assert that in the exercise of this power, he has decreed some to everlasting life, and others to endless misery. And some expressions of the apostle Paul seem to warrant the idea, when considered independent of other of his expressions, viz.: "Therefore hath he mercy on whom he will have mercy, and whom he will be hardeneth," &c. But he has furnished a solution of that, where he says, that "it is impossible for God to lie." And it is no more impossible for him to lie, than it is to do any act contrary to equity and justice; for, I conceive, that power in the Divine Being is always governed by his equity and justice.

But contrary to this, most men, not taking into view his other attributes, suppose that he may and can do any thing, according to his Almighty power, and his doing it makes it right. As a Friend of high standing once argued with me, in regard to his power to save all mankind, that, if it was agreeable to his pleasure, he could convert and save all mankind in a moment. To which I objected the impossibility of the Divine Power, *consistently with his own attributes*, saving any rational, immortal soul, by an act of mere coercion, that had, in its own will and choice, fallen into a state of death and condemnation: for if he could, contrary to the choice and will of one immortal soul, that had fallen by transgression, restore it again, by a mere act of power, against the will of the creature, then I had no doubt but all would be saved, because perfect justice could not, consistently with its own nature, save one and reject another, as all are by him considered in one predicament, that is, in a state of unbelief, that he might alike have mercy upon all.

I hope ere now my letter of last month has come to hand; if so, any further addition, at present, will not be necessary. I should be glad to hear from thee, after the reception of this. Please write by mail, and leave the postage unpaid.

With love to thee and thine, I rest thy affectionate friend.

ELIAS HICKS.

TO PHEBE WILLIS.

Dear Friend,
New York, 9th mo. 23d, 1820.

I have read thy communication with attention and candour and am very sorry that any thing that I have said or done, should have given thee so much trouble or concern. But I can assure thee, that if I am any way faulty in the premises, it is altogether unintended by me; and did I not believe that thou hadst acted intentionally the part of a sincere friend, I should not have noticed thy letter so far as to have made any reply, as the greater part is entirely irrelevant to the subjects, or to my real case. For if people that hear communications, or read writing, will take the liberty to divide and dissect communications, so as to make them say what they were never intended to say, who is the most blameable, the speaker or writer, or hearer or reader?—And this is often done, I believe, by some, on purpose to find fault, though I don't mean to apply this disposition to thee in the least, and yet, I believe, there are many such, and not a few only, in our own society.

Thy greatest concern seems to be what I have said, or what my sentiments are, respecting the Scriptures, and "that I am of a different opinion concerning them, than I was in the early part of my exercises, in a religious way." But this is entirely a mistake, for my belief concerning them has been uniformly the same from my youth up, even before thou hadst seen the light of this world:—for a communication I trust I was led to deliver in a public meeting in Oysterbay, between forty and fifty years since, is very fresh in my remembrance, as it then opened in my mind; that the professors of Christianity generally idolized them as much, or even more, and that to their hurt, than ever the Israelites did the brazen serpent; which simile I then noticed to the people, and gave it as the opening view of my mind, that the time was drawing near when the Lord would raise up Hezekiahs, who should be led to take hold of that idolizing spirit and disposition, and grind it to powder, and it would be swept away into annihilation by the power of Shiloh's Brook, and its remembrance would cease as to its reality. For is it possible that men can be guilty of greater idolatry, than to esteem and hold the Scriptures as the only rule of faith and practice, by which they place them in the very seat of God and worship them as God?—Thus did the Israelites with the Brazen serpent ; and although that had been an instrument of so much good to that people, while they looked beyond it, to the power and presence of God, yet, when they left their hold of his power and presence and looked only to the power of the Image, it did them more hurt than good. The Lord [therefore] saw meet to take it away, although if the Israelites had kept up the true faith in the immediate presence, it might have been continued through their generations until the antitype came, which is Christ, as God in spirit ; but not Christ as man. And to this Christ and God which is one. I ascribe all true divinity, and to those immortal spirits that are in unison with him and partake of his divine nature, but to nothing else do I ascribe any real Divinity ; and surely it cannot be ascribed to any corporal matter, only in similitude or shadow.

The next thing I would observe is, " that I have said that it would be better that they were entirely annihilated." But this is not the case ; as I have never said it, as I remember, except I might when in pleasant conversation with my particular friends, who are in full unity and knew how to understand me, I might have said that I did not know but it might be as well that they were entirely done away, but never expressed this as my settled belief. But I may add, that I sometimes think, that if they are really needful and useful to a few who make a right use of them, yet as, I believe, they are doing great harm to multitudes of others, whether it would not be better for the few who find some comfort and help from them, to give them up for a time, until the wrong use and abuse of them are done away, in the same manner as, in a moral relation, it might be better for the inhabitants of the world, if distillation, and the means of making spiritnous liquors, were, for a time, given up and done away, until the wrong use and abuse of them are done away and forgotten; although it might deprive some of the benefit of them who use those articles only to their comfort and help; for if after a time it might be thought right to renew the making it, when the intemperate use and abuse was done away, it would be a very easy thing for man to make it again.

Just so in respect to the Scriptures; it would be a very easy thing for Divine Wisdom and Goodness to raise up and qualify some of his faithful servants to write scriptures, if he should think best, as good and as competent for the generation in which they lived, and likely would be much better than those written so many hundred years since. For would not some of us be very glad, if we could have immediate access to Paul and some other of the apostles, who contradict one another and sometimes themselves; by which means we might be informed of the true meaning of what they wrote and cause us all to understand them alike.

Another complaint thou mentionest is, "that I counteract our discipline respecting reading the Scriptures," which is also a mistake, as my mind is the same to encourage Friends, especially the younger class, as I have always done in that respect; but I have only endeavoured to counteract the innovations that appear in many Friends, by fixing times beforehand, some at tables, and a great stir there is in England, since they joined the superstitious Bible societies, to bring Friends into a poor, lifeless form of calling their children and families together in the afternoons of the first day of the week, by which they join with others in establishing a seventh-day Sabbath, and by that means would, if given way to, bring the Society under an old Jewish yoke of bondage, which the apostle informs us was even too heavy for them to bear; that all that is good within me abominates such superstitious conduct. I consider our discipline goes no further, and means no more, than that Friends carefully endeavour by every right means to inculcate right ideas of morality and religion in the minds of their children and their families; and believing, that by sometimes reading the Scriptures and other good books at intervals, when nothing better offers, they prove as an auxiliary, they recommend them accordingly; but have fixed no times for it; and which, in my opinion, would be very improper. But that Friends, especially heads of families, live under a right concern, so that they may be ready, whenever they feel their minds secretly drawn into a solemn state, that they yield thereto and wait to be instructed how to act and what to do, and, I believe, were this the case with parents of children, they would often be furnished with a word of counsel and encouragement, although contained in but few expressions, that would be more effectual to the help and encouragement of their children and families, than the reading of all Paul's epistles without being under the right covering ; for it will remain an eternal truth that the letter killeth, but the spirit only giveth life.

I shall notice one thing more in thy letter, that respecting the atonement; and as time will not admit me to write much more, I shall in a short way give thee my view on the subject. And first, I may say that our primitive Friends stopped short in that matter, not for want of faithfulness, but because the day, that was in some respects still dark, would not admit of further openings, because the people could not bear it, therefore it was to be a future work. But to suppose, in this day of advanced light, that the offering of the outward body of Jesus Christ, should purge away spiritual corruption. is entirely inconsistent with the nature and reason of things, as flesh and spirit bear no analogy with each other, and it likewise contradicts our Lord's own doctrines, where he assured the people, that the flesh profiteth nothing, and many other of his sayings it contradicts. And I believe nothing ever did or ever will atone for spiritual corruption, but the entire death of that from whence that corruption originated, which is the corrupt will and the life that the creature has generated in him by that will; both which must be slain by the sword of the spirit, which stands in the way to Eden, and must die and be annihilated on the cross; and this is the true atonement, which the creature cannot effect for himself, only as he submits to the operation of the life and spirit of Christ, which will enable the willing and obedient to do it. And the outward atonement was a figure of it, which, with the outward example of Jesus Christ in his righteous works and pious death, gives strength to be faithful to make this necessary offering and sacrifice unto [God], by which his sins are blotted [out], and he again reconciled to his Maker.

I must now close, as time calls me away; thou must excuse the scribbling way in which I have written, as the shortness of time made it necessary to write in much haste.

In love to you all, I rest thy affectionate friend,

ELIAS HICKS.

TO WILLIAM POOLE, WILMINGTON.

Jericho, 12th mo. 28th, 1820.

DEAR FRIEND,

Thy letter of 8th mo. 21st, and that of 9th mo. 20th, as also a note by Stephen and Edmund Willets, were all duly received. In the latter, thou accountest correctly for my not answering the two foregoing ones, ere now. I left home the 22d of 9th mo. to join a committee of our yearly meeting, in visiting the monthly meetings within its compass, on a concern that originated in said meeting, in consequence of the many deficiencies stated in the reports from the Quarters. Previous to this time, I was for some days taken up in attending on my son-in-law, who had a severe attack of indisposition, and as soon as he mended, so that I felt easy to leave him, I left home, the committee having proceeded a few days previously. He is now pretty well restored to usual health: but he, and his wife and surviving children, have recently had a close trial, in the decease of his youngest daughter Elizabeth, about eight years of age;—she was a precious, promising child. Since which, Sarah, the widow of Isaac Hicks, has had a similar trial, in parting with Mary, her youngest daughter; and although it was like rending bone from bone, yet by labouring after patience and due resignation, they appear again pretty well composed.

What thou farther observes, of Heaven being a state and not a place, is perfectly congenial to my views; and, I conceive, it would be the sentiment of every intelligent person, did they rightly improve the means dispensed to them by a wise and gracious Providence, freed from the shackles of superstition and tradition, which have been riveted on their minds by an erroneous education.

> " 'Tis education forms the common mind,
> Just as the twig is bent, the tree's inclined."

What very great responsibility attaches to parents, and how

very necessary it is for them to use every right means in their power, to establish in the minds of their children, in early life, correct principles and right views, in order that the rising youth under their charge, may be educated in the path of rectitude, and have right ideas of the Divine character.

As to the unchangeable unity of the Divine Power and great First Cause of all created existence, as declared to Moses, viz. " I am, that I am," we must believe he is incapable of division ; for as there can be but one will in Heaven, to render it a state of perfect happiness, so there can be but one will in God, who is the King immortal, invisible; "whose dwelling is in the light, which no man can approach unto ;" and who saith by his prophet Isaiah, "Who hath told this from that time ? Have not I the Lord ? And there is no God else besides me; a just God, and a Saviour; there is none beside me. Look unto me, and be ye saved, all the ends of the earth ; for I am God, and there is none else." Isaiah xlv. 21, 22.

I apprehend that all those erroneous ideas, that have got a place in the minds of most of the professors of Christianity, (some of which thou hast hinted at,) as it respects the unity of God, have arisen from the want of being rightly instructed in the design and purpose of Jehovah, in dispensing that outward figurative covenant, and letter, or written law, to the people of Israel ; and therefore, they have blended it with the Gospel, and endeavour to unite Flesh and Spirit, Heaven and Earth : and which has given rise to most of the disputes and dissension among those that go under the Christian name. Hence the necessity of keeping the two dispensations or covenants separate and entirely distinct, one from the other ; giving to the outward law dispensation all its claim ; that is, all that is outward, all that is visible ; every thing discoverable by the outward or external senses, such as outward circumcision, an outward bondage and captivity, an outward deliverance and salvation, an outward Jerusalem, an outward Heaven, an outward God [or representative of him,] outward legal sins, and an outward Saviour to redeem from those outward legal sins and transgressions;—all these joined together in an outward covenant, make one complete whole, all open to the view of the external senses.

And as this first covenant was outwardly suited to man's animal nature, so likewise the Heaven was suited to man's animal nature; as all its bread and all its wine, and all its water, could only nourish, comfort, and satiate the thirst of man's animal nature, likewise its God was outward and its Saviour outward,—all applying to man's animal nature, and could rise no higher. The apostle Paul correctly declares, "That was not first which is spiritual, but that which is natural, and afterward that which is spiritual;" and he further says, "For if that first covenant had been faultless, then should no place have been sought for the second." Therefore, the first must altogether pass away, not only in part, but the whole, even its heaven; for otherwise there would be no place for the second.

Such was the ignorance and carnality of the Israelites, that is, the generality of them, that they did not look to be instructed in any other way, than through the medium of their external senses; therefore the Lord condescended to meet with them and instruct them in that way through his servants, viz. Moses and the Prophets, and finally by his Son Jesus Christ, who, when he had fulfilled the law of the outward covenant, and all the righteousness of that external testimony, told his disciples, that it was expedient for them that he should go away, assuring them, that if he went not away, the Comforter would not come. By which we clearly discover, that that outward body of Jesus, together with all those outward miracles, wrought in and through that body of flesh, and blood, such as healing the sick, cleansing the leper, causing the blind to see, the deaf to hear, the dumb to speak, the lame to walk, &c., are all a part of the figurative dispensation, and that Jesus of Nazareth, with all his outward, visible, mighty works, acting on the animal bodies of men, was the top-stone of that shadowy dispensation, given only to the people of Israel, as Jesus with all his mighty works was sent but to that people, according to his own declaration; "I am not sent but unto the lost sheep of the house Israel." Matt. xv. 24.

But in and under the Gospel dispensation, the law and covenant is spiritual and universal, written in the heart of every rational being under Heaven; and is, therefore, invisible to all the external senses, and is only manifested by its fruits. And as the law and covenant is spiritual and internal, so likewise, the Messiah and Comforter of the Gospel dispensation is spiritual, and only internally and spiritually known and manifested, and is *universally* manifested to all the children of men, the world over; and by whom the Gospel is preached in every rational creature. For every one that has pierced him shall see him; and as all have pierced him with their sins, so every eye shall see him, inwardly, but not outwardly, for only one man pierced the outward Messiah, but all have pierced the spiritual Messiah, and borne him down as a cart with sheaves, and for which all will have to weep, and howl, either in mercy or judgment.

But some may object and say, who is this spiritual Messiah, or Comforter? To which I answer, he is the Holy Ghost, or Spirit of Truth, the one God, and only self-existing First Cause, by which the worlds were made, and who is the Author of all created existence,—one God over all, and through all, and who graciously condescends to teach his people himself, for the "Lord's children are all taught of the Lord, and in righteousness are they established, and great is the peace of his children." For as the mind or soul of man is visited and acted upon by the Holy Ghost, or invisible power of God, and is united with this divine visiter, and becomes passive to its influence, there is a conception witnessed, and a new birth is brought forth, which the miraculous conception and birth of the blessed Jesus was a figure of. And as Mary nursed and brought up the child Jesus, from his infancy to manhood, by the aid of her husband, so the soul, under the direction of its Heavenly husband, nourishes up this new born child of God, until it comes to the state of a "young man, and has overcome the wicked one;" that is, the old earthly or first nature, by which it witnesses the resurrection from the dead, being raised up from dead works, to serve the living God in newness of life, which is the second birth, whereby it regains paradise. Hence is fulfilled, spiritually, all that Jesus passed through outwardly; the one the figure, and the other the substance; and as Jesus did all, in the outward, by the power of his Heavenly Father, so this spiritual birth likewise does all, by the power of its Heavenly Father. Hence it is one God, working all in all, both in the outward, and in the inward and spiritual Covenant, and hence all is given up to him, and he becomes all in all, one God over all, unchangeably the same, yesterday, to-day, and for ever.

And, although God was in Christ in the fulness, even in that very man called Jesus of Nazareth, and through him, as a proper vehicle, wrought all those mighty works, yet, at the same time, he was also every where else, as he pervades all space, and is a complete, indivisible, omnipresent, unchangeable God, and who only is worthy to be worshipped, honoured, and obeyed by the children of men, throughout all ages, world without end. And as the holy man Jesus possessed the divine nature of his Heavenly Father in the fulness, so his children, born anew by his spirit, become partakers of his divine nature, and, as Paul says, these are "heirs of God and joint-heirs with Christ."

Finally, my dear friend, farewell.

ELIAS HICKS.

TO WILLIAM POOLE, WILMINGTON.

Jericho, 2d mo. 14th, 1821.

DEAR FRIEND,

Thine of the 16th ultimo was duly received, and read with satisfaction; and for my not giving a more full explanation of some of my views, in my last, please to forgive the defect, when I make the following apology, viz.: having been from home, most of the time, for a number of months past, attending to various religious engagements; while absent, many letters were received from a number of my friends, from various parts of the country, and, as thou knowest that friendship is a sacred tie, and involves mutual obligations, I was desirous of filling up my part, by answering my friends' letters seasonably, lest I should incur censure for neglect. I have found it expedient, when thus urged, to forward the first rough draft, most of which are written in haste; this was the case with my last to thee; but believing that thou wouldst construe charitably such omissions, or errors, as I might have overlooked, I ventured to send it, (although not fully satisfied with it myself,) and had rather, if time had permitted, given it another investigation. But it may be best as it is, as thy remarks thereon, may enable me more fully to give thee my views on those subjects not so fully explained.

In regard to an outward [representative of] God, (to open this subject,) it will be proper to have reference to a number of passages of Scripture, and also to begin with the opening of the law dispensation by Moses: " Even he shall be to thee instead of a mouth, and thou shalt be to him instead of God."—Exodus, iv. 16. " I will raise them up a prophet from among their brethren, like unto thee, and will put my words in his mouth; and he shall speak unto them all that I shall command him. And it shall come to pass, that whosoever will not hearken unto my words, which he shall speak in my name, I will require it of him."—Deut. xviii. 18, 19. " For Moses truly said unto the fathers, a prophet shall the Lord your God raise up unto you of your brethren, like unto me; him shall ye hear in all things, whatsoever he shall say unto you. And it shall come to pass, that every soul which will not hear that prophet shall be destroyed from among the people."—Acts, iii. 22, 23.

It is very evident, from these passages and many others, that might be quoted, that the Israelites were reduced to such a state of sensuality and ignorance by their bondage, that the height of their desires, generally, as a body of people, in regard to happiness, was comprehended in a deliverance from their outward captivity, and being placed in the full enjoyment of temporal blessings. And we do not find that any reward was offered as an inducement to their fulfilment of the outward law and commandment, but the outward promised land, with outward advantages, comprehending every thing necessary to complete the happiness of the animal man, as they were faithful to the law and testimony of that dispensation; (although it made none of the comers thereto perfect, as pertaining to the conscience,) and thus we are furnished with a complete figure of the invisible heaven, or state of happiness to the immortal soul; and as the invisible God, who is an eternal, self-existing, undivided. unchangeable spirit—the alone Creator, and First Cause of all things, becomes the sole Ruler and Governor in any immortal soul of man, and the creature becomes wholly passive, here the divine will governs in all things, and this constitutes Heaven to the soul. And although there may be ten thousand, or any other number of souls, yet if all are passive as above, and as meal to the leaven, still, there will be but one will, that rules and governs all; and this state, and this only, constitutes Heaven, where there is perpetual and universal harmony.

And it is clear, from the history of Israel's redemption from Pharaoh's yoke, that this complete passive state of the will, was the principal requisite in effecting their deliverance, for when there was the least appearance of the Israelites' exerting a will, contrary to this entire passive state it immediately stopped their progress. But where there are two contrary, wills, even in a family outwardly, there is always a want of right harmony. Thus when our first parents set up a will, and turned away from that passive state, they ought ever to have stood in to the divine will, God graciously ordained, that the woman should be subject to her husband, and he should rule over her, and this subjection ought to continue until both surrender their wills again to God, as in the beginning, and then male and female are one in him, and then man's sovereignty over the woman is entirely done away, and God's will becomes all in all.

And to make the outward law and dispensation a complete figure of the inward, there must be not only an outward circumcision, but an outward moral law, to regulate the outward conduct, likewise an outward ceremonial religion; and as religion is to pave the way to Heaven, therefore, to make the figure complete, there must be an outward Heaven. This the Jews had, and as Heaven cannot be such without a God, so, as all the rest are outward, there must be an outward God, or representative of God, to complete the figure. And by the foregoing quotations, it appears to me, that Jesus Christ was to be the sole Director and Governor in Israel, during the time of his outward ministration; as all were to hear him, under the penalty of being cut off or destroyed from among the people. And this view seems verified, by the implicit obedience of his disciples to his commands, by which their wills were entirely subdued to his will; and although he often, in his communications, endeavoured to raise their views, yet it is very evident that their attachment was so fixed on the outward manifestation, and their attention so wholly turned to be instructed through the medium of the outward senses, that, I conceive, it requires no forced construction to conclude, he stood in relation to them as a God, in the same sense as their outward good land was a type of Heaven, or an outward Heaven, and their outward Jerusalem as the city of God and type of the spiritual Jerusalem. Jesus Christ, in his *outward manifestation*, was more blest, and abundantly more glorified, than any other man, and was above all, and therefore was the representative of God on earth, visible to the external senses, although the power by which he did all his mighty works, was the invisible power of God, conferred upon him for that end, he being the instrument through whom God, by his power, wrought all those mighty works, that declared him to be the Son of God with power; but it was only the effects of the power, and not the power, that was visible to the outward senses of his disciples and the people.

Hence it was expedient that he should leave them, as to his *visible* appearance, as nothing short of that, could open the way for their reception of the Holy Spirit as a leader. And, in another respect, he stood in place of God to that people, in raising their dead outwardly, and healing all their outward maladies, and forgiving those he healed of all their legal sins, by which he qualified them to enjoy all the privileges and good things of their outward Heaven, and all the happiness it comprehended. In which, he and his mighty works, outwardly wrought, were a complete figure of the work of God on the believing soul; raising it from the death of sin, healing it of all its spiritual maladies, and fitting it for the enjoyment of the divine presence, which is Heaven in the substance. And as he stood in place of God outwardly to Israel, so he was likewise a real and true man, as the scriptures abundantly assure us, being the son, or offspring, of Abraham and David after the flesh; born of an Israelitish virgin, brought up and nursed by his parents, and was subject unto them, until he arrived at the state of manhood; complying faithfully with all the requisitions and ordinances of the Jewish law, by which he justified his Heavenly Father in giving that law and those commandments, proving, by his faithfully fulfilling all of them, that it was within the capacity and power of every Israelite to have done the same, had they faithfully improved the ability they had received for that end; and, by which, he condemned their unfaithfulness. And the last ritual was John's water Baptism, by complying with which, he fulfilled all the righteousness of the outward law and testament, and was then prepared for entering upon his mission by the more full diffusion of the Holy Spirit, which descended upon him as soon as he had finished all the work of shadows, relative to the law state, and which qualified him for his Gospel mission, in which he went forth, clothed with power from on high, preaching the glad tidings of peace and salvation; very few, however, understood or believed his doctrines, the people being so outward and worldly-minded. And, when he had finished his ministration, in which he fulfilled the righteousness of both the law and the Gospel, setting thereby an example to all his followers,—showing them that by faithfulness to the operations of the same spirit and power, according to the measure received, they might do the same; yea, he assured his immediate followers, that even greater works than these which he had done, should they do. When he had thus finished his course, he surrendered himself to his enemies, who crucified him, that is his outward body, which was all they could do. But when he gave up the ghost, his immortal spirit rose superior to all their malice, and ascended immediately into Paradise. This ascension was not visible to the outward senses; his body was laid in the tomb,—and to complete the figure of our redemption, it was raised again outwardly, by which is typified the crucifixion of the old fallen man, with all his deeds, which is effected by the cross of Christ; as saith the apostle, "Know ye not, that so many of us as were baptized into Jesus Christ" that is into the spirit and power of God "were baptized into his death? Therefore we are buried with him by baptism into death; that like as Christ was raised up" outwardly "from the dead by the glory of the Father, even so we also should" be spiritually raised up to "walk in newness of life."

And this outward ascension, as it was manifest to the external senses of his disciples, must have been the outward man, as the immortal spirit of the Saviour never was, nor ever could be, seen by outward eyes;—hence this outward ascension was a complete type of the inward or spiritual ascension, of the immortal soul of man, from an earthly to a heavenly state; by which it regains Paradise, and which must and will be regained by every redeemed soul on this side the grave.

I have the same view as thou hast, in regard to the expression of Jesus on the cross, when he said "It is finished," that it not only related to his finishing and abolishing the law, but equally so to his ministry of the Gospel; for his Gospel doctrines supersede the law, in my opinion, entirely. By these we are required to do good for evil, and when smitten on one cheek to turn the other, to cease from oaths, to love our neighbour as ourselves, and to love our enemies and to pray for them; and to do unto all others as we would they should do unto us, &c. &c.

I conceive that those who have these divine precepts, and understand them, have no absolute need of any part of the law of Moses for instruction. As the inward Divine Law comprehends much more, and its moral precepts are much more extensive and dignified, than those of the outward law and testimony, and therefore, it not only supersedes them, but renders them entirely nugatory to the Christian, as he must know them all fulfilled, before entering the Christian state.

I agree with thee, that unbelief in the creature more generally arises from the want of a willingness to believe plain truths, than from the want of knowing what those truths are, and for the reasons thou hast given, for they find if they yield to plain truth, it will take from them what they want to retain, or stand in the way of what they wish to gain, as in the case of Balaam.

As to my saying there can be but one will in Heaven, I had no other view, than to consider it a state and not a place; and I apprehend that the premises on which I founded the expression, would have explained it in that way; but as I have no copy of that letter, and do not remember the wording of it, I conclude it escaped my notice. But as all my knowledge of Heaven arises from an inward sense in my own soul, and that sweet enjoyment that I sometimes feel and believe to be of a heavenly nature, because it satiates all the desires of the soul, and which is only witnessed when the soul is entirely swallowed up in the Divine will, and wholly passive to the Divine power; this has brought me to believe, that there can be but one will in the soul that is in a heavenly state, or a state in which God only rules and reigns.

Other parts of thy letter that I have not particularly noticed, are in unison with my views, and as my paper is now nearly full, I must draw to a close. Therefore, with the salutation of love to thee, thy dear wife and children, in which my wife joins, I conclude thy affectionate friend, ELIAS HICKS.

TO WILLIAM POOLE, WILMINGTON.

New York, 4th mo. 26th, 1821.

MY DEAR FRIEND,

Thine of the 16th instant was handed to me yesterday by a friend at the close of our Select quarterly meeting, and the sight of it only was truly consoling, having, from a report of thy indisposition that was circulated among us, let in a fear, that I should never see another letter in thy own handwriting :—that truly, my dear friend, the sight of it, and the contents when read, were a feast of fat things, to find that thou wast improving in thy bodily health, but more especially that thy mental tone of reflection, and consideration was returning in its usual vigour. Have we not often cause to say, with David, "What shall we render unto the Lord for all his benefits?" for he often wounds to heal, and sometimes brings a dark shade of affliction and trial over us, purposely for our brightening and more full purification from the dregs of our fallen nature; and to give a more enlightened view of the excellence of his wisdom and power; and of his never failing, unchangeable goodness and mercy; therefore, dear friend, we have abundant cause continually to thank him and take courage.

As to the subject thou mentionest relating to a sentiment of mine, that a preparation for Heaven and happiness must be witnessed on this side the grave; this sentiment I conceive is unchangeably correct; as reason and truth corroborate the scripture testimony, that there is no repentance in the grave, nor are we, from these sources, permitted to believe the Romish error of a purgatory after death, nor have we any ground from reason or revelation to believe we shall have another state of probation when this has passed away; but what most forcibly establishes my belief in the premises, arises from a consideration of the state in which Divine Wisdom has placed his **rational creatures, formed** by his own power, innocent and clean from any defilement; but placed in a state of probation, endued by their gracious Creator with a sufficient portion of wisdom and understanding, if rightly improved under his wise direction and guidance, to rise out of this innocent state, to a state of experience in knowledge and virtue, and, by a steady perseverance in this way, to a state of glorification with their heavenly Father.

And as all man's defilement arises from his own acts, by making a wrong use of his liberty, while endued with sufficient power and understanding to have stood, had he made a right use thereof, so this power and ability is continued to him, to enable and lead him in the way of return, during the time of his probation; but if still he goes on in his wrong choice, and in the gratification of his own will and sensual lust, in opposition to the strivings of the divine light in his mind, during the day of his probation here, he becomes so swallowed up in the vortex of darkness and hardness of heart, that, if hereafter he had an eternity of probation, we have no reason to suppose he would ever change his course. And when man makes his election and choice to do right, and improves his ability so to do, under the direction of his gracious Benefactor, he becomes so wedded to it, and so swallowed up in the Divine Nature, that all the ground of temptation in him is removed and done away; and this agrees with the doctrine of the apostle respecting those who are born of God. Therefore the circumstance of Israel's having enemies to encounter after they entered their promised land, will not hold good as a figure to the righteous after death, but may, in some degree, while passing through this scene of trial; because it would prove too much, as Israel so revolted after they had entered, as to become entirely dispossessed; which, to admit as a figure to those who die in a heavenly state, or state of acceptance with God, that they might afterwards fall away, or be farther tried, would be a cause of great discouragement, and tend to destroy all our hope. And although I believe, that the righteous after death are established beyond the reach of danger, or trial, yet not beyond a state of continual advancement in glory and joy. For, as by experience, we learn that the continued possession and enjoyment of any favour or blessing, tends to lessen, in some degree, the happiness we derive from it; so the continued accession of new favours, tends greatly to augment our happiness. Therefore, as the Divine perfections are infinite, and without end, I consider it altogether reasonable to suppose, that God, in his unsearchable wisdom and goodness, will continually advance his dedicated children and servants, in the new enjoyments of his infinite perfection, through all the eternal ages.

I this morning received thy letter of the 10th instant, which was also acceptable.

My dear wife has been a house-keeper most of the past winter and spring, through bodily indisposition, though mostly able to be about house; the rest of my family, and those of our children, are in usual health. Thou mentionest a little view of a visit to us, but rather despairs of effecting it. But should thy health improve, and way open for it, it would be very cordial to us, and might be a real improvement to thy state of bodily health.

I may now draw to a close, and, in much love and affection to thyself, wife, and children, rest thy sympathizing friend.

ELIAS HICKS.

AN ESSAY

ON THE BIRTH AND OFFICES OF CHRIST.

Wisdom is justified of her children—The fulfilment of the Law, and the Introduction of the Gospel, &c.

THE following prophecies and scripture testimonies, concerning Jesus of Nazareth, fully show, that he was born of the Virgin Mary, and brought up and educated in all the precepts, statutes, and commands of the law, given through Moses to Israel, by the pious care of his mother, and Joseph her husband, and was subject and obedient to them until he arrived to man's estate; thereby setting a perfect example to children, agreeably to the requirings of their law. And, after he had arrived to the state of manhood, he entered upon, and performed, all the duties of that covenant, as a real, true Israelite; fulfilling all the commandments and ordinances of their law, blameless; by which he set a perfect example to all the Israelites, showing them, how by faithfulness to the manifested will of the Heavenly Father, and a right improvement of the ability received from him for that end, they might likewise have fulfilled all the righteousness thereof as he had done. And by which, he condemned their unfaithfulness and hardness of heart; as we believe it is impossible, that the all-gracious Creator, should ever require any thing of his rational creation but what he furnishes them with ample ability to perform, as they are faithful to the clear manifestations of his light in their own hearts.

The first Prophecy that appears clear on this subject, is that of Jacob, when blessing his sons: "The sceptre shall not depart from Judah, nor a law-giver from between his feet, until Shiloh come; and unto him shall the gathering of the people be."—Gen. xlix. 10. What an excellent display of infinite wisdom, is to be seen in the manner in which God hath meted out his varied dispensations, as a means for the recovery of his poor lost creature man from the bondage of sin and death; not opening two dispensations at the same time, nor a new one, until the former is at an end. Neither doth he require his servants to do two things, or walk two ways at once, although both are right; but every thing singly in its right place and time, and this wisely, to prevent all confusion. As where there are two heads of equal power, or two wills to be satisfied, in a family or nation, there will always be confusion. And, therefore, the Shiloh of Israel was not to come, until the outward sceptre, and last King of Israel, that sprang from Judah's loins, should first pass away; which was accomplished in the death of Herod, who died not long after the birth of Jesus; and this in order that the people should have but one head to look to. For, if there were two, their ideas would be confused; and it shows the correctness of the parable, that no man can serve two masters.

The second Prophecy is that of Moses, confirming the former: "The Lord thy God will raise up unto thee a Prophet from the midst of thee, of thy brethren, like unto me; unto him ye shall hearken." " I will raise them up a Prophet from among their brethren, like unto thee, and will put my words in his mouth, and he shall speak unto them, all that I shall command him."—Deut. xviii. 15, 18. "Therefore the Lord himself shall give you a sign; behold, a virgin shall conceive and bear a son, and shall call his name Emanuel."— Isaiah, vii. 14. " Behold my servant whom I uphold, mine Elect in whom my soul delighteth; I have put my spirit upon him: he shall bring forth judgment to the Gentiles."—Isaiah, xlii. 1. " Behold my servant whom I have chosen; my beloved, in whom my soul is well pleased; I will put my spirit upon him: he shall show judgment to the Gentiles."— Mat. xii. 18. " Philip findeth Nathaniel, and saith unto him, we have found him of whom Moses in the law and the Prophets did write, Jesus of Nazareth, the son of Joseph."— John, i. 45. " Ye men of Israel, hear these words; Jesus of Nazareth, a man approved of God, among you, by miracles and wonders and signs, which God did by him in the midst of you, as ye yourselves also know."—Acts ii. 22.

This brings us to the end of the outward advent and ministration of the Jewish Messiah; I say Jewish Messiah, because he was not permitted to visit, outwardly, the Gentile nations, in that outward nature, in which he was a complete Israelite, proceeding from the loins of Abraham and David, as the Scriptures clearly testify. Nor did he suffer his disciples to do it, when he sent them forth to preach, while he was personally with them. Which shows that the end of his coming, agreeably to the foregoing prophecies, was, first, as a real Israelite, to prove, by fulfilling all the righteousness of their outward law and covenant, that the Lord was not a hard master, by requiring obedience to the outward statutes and judgments that he had given them to perform, and to put an end to that covenant, and do it away; as was effected when he gave up his outward or bodily life on the cross, saying, it is finished. And secondly, after having finished the law, John's water baptism being the last ritual he had to conform to, he immediately after this received the descendings of the Holy Spirit of God upon him, agreeably to the above prophecy of Isaiah, by which he became a partaker of the Divine Nature of his heavenly Father, and by this spiritual birth, became the Son of God with power, and thereby fully qualified for his Gospel mission, and went forth, clothed with the spirit and power of God, preaching the Gospel to the poor. Hence we see another instance of the consummate wisdom of the Highest, in sending his beloved Son, qualified only as a real and true Israelite, first to fulfil, in that state, all the righteousness of the law, before the full pouring forth of the Holy Spirit upon him, which is the peculiar privilege of the Gospel state; but which no individual is prepared to receive, until, like the blessed Jesus, he has fulfilled all the righteousness of the moral law. For had this full diffusion of the spirit been conferred upon him, while engaged in the fulfilment of that outward covenant, he would not have been any example to that people, as it would have proved that it required greater ability than the Israelites had received, to perform the same; and thereby impeach the Lord of being a hard master, in requiring more than he had given them ability to perform.

But by withholding this full diffusion of the spirit, until he had fulfilled the law of the outward covenant, with the same ability that every Israelite had conferred upon him for the same purpose, he thereby justifies his heavenly Father, and proves his impartiality towards the children of men, and stands as a perfect example, in that relation, to all succeeding ages, who come to the knowledge of it. And then by the pouring forth of his spirit upon him, he shows his readiness to do the same to every other of his rational creation, according to their several needs, to enable them to fulfil, as Jesus has done, all the righteousness of the Gospel: who have previously come up in the same way of faithfulness in fulfilling the righteousness of the law.

And when he had finished his outward ministration, he then gave himself up to the power of his enemies, although it was a very severe and trying baptism for his human nature to bear, having a clear prospect of his sufferings and death, saying "O my Father, if it be possible, let this cup pass from me: nevertheless, not as I will, but as thou wilt." By his willing surrender to his heavenly Father's will, he has set us a perfect example, that we should count nothing too dear to surrender, not even our bodily lives, for the Gospel's sake and the testimony of a good conscience.

And when he had sealed his testimony with his blood, outwardly, he was raised up again, by the power of God, and showed himself to his disconsolate disciples, who were now witnessing the fast he had foretold them of. Mat. ix. 15 Mark ii. 19, 20. And after having several times shown himself to them, and instructed them further in those things relating to the Gospel dispensation, he left them his farewell command, to tarry at the city of Jerusalem, until they should receive power from on high, "For John," says he, "truly baptized with water; but ye shall be baptized with the Holy Ghost, not many days hence." "But ye shall receive power after that the Holy Ghost is come upon you: and ye shall" then, but not till then, "be witnesses unto me both in Jerusalem and in all Judea, and in Samaria, and unto the uttermost parts of the earth."

Hence we have the example and testimony of Jesus Christ and his disciples; who never attempted to preach the Gospel until they had received the Holy Ghost, to prove that nothing short of the Holy Spirit of God, immediately received, ever did, or ever can qualify any man to preach the Gospel. Therefore, if any undertake to do it, without this qualification, they ought all to be considered as intruders, and ministers of Anti-Christ.

For it is "not by might, nor by power," that depend upon the associations or wisdom and science of men, nor yet by their money, though the professed ministers of Christendom, who preach for hire and divine for money, seem to consider the latter the principal thing by which the Gospel and Kingdom of peace is to be exalted and advanced in the earth, " but by my Spirit, saith the Lord ;" that is, by the little stone that Nebuchadnezzar saw cut out of the mountain without hands, viz. without the help, the power, the wisdom, or contrivance of any man, or any associations of men. And this little stone, that brake in pieces, that mighty image that Nebuchadnezzar saw in his dream, was not cut out, nor sent into the world, until all the outward Kingdoms that God had set up and finished had come to an end ; then, in the fulness of time, he came to effect the glorious end of doing away, and utterly destroying, all the Kingdoms of the world, that man sets up in his own wisdom and power, for his own glory and aggrandizement.

Take it in the prophet's words, Daniel ii. 44, 45, " And in the days of these kings, shall the God of Heaven set up a Kingdom, which shall never be destroyed ; and the Kingdom shall not be left to other people," that is, not to those who would make use of it to their own glory and aggrandizement, " but it shall break in pieces and consume all these Kingdoms, and it shall stand for ever. Forasmuch as thou sawest that the stone was cut out of the mountain without hands, and that it brake in pieces the iron, the brass, the clay, the silver, and the gold ; the Great God hath made known to the king, what shall come to pass hereafter ; and the dream is certain, and the interpretation thereof sure."

TO WILLIAM POOLE, WILMINGTON.

Jericho, 7th mo. 7th, 1821.

DEAR FRIEND,

Thy acceptable letter of the 10th ult. was duly received, and the information it contained of the continued improvement of thy health, was very satisfactory ; although it also contained some alloy, by stating the indisposition thy wife has lately experienced—but it was grateful to hear she was better. And seeing this is allotted to all mortals, in passing through this checkered scene, I know of no way better for us, than continually to endeavour quietly to submit, and cheerfully to acquiesce in the allotments of a Gracious Providence, who certainly knows what is best for his creatures; and does not afflict willingly nor grieve the children of men, but designs that all his dispensations, however various, shall work together for their real good, and will accomplish his design to all those who love him and keep his commandments.

Therefore, it behooves us, at all times, to endeavour to be in the condition in which we can continually thank God and take courage, for this is well pleasing to him.

The account of the burning of my son-in-law's barn by lightning, was correct. It being a providential circumstance, was quietly acquiesced in; and especially when we consider, that had it not been for the heavy rain that fell at the time, there is no doubt but that his house and mine, together with all my other buildings, must have fallen a sacrifice to the devouring flames; as the wind sat directly to them, and they were for some time almost continually more or less covered, as I was informed by those present, with large flakes of fire; but the rain falling so fast, they did not kindle so as to do any damage. It happened when we were from home, attending our yearly meeting.

I also received the papers thou alludest to, and I am really astonished at the ignorance and weakness of the individual who, under the signature of Paul, has made a public attack upon our Society, and especially when we consider the manner of his movements, in his fourth number. In reply to Amicus, he says, "To his essay I have the same objection, as to the Society of which he is a member. He makes too much of little things; is employed, like the Pharisees of old, in tything mint, anise, and cummin, and has omitted the weightier matters of the law:" but what these weightier matters of the law are, he omits telling us, because they are directly in opposition to his purpose. And therefore, after passing on a little, he brings in his substitutes for them. And what are they? Why, nothing more or less, than two mere, old, wornout, antiquated ceremonies of the Jewish law, water baptism and the Jewish Passover, which he seems to put in place of justice, mercy, and faith, the principal essential things, both of Law and Gospel. But what subterfuges will hirelings flee to, to support their hire! for in the beginning of his catalogue of non-essentials, (that nevertheless seem uppermost in his mind,) is this: "Whether the ministry be supported by previous or subsequent, by express or implied contract." These he supposes parallel with the Jews' tithing mint, anise, and cummin; and although it may be non-essential to him, which of those ways is substituted, provided his pay for preaching is secured to him; yet, let us suppose that none of those ways were substituted to ensure the wages of the hireling; would he then consider it non-essential whether he was paid or not, and was left to the necessity of preaching freely, as Jesus commanded, and as he and his disciples practised? I apprehend he would then consider it essential, as I do tything of mint, anise, and cummin, in the days of the outward advent of Jesus Christ: even more essential than what he calls, though very untruly, the sealing ordinances of the Gospel, viz. water baptism, and the partaking of a little bread and wine, corporeal things, that many wicked men partake of in abundance to their own hurt. And yet I fear that many of those who partake of them in a ceremonial way, as a religious act, are really injured by it, as it keeps them under bondage to ignorance and superstition, and therefore becomes wounding to their immortal souls.

The plain grammatical language of thee and thou, to a single person, being the only correct and plain language of truth and of the Scriptures, I deem much more essential than water baptism, or the partaking of bread and wine in a ceremonial way.

First, It is the only language of plain truth, and the holy men of old use it throughout the Scriptures, which I consider an unequivocal testimony of its essentiality; because it is contrary to the reason and nature of things to suppose that they should have always thus kept to it, had they not thought it essential.

Secondly, I have found it to be the testimony, may I not say the undeviating testimony, of every class of Christian professors I have ever conversed with, that water baptism, and what is called the Supper, are non-essentials. And they say, moreover, that they do not make use of them as things essential; and allow that those who do not use them, may be effectually saved without them, if they attend to those things that are essential, viz. justice, mercy, and faith.

And I further assert, that the tything of mint, anise, and cummin, under the Jewish dispensation, was much more essential to that people, than water baptism, or the ceremony of the Supper, is to the Christian; as they can bear no other comparison than that the first was essential, and the latter is non-essential. And when Jesus Christ reprehended the scribes and Pharisees, for tything mint, &c., it was not because it was non-essential to them, but because they preferred the shadow to the substance; which the closing paragraph on that subject clearly proves, viz. " These ought ye to have done, and not to leave the other undone." Matt. xxiii. 23.

And I have often been surprised at the ignorance of many of the advocates for water baptism, in their bringing forward the apostle Paul, as a witness on its behalf; seeing he has left on record such a plain and unequivocal testimony against the use of it. " I thank God that I baptized none of you but Crispus and Gaius; lest any should say that I had baptized in mine own name. And I baptized also the household of Stephanus: besides, I know not whether I baptized any other. For Christ sent me not to baptize, but to preach the Gospel: not with wisdom of words, lest the cross of Christ should be made of none effect." 1 Cor. i. 14, 15, 16, 17.

Now if it be as Paul declares, that Christ sent him not to baptize, how can any real or pretended minister of the Gospel presume that he has any commission therefor. As I understand, they found their principal authority for baptizing with water, on the 19th verse of 28th chapter of Matthew. And if that command is considered to have binding authority on any one of the ministers of Christ's Gospel, it must certainly be binding on every other, as it comprehended all his disciples. Hence if any one of his ministers is brought under a binding obligation, from that command, to baptize with water, every other must lie under the like obligation, and, of course, Paul among the rest; who nevertheless assures us, he was under no such obligation, and manifested his sorrow for having spent the little time he did, about such a non-essential thing; believing, no doubt, as I do, that it is impossible that a wise and holy God should at any time command his rational creature, man, to do a non-essential act, as it would cast an indignity upon his Divine character.

I further note what thou observes of my being attacked on every side, by the advocates of Bible and Missionary Societies, and a hireling ministry. I freely acknowledge it is so, and was this all I had to suffer, I should account it a very light thing. But I have been assailed by those of our own household, and that without any reasonable cause; and even some with whom, in days past, I have taken sweet counsel; but who, by dwelling on back ground, have too much settled on their lees: and when any are called to advance reformation, and exalt truth's testimony over tradition and error, they cry out novelty! and schism! and seem disposed, unless these settle down with them on their beds of ease, and rest in the labours of those who have gone before, to prepare war against them, and persecute them, as did the priests and rulers in Israel formerly persecute and kill their prophets, and even Jesus Christ. And no doubt, as these rise up, in the same spirit, in the present day, to oppose the progress of truth, they will as effectually, in a spiritual sense, kill the prophets, as the Jews did theirs outwardly, that is, they will so discourage and block up the way of the Lord's messengers among the people, by their opposition, as to cause them to cease from their labours, seeing no way to go forward: for the time appears to have come, long since spoken of, when men "will not endure sound doctrine," and even is come home to us, in this favoured Society, and "if they do these things in a green tree, what shall be done in the dry?" Is it not with us, as it was with the Lord's people formerly, when the prophet was led thus to exclaim, "Let the priests, the ministers of the Lord, weep between the porch and the altar, and let them say, Spare thy people, O Lord, and give not thy heritage to reproach, that the heathen should rule over them: wherefore should they say among the people, where is their God?" Joel ii. 17.

I must now draw to a close, lest my letter should be too long and tedious; and as the time is near at hand for the mail to close, I have no time to copy, therefore please to excuse the errors that may occur, as I send the first draft.

With love to you all, I rest thy sympathizing friend.

ELIAS HICKS.

TO WILLIAM POOLE, WILMINGTON.

Jericho, 12th mo. 26th, 1821.

MY DEAR FRIEND,

Thy letter of 10th mo. and that of 12th mo. 1st, are now before me. I have read them with satisfaction and interest, several different times, and with a view to have answered them ere now; but before I set pen to paper something has intervened, which diverted me from it until the present time.

I conclude my last letter to thee has miscarried, as thou hast not noted the reception of it, and as I seldom have time to copy my letters, I do not now remember the time of its date.

In regard to the controversy between Paul and Amicus, I am willing to say to the latter, I wish him good speed, and that Paul, according to my judgment, has gained no advantage over him; but on the contrary, doubt not, as Amicus keeps a single eye to the right director, he will maintain and advance the cause of truth. And I am led to hope, that through this and some other like controversial investigations, now going on with us and in some other places, that some of the main pillars of anti-christ's kingdom will be shaken to their very base.

I remember in one of thy former communications, thou mentioned hearing of some dissension among Friends in New England, and requested, if I was in possession of the cause, I would inform thee of it. And although I have made inquiry at different times in regard thereto, I have not found any thing worthy of notice, so far as to trouble thee with it; but thy request at the present time being brought to remembrance, I felt a freedom to mention two circumstances that, I believe, have given occasion for a diversity of sentiment among some Friends in the east, and which, I apprehend, they have suffered to rise too high, for want of abiding in the everlasting patience.

The first was occasioned by a new member, who had, at his request, been admitted into Society. He was one who stood high in a political point of view among the people, having filled several high offices, both in the civil and military department, in pretty early life; but being made sensible of the impropriety of those things, and the inconsistency of such a course of life with the precepts of the Gospel, he made a full and pretty sudden surrender of all his worldly honours and offices, and turned his attention towards Friends, and soon became a member, and not long after began to speak in public meetings, and was pretty well approved by some Friends of the foremost class: some others were fearful he was running too fast, and for want of prudence they manifested their different views to him, which raised a jealousy in his mind towards those he considered as his opposers, which tended very much to break the unity in several of their meetings. Before this disturbance subsided, the other made its appearance, which was in this wise: A certain young man, whom the Presbyterian association had admitted into one of their seminaries of learning near Providence, in order to be educated for the ministry, on the charity funds of the society under their control, as I have understood; having his eyes opened to see the inconsistency of their doctrines, he left them and turned his attention towards Friends, and occasionally attended their meetings, and manifested a very orderly and sober life. Apprehending it right to inform his old friends of the reasons for leaving them, he took up his pen and in a pamphlet, which he styled the Celestial Magnet, gave them his reasons, founded on scripture testimony, and showed that the Divine light in the soul of man is a sure guide and sufficient teacher in the way of salvation, without the necessity of any other means, as man gives up in full obedience thereto. This gave great umbrage to his old friends. In addition to this, he wrote four other pamphlets under the same signature; all which, through the kindness of a friend, I had the opportunity of reading.

The first and the third, I considered to manifest pretty clear evidence that his mind, in a degree, had been divinely opened. His second number, as I had but a slight opportunity of considering it, I have entirely forgot the contents of; but his fourth and fifth numbers I should have been much better pleased if they had never been written. These pamphlets have also been a bone of contention among some Friends, not only in the east, but even among some this way; which, in a clear manner, evidences the exceeding weak state of our Society.

Neither of these cases, I conceive, was of moment sufficient to unsettle the minds of Friends; the latter especially. The young man not being a member, Friends were not amenable for his conduct, and he in no wise accountable to them. And yet, some Friends have let themselves out against him in a very harsh manner, setting him down publicly as a deist, and his book a deistical performance and a very pernicious one. Some of these have never seen him or his book, but are altogether acting on mere hearsay, which I consider a stain upon Society. If I should meet with the first and third numbers, I intend to forward them for thy perusal.

Some things, that have been subjects of our former communications, have caused me considerable exercise, by the opposition I have met with from some, who may be accounted wise in their own eyes. Such as that of Heaven being a state and not a place; and also the Garden of Eden being a state and condition of the soul, in union and communion with its Maker, rather than a mere local spot on the surface of this earth; and that of Jesus of Nazareth being a real and true man, and placed in a state of probation as we are, having our real and true nature, *as to his manhood*, and tempted in all points as we are, yet by his faithfulness to his Heavenly Father he overcame every temptation and lived free from sin, and by the pouring forth of the divine spirit upon him, and he uniting with it, he became a partaker of the divine nature, and was born of God, and was then the Son of God with power: as no created being can be, *strictly speaking*, a son of God, but by being born of the spirit of God.

But spirit and corporeal matter cannot unite together and produce a birth; but the spirit of God can command matter and *create* material substances, such as an animal man, &c.; as in the case of the blessed Jesus. But a real son of God is only produced by a union of the spirit of God with the rational spirit of man; as these are united in marriage covenant, there is a birth brought forth: this is the new birth that Jesus spake of to Nicodemus, and this is that which is born of God, and cannot sin, as saith the apostle, "Whosoever is born of God doth not commit sin, for his seed remaineth in him; and he cannot sin, because he is born of God." This is that son that knoweth the father, as Jesus Christ said. This is the Christ, or Son of God, that Paul travailed in birth, or in prayer, that he might be formed in the souls of his newly converted children. This is that child born, and son given, that the prophet speaks of, and which is born in every converted soul, and upon whose shoulders the government rests; and here now is known the wonderful Counsellor, the mighty God, the everlasting Father, and Prince of Peace. Here it is that the Father and the Son are one, and now it is that the Son becomes the head of all principalities and powers, thrones and dominions, and having conquered all, even death, the last enemy, the Son surrenders all up to the Father, and God becomes all in all. All this must be known, and is known, in every truly redeemed and completely saved soul. Here it is that God only reigns, and all the hosts of Heaven are made to rejoice with this holy anthem, without any corporeal jar or noise, "Alleluia, for the Lord God omnipotent reigneth." Here we are brought to understand Paul, where he says, "Wherefore, henceforth know we no man after the flesh: yea, though we have known Christ after the flesh, yet now henceforth know we him no more." All external evidences are at an end, by the revelation of the Father, by and through the Son, or this new birth of the spirit of God in the soul of man, which knows and calls God, Father, and is in unity and oneness with him. Here the mystery of our salvation is opened by the pure, unchangeable light in the soul, and becomes as self-evident as the most plain and simple truth, on which the soul rests with entire confidence, as on a rock that cannot be shaken; against which, Jesus said, "the gates of hell shall not prevail."

I should like to have thy views on the foregoing subjects, when opportunity offers.

In love to thee and thine, I rest thy affectionate friend.

ELIAS HICKS.

TO WILLIAM WHARTON.

Jericho, 1st mo. 14th, 1822.

DEAR FRIEND,

Thine of last month was duly received and was very acceptable. It is, as thou justly observes, a day of much inquiry, and happy would it be for them did the members of our highly professing society keep a single eye to our foundation principle, the light within, and walk agreeably to its dictates, and cease from all speculation and disputation on nonessentials, which comprehend every thing that has no other foundation of belief than external evidence, which never did, nor ever can give a true and living faith in God, nor manifest to us his will relating to the salvation of the soul; for this is reserved as the sole privilege of the light within, or spirit of truth, which teacheth us all things that we need to know in the way and work of our salvation; and as we obey him he leadeth into all truth, and is the only infallible teacher. And all those who walk by this light are delivered from all the bonds and shackles of tradition and superstition, and place no dependance on any outward sacrifices or offerings, not even on the offering of Jesus Christ on the outward wooden cross, except as an example of faithfulness to the requirings of divine truth; being strengthened and encouraged thereby to surrender our lives as a willing offering to God, as he did, rather than balk our testimony to his truth. Were the members of our Society generally brought into this state, it might then be said of us as Jesus said of his disciples, " Ye are the light of the world," and others seeing our good works, would have cause on our behalf to glorify our Heavenly Father; but a state very dissimilar to this, I fear, is more consonant with our present state, even like that the apostle expressed concerning Israel, that blindness in part had happened to them; for many, yea, very many of our society appear to be little more than traditional members, being very void of any right sense of true spiritual religion, and doating about names and historical testimonies, which never can produce that true and living faith that works by Love to the purifying of the heart; which is the gift of God, created in the soul of man by his faithfully attending to the teachings of his grace or light within, and by nothing else. But many among us, for want of a right and entire dependance on this guide, are too much settling in a form of godliness, without experiencing the power thereof to raise them out of their traditional death. These are as dead weights, that greatly hinder the progress of right reformation; and are in the same spirit with the scribes and Pharisees of old, ready to rise up in opposition to every right and necessary step for promoting the righteous cause of truth in the earth. These are such as cry out "heresy," against those whom the Lord is raising up and qualifying by his grace to advance his kingdom of peace and righteousness in the earth, branding them with the degrading epithet of being the disturbers of the church's peace, whilst the beam is in their own eye.

In love I conclude, thy friend.

ELIAS HICKS.

TO WILLIAM WHARTON.

Jericho, 2d mo. 18th, 1822.

My Dear Friends William & D. F. Wharton,

Dear D's. very acceptable letter of the 3d instant was duly received. Your opening this medium of correspondence is truly grateful to my best feelings, as my sympathy is often strongly excited with and toward the youth and younger members of our Society, attended with a hope that, through the powerful influence of divine love, and the inspirings of divine light in their minds, many of them will be strengthened, as they are faithful thereunto, to break asunder the strong bands of tradition and education, under the implicit leading of which our poor Society has been doing little more for a century past than, like Israel of old, encompassing a mountain in the wilderness, without making any advancement.

And as what was written aforetime was written for our learning, let not my young friends be dismayed, although they should see but here and there one of their elderly friends who are enough alive in the travel to lead the way for them, when the command is heard in the camp, go forward, for ye have tarried long enough in this mountain. Seeing that among the thousands of Israel, none but their leader, Moses, and good Joshua and Caleb, were prepared to go forth and lead the youthful army; the rest died in the place where they were, just going the round of former experience.

I noticed the addition to your little family, and, if consistent with Divine Wisdom, may it increase to many more, and by your faithfulness to the pointings of truth, may they be brought up in the nurture and admonition of the Lord, and grow up like olive plants about your table; then will they be a blessing and a crown to you.

Except my wife and myself, who are more and more feeling the infirmities of age increasing upon us, with some attendant bodily pains, which nevertheless does not hinder our being about amongst our friends, all the branches of our family are in usual health.

Please to present my love to your father, my truly valued friend, S. R. Fisher; to your sister Sarah and brother Thomas; and with a large share to yourselves, I conclude affectionately, your friend.

ELIAS HICKS.

TO WILLIAM POOLE, WILMINGTON.

Jericho, 11h mo. 8th, 1822.

My Dear Friend,

Thine of the 3d ult. was duly received, and is now before me: I have perused it several times. It came to hand in a favourable time to excite my sympathy, as I was then and for some time after, under very considerable bodily affliction. Add to that, the many false reports and unjust insinuations that have been spread concerning me. I have been slandered, reviled, and defamed, by pulpit, press, and talk, not only by open opposers, but also by some more privately, who profess to be my friends, terming me a deist, a seducer, socinian, unitarian, denying the divinity of Christ the Saviour, and what not. And all because I have faithfully and honestly borne testimony against those false and unscriptural, though generally acknowledged and applauded doctrines, of one God subsisting in three distinct and separate persons; the impossibility of God's pardoning sinners without a plenary satisfaction; and the justification of impure persons by an imputative righteousness, &c.

That which, as I am informed, is the principal reason of the great noise which hath sounded in so many ears of late, is, my denying the divinity of Christ, and divesting him of his eternal God-head, which has been most busily suggested, as well as maliciously insinuated among the people; but which is one of the greatest falsehoods that the malicious spirit of the slanderer ever fabricated. The Proverbs, which as most agree intend Christ the Saviour, speak in this manner, (viii. 15, 20, 23); "By me kings reign, and princes decree justice." "I (wisdom) lead in the way of righteousness; in the midst of the paths of judgment, I was set up from everlasting." To which Paul alludes, (1 Cor. i. 24), "Unto them which are called," we preach "Christ the power of God, and the wisdom of God." Which doctrine, thousands can bear me witness, I have often held forth and urged on my hearers, in my public communications, and from whence I conclude, that if Christ is the power of God, and wisdom of God, then certainly Christ the Saviour is God, in as much as it is impossible God's power and wisdom should be distinct or divided from himself: Therefore Christ is not distinct from God, but entirely that same God, and which the Evangelist also asserts concerning Christ, the word, that was in the beginning with God and was God.

David and Isaiah speak thus: "The Lord is my light and my salvation:"—" I will also give thee for a light to the Gentiles;" and to the Church, he says,—For "the Lord shall be unto thee an everlasting light." From which plain testimonies, I assert the unity of God and Christ; although nominally distinguished, yet essentially the same Divine light; and I have ever believed that the divinity of God and of Christ are one—but I do not believe in two divinities.

The foregoing, thou will observe, is mostly taken from "Innocency with her open face," written by William Penn, who, in stating his own case and sentiments, has clearly described mine.

I will now return to thy letter, and in near sympathy and fellow feeling with thee, in thy present exercises and tribulations, and in order for thy encouragement, inform thee of my place of retreat and sure refuge, in times of trouble; when the old accuser lays close siege to me, in order to raise in me, if possible, a spirit of murmuring, that he might lead me to despair of the never-failing mercies of our all-sufficient Helper. In order to blunt the sharpest darts of the enemy, I enter into a close and inward investigation of my deepest sufferings, to know, with clearness, whether they are real or only imaginary. By this search, I often find the enemy has greatly exaggerated them; and having obtained a pretty correct view of them, I then compare them with my present deserts, and here all my uneasiness subsides; as I find myself better dealt with than I really deserve, even in the midst of my sharpest conflicts. I then take a more enlarged view of my friends and fellow creatures around me, and I see none so happy and free from trouble as to induce me, even if it were possible, to change situations with them: but I see many others, whose troubles appear much greater than mine, although as deserving an exemption therefrom as myself. By this time, thou wilt begin to discover, my state of suffering and sorrow is turned to a state of rejoicing, and in which I am renewedly strengthened to thank God and take courage: and this I crave, in sympathetic desire, through the divine blessing, may be thy happy experience, my dear tribulated friend.

Thou seemest somewhat alarmed at the stir and dissension

that are manifested in divers parts of our favoured, though at the same time, lukewarm and lethargic Society. But I account it rather a favour, as it is only when Zion travaileth, that she bringeth forth her healthy and well-favoured children; and, in my view, it seems like one of those times the apostle alludes to where he says, "Yet once more I shake not the earth only, but also Heaven." And is not the heaven of our Society become almost like the old Jews' heaven, a mere traditional one ? "And this word, Yet once more, signifieth the removing of those things that are shaken," or may be shaken, "as of things that are made, that those things which cannot be shaken, may remain."

And a great many of the members of our Society, are not only little more than traditional ones, but some of them seem even to be cleaving to some of the old doctrines of the Romish Church, that truth and righteousness cannot warrant nor approve; and I hope that these shakings will remove those quite out of the way, by opening their unsoundness and inconsistency to the right-minded and honest seekers in Society, whose immortal spirits cannot be satisfied on the old, mouldy crumbs of tradition and education.

My wife joins me in love to thee and thine, and in which I rest thy sympathizing and affectionate friend.

ELIAS HICKS.

TO EDWARD HICKS, NEWTOWN, PENN.

DEAR FRIEND, *Jericho, 4th mo. 9th,* 1822.

I have been for a considerable time past, almost every day, anticipating the pleasure of communing with my beloved friend Edward Hicks, face to face. This I was induced to expect, by information received both by letter and verbal communication, that he had obtained the concurrence of his friends to make another transit on some part of the disk of poor Long Island; and as my information appeared very correct, it made the disappointment greater. And as days, and weeks, and even months, passed away without meeting the anticipated gratification, I was led to query with myself, what should be the cause, and whether the remembrance of the Bulls of Bashan, or the scurrilous reports of long-tongued lying fame, had shut up the way. But while ruminating on those things, I was recently, or not very long since, informed, that an accident by fire, had consumed his covert of temporal amusement, and place of industry, (where, like Paul of old, he laboured with his hands for his own and his family's comfortable support,) as also his implements for carrying on his work, with other materials of considerable amount, and therefore not a small loss. Add to that, I have been lately informed, that while engaged in labour in his master's vineyard, he was seized with such bodily affliction as to unfit him, for the present, to proceed in his religious labours, and also to render him unable for bodily exercise and labouring with his hands in his workshop, had it escaped from the flames.

Now, my dear friend, are not these lessons of very deep instruction? They show how very unfit and incapable we are of laying out, or making any appointments of our own, that will insure to us any real good, either in temporals or spirituals, and even when we proceed in his counsel, and enter into concerns, either of a temporal or of a religious nature, he does not leave it for us to judge how long, or how far we may proceed therein, but he keeps the reins in his own hand, like the well-advised husbandman when breaking the horse, that noble, and when broken, by his will being fully subjected, useful and docile quadruped. His first business is to learn him to lead, so as to follow his master cheerfully, contrary to his own will. But this he seldom does until he has made himself very sore by his obstinate hanging back and refusing to go; but after a considerable struggle, he yields and follows his master wherever he pleases to lead. But he has still another important lesson to learn, and that is, to stop when and wherever his master directs. To effect this, the bridle is necessary, with the bits in his mouth, against which he presses in his own will until he makes himself sore again before he is passive, and then instead of standing still as he ought, his will not being fully subdued, he runs backward. Here again the whip or the spur becomes necessary, in order to make him stand still at command, or even at the beck of the finger. This effected, he is now well broken, and becomes wholly passive to his master's will, and stands in his favour, and is highly prized by him.

But how very seldom is man brought to this complete passive state. We read of but one who came completely to it, viz. Jesus Christ, our great pattern, and he was brought to it by the things that he suffered. And I have often thought, and do most surely believe, that did men and women attend strictly and faithfully to the inward manifestations of truth in their own minds, when arrived to years of understanding, without regard to tradition and custom, thousands would be soon brought into this happy, passive state; for no other state can be truly happy. Then would the children of men be brought down to that state of equilibrium, that, undoubtedly, must have been the design of the Creator in the beginning. But man having swerved from this state of filial and complete passive obedience to the will of his all-wise and gracious Creator, it has led him into those many and great inconsistencies and inequalities, which cause all his present misery and distress. And many there are, I believe, who, in their setting out in life, may be rightly directed in their choice of business by which to obtain a comfortable livelihood for themselves and families, and at which time they neither thought of, nor coveted more; but, through the corrupt custom and course of trade and business among men, in their fallen state, some increase in their wordly possessions in such a rapid way, they soon obtain and amass together much more than they either desired or expected in their first setting out. And for want of keeping a single eye to their Divine director, who, if rightly attended to, would as clearly have showed them where to stop, as he showed them where to begin, they have continued on, by which means their desires after more have increased with the increase of their possessions, and finally they lose all sense of what is right for them, and by grasping after more in their own dark wisdom, they bring a blast on all their designs, and plunge themselves and families into irretrievable poverty and disgrace. While some others are permitted to proceed on until their minds are wholly swallowed up in their abundance, the care of which becomes such a load and burden, that they have no rest, and it eventually terminates in the utter ruin of themselves and families, and their temporal abundance soon becomes squandered and lost by the licentiousness and extravagance of their offspring or heirs, as such estates, thus gotten, seldom last longer than the second or third generation.

And as in temporals, so in spirituals. Many we see, who appear to set out right, for want of attending to their right guide, have not been able to endure those fiery baptisms that are necessary for the entire crucifixion of the old man. And although they may have been partly broken, so as to lead in a tolerable degree, yet, when put forward, for want of being wholly subject to the bit and bridle, they run away, and so make shipwreck of faith, and lose their little beginning. But I hope better things of my dear Edward, who has passed through the ordeal of many fiery baptisms, and has been thereby induced to dig deep, through the sandy superficial surface of tradition and superstition, to the imperishable foundation, the rock that is immovable. Therefore stand fast, my dear friend, in that liberty, in which the truth has made us free, and be not entangled with any yoke of bondage; for such shall assuredly reap if they faint not. And thou hast the seal of a son, if the apostle is correct; for, says he, "Every son that the father loveth, he chasteneth;" and he further says, that "if we are without chastisement, we are bastards and not sons."

By letter from Hugh Judge, I am informed that W. F., the English Friend, revived in their Yearly Meeting last fall, the old subject, namely, the appointment of a congress, as proposed by your Yearly Meeting some years past. And although that Yearly Meeting, the year before, had unitedly laid it quietly asleep, yet W. F., as Hugh informs, pressed the matter so much, that Friends, although contrary to the sense of the Meeting, condescended to take it on minute, and appointed a committee to consider it and report, and called on the women to join them in it. But the women were wiser than the men, and dismissed the subject without further troubling themselves with it; and the men's committee reported that no way opened to take any step, and the Meeting was for dismissing it; but W. F. urged the matter so hard, that he prevailed with the Meeting to refer it over to the next year for consideration. I thought it might have been well if my friend E. H. had been there, to have taught the Friend better.

My wife and daughter Elizabeth unite with me in love to thee and thine, and in which I rest thy sure and affectionate friend.

ELIAS HICKS.

TO WILLIAM POOLE, WILMINGTON.

New York, 5th mo. 25th, 1822.

MY DEAR FRIEND,

I now take my pen to acknowledge the receipt of thy five last kind letters, received since my last to thee, and shall make no other apology for deferring an answer till this time, than that a full belief pervades my mind, that our friendship is not only mutual, but is established on its right foundation, so as to banish all suspicion and jealousy from our minds, in regard to any neglect of right attention to each other's communications.

Thy several letters, above alluded to, were all pleasant and very acceptable, especially the one dated 4th month, 13th; for the length of which thou makest some apology, but which was altogether unnecessary, as it was none too long. The doctrinal points it treated of were exactly in accordance with

14

what has long been my settled belief; and the encouragement and fellow feeling it contained was truly grateful.

We have just entered on the concerns of our Yearly Meeting; I therefore can say but little about it, saving that we have the company of divers Friends from yours, viz., R—— J—— and J—— W——, from Jersey; E—— H—— and several others, from Bucks county; N—— S—— and S—— P——, from Concord; T—— P—— and wife, from Baltimore, &c.

The papers containing the controversy between Paul and Amicus were duly received, and on reading some of Paul's communications it was really distressing to think, that a rational being could possibly be so grossly ignorant, as his assertions on divers subjects manifest him to be; especially where he assures us, as his belief, that all the human species that are not furnished with the Bible, and history of the outward advent of Jesus Christ, must perish, or be eternally lost. Can any believe a rational being sincere when making such assertions?

Not being furnished with much to communicate at this time, may now draw to a close.

Thy affectionate friend.

ELIAS HICKS.

TO WILLIAM POOLE, WILMINGTON.

Jericho, 8th mo. 8th, 1822.

My Dear Friend,

When I inform thee, that the day after the close of our Yearly Meeting, after returning home, I was seized with severe indisposition, it will serve as an apology for my not writing soon after the close of it. Such was the severity of my pains, which came on by intervals of from three to five hours, and sometimes more, between the turns, which held from ten to forty or fifty minutes at a time, and sometimes an hour or more, that it disqualified me for almost all kind of action for several weeks; so that I could neither write nor talk without bringing on those severe spasms of pain, which ran through the upper part of my breast in a direction to each arm, and so down to my elbows; which at times was so excruciating, that I lack words to give to another a full idea of it. But in the intervals I felt pretty well, so long as I kept quite still, which I accounted a great favour, as I could then meditate and improve the time. Upon the whole, I consider it in a good measure verified, as expressed by one formerly, that all things work together for good to those who truly love God, and delight to meditate in his law.

Thy letter of the 22d ultimo is now before me, by which it appears, that various and many are the reports that are spreading, not only concerning my bodily indisposition, but also concerning the infirmity of my mind. But thanks be to God for his unspeakable mercy, who has been pleased in the riches of his love, to keep me sound within, and is strengthening by his own power my inner man, and enabling me to walk cheerfully on amidst evil report and good report, and will not suffer any of those things to move me off the ancient foundation, the inward revelation of his own blessed spirit, who is over all, God, blessed for ever.

"Neither count I my life dear unto myself, so that I might finish my course with joy, and the ministry which I have received of the Lord Jesus, to testify the Gospel of the grace of God."

As to the two natures in Jesus Christ, I conceive that if any should deny that, they are justly to be accounted deists, as they make void every scripture account concerning him, for his human nature is as fully established as his Divine nature. There are some who are accused of denying his Divine nature, but I don't recollect of ever hearing of any who dare deny his human nature; for that would contradict every scripture testimony that declares him to be the son of the Virgin Mary; for nothing but the human nature could ever be produced from the flesh and blood of Mary. This, Jesus himself testifies, when speaking to Nicodemus. "'That," says he, "which is born of the flesh is flesh; and that which is born of the spirit is spirit. The wind bloweth where it listeth, and thou hearest the sound thereof, but canst not tell whence it cometh, and whither it goeth : so is every one that is born of the spirit." Hence we discover the cause of the ignorance, and consequently the unbelief of Nicodemus; being ignorant of the spiritual birth he could not believe in it, for none can believe what they do not understand, and this is the reason why so many disbelieve the divinity of Christ. For none can believe it *really* and to profit, but such as are, in a greater or less degree, themselves born of the spirit; for it is the spirit of God only that quickens an immortal soul; the flesh profiteth nothing in the things of God. Although we cannot see wind, yet we know and feel self-evidently its power and operation ; just so, those who feel the power and operation of the spirit of God upon them, self-evidently know that it is; and as they yield and unite with its operation upon them, then is a birth of the spirit, according to their surrender to its power, begotten in them, and these, and these only, can savingly believe in the divinity of Christ, and know that he is born of God, and is truly the son of God ; " for as many as are led by the spirit of God," as saith Paul, " are the sons of God." But none can believe this doctrine but those who know it effected in themselves.

I find by thy letters, that thou despairest of seeing Long Island this summer ; nevertheless, should it be consistent with the ordering of Best Wisdom, that thou and I should be permitted to continue in this mutable state a few months longer, and be preserved in health, we may probably see each other and witness the satisfaction of speaking face to face, and have the pleasure of communing on those things verbally which now make use for our pens. I am ready to conclude that ere this comes to hand, thou wilt have heard that our Monthly and Quarterly Meetings have set me at liberty to visit, in a religious way, some parts of your Yearly Meeting, and I think Brandywine and Wilmington will likely be comprehended in the limits. Until when, I remain thy sincere and very affectionate friend. ELIAS HICKS.

TO WILLIAM POOLE, WILMINGTON.

Jericho, 9th mo. 23d, 1822.

MY DEAR FRIEND,

It appears, by a letter Valentine lately received from thee, that I had omitted informing thee of the reception of the last numbers of the Christian Repository thou hadst forwarded; these may certify that they came duly to hand, and the one thou lately forwarded to Valentine, I was well satisfied with.

Thou desirest to have seasonable notice of the time when I may likely be with you at your meeting. I shall willingly comply with thy request, as far as way opens for it. But it is not likely I shall see you until after Baltimore Yearly Meeting, and my visit is finished to the southward. I propose proceeding through the upper part of Jersey, into Bucks county, taking meetings through that county, as way opens, and after that proceed pretty directly to Baltimore.

I find I shall not leave home as soon as in an early period of my concern I had contemplated; for as the time drew near, and I was brought to look into the state of my accounts about home, in order for a full settlement, I found myself somewhat in debt in some neighbourhoods, in a religious way; and I have been closely engaged for some time endeavouring to pay all off. I had two large meetings the day before yesterday, principally among those not of our Society, about ten or fifteen miles distant from my place of abode. They were truly strengthening, encouraging seasons, in which the Lord's power was felt to preside to the humbling and contriting many hearts; for which my mind was inspired with gratitude, and made humbly thankful for the unmerited favour. Two or three more such opportunities will, I believe, close my accounts about home, that it appears probable I may proceed on my western and southern journey about the middle of next week.

I shall now, as I feel but little ability for writing at present, conclude with just informing that my health, and that of my family, is pretty much as usual; although I frequently feel some returns of the pain in my breast, and which I hardly expect ever to get clear of, considering my advanced age.

With love to thee and thine, I rest thy sympathizing and affectionate friend.

ELIAS HICKS.

TO WILLIAM POOLE, WILMINGTON.

Upper Dublin, 10*th* mo. 16*th*, 1822.

MY DEAR FRIEND,

Having a little leisure this morning, whilst waiting for the time of meeting here, and having thee frequently in remembrance since I left home, and finding our friend Isaac Parry, who is now with us, intends going in a day or two to Philadelphia, to attend your Meeting for Sufferings, and who expressed a hope he should see thee there; I was induced to take my pen, and salute thee with a few lines, desiring that grace, mercy, and peace may be with thee and abound.

I left home the 2d instant. Left my family and friends, generally, in usual health; and passing on through New York and the upper part of Jersey, into the upper part of Bucks county, taking meetings in our way, we arrived here last evening. We have abundant cause to bless the name of Israel's unslumbering Shepherd, who hath graciously manifested his power and presence for our help and preservation; opening a way for us in the hearts of the people, among whom we have been exercised in Gospel labour, for the promotion of his noble cause of truth and righteousness in the earth; breaking down and silencing all opposing spirits, and causing his truth to reign triumphant over all, to the praise of His grace, who is over all, blessed for ever.

We are now pressing on towards Baltimore, taking such meetings in the way as the time will admit of. After attending the Yearly Meeting, we have a view of seeing Friends on the Eastern shore of Maryland; after which we shall bend our course towards Wilmington.

If thou feelest the way open for it, I should be pleased to hear from thee, while at Baltimore. I shall likely lodge with Gerard T. Hopkins.

Finding nothing further at present to communicate, I shall now conclude, with much love to you all, thy affectionate friend.

ELIAS HICKS.

TO WILLIAM POOLE, WILMINGTON.

Head of Chester, 11th mo. 8th, 1822.

DEAR FRIEND,

We came here last evening in our way from Baltimore to Easton, on the Eastern shore of Maryland. We have a meeting appointed here to-day, to-morrow at Cecil, and the next day, the first of the week, at Old Chester Neck; from thence we shall proceed on towards Easton, and after taking the meetings in that quarter, turn towards the Delaware. But whether we shall take all the meetings on the Delaware side below Wilmington, or proceed pretty directly on to that place, taking only such as fall in our way, is not yet determined. If the latter course is pursued, we shall get there in two or three weeks; if otherwise, it may be four weeks or more.

But I feel myself as a day labourer, and of course do not see far ahead.

The yearly meeting we have recently attended, was acknowledged by Friends who were there, to be the largest and most favoured of any they have had in that place for many years past. The latter I can concur with, at least as far as my own feelings and observation will warrant; as I have not been in a Yearly meeting, where Friends, in the public service, and also in the ordering of discipline, were so fully harmonious; and the almost universal unity and regard both old and young manifested to me through the course of the meeting, and at our parting, bowed my mind in an humbling sense of the unmerited favour and inspired it with thanksgiving and gratitude to the gracious and benevolent Author of all our rich mercies and blessings.

It has been somewhat remarkable, considering the abundant reports that were widely spread before I left home, calculated to make an unfavourable impression, that there has not a single circumstance transpired, that has been attended with any unpleasant aspect: but, on the contrary, scarcely a dog has opened his mouth against us, unless he has done it behind the door in secret.

But, it may be, the worst is yet to come:* but thanks be given to the great Preserver of men, who hath in mercy led me into that place of safety recommended by Paul, that is, to be entirely without carefulness about any of those things. Being reduced into that state of nothingness of self, that the sharpest shafts and arrows of professed friends, or open foes, cannot hit me; for thou very well knowest, that where there is nothing, there is nothing to hit; of course they are all shot in vain.

It is now near meeting time, I must therefore draw to a close; and in much love to thee, thy dear wife and children, and inquiring friends, subscribe thy affectionate friend.

ELIAS HICKS.

TO WILLIAM POOLE, WILMINGTON.

Camden, 11th mo. 23d, 1822.

My Dear Friend,

Thy letter of the 14th instant is now before me, and its salutary and encouraging contents are truly grateful; stimulating to faithfulness in the path of duty. It came duly to hand at Easton, and it was my intention to have written thee

---

* Information of the fact of the combination which was forming against him in Philadelphia, and the publication of T. E's. letter, developing some of the features of that combination, had a little before this time reached E. H.

from that place, but my time being pretty much occupied when I first received it, in writing to some other of my friends, when I was about to put pen to paper I discovered that my companion, to whom I had shown thy letter, had written to thee, and given the desired information; I therefore deferred writing for that time, but coming here last evening, and having some leisure to-day, I feel inclined to address a few lines to thee, to inform thee where we are and how we are to be disposed of for a few days to come, &c.

We have a meeting appointed to-morrow at Mother Kiln; the next being first day, we propose attending Friends' meeting here in the morning, and at three in the afternoon we have a meeting appointed in the town of Dover; and on second day at Little Creek, and the next day the Quarterly Meeting will begin, where I anticipate seeing thee and thy wife, and being comforted in conversing with you face to face, that our joy may be full. Therefore I shall not at present write much, especially as the time is near at hand for the mail to leave this place. We have attended all the meetings of Friends on the Eastern shore, and had two large meetings with others—one at Chestertown and one at Easton. I think they were favoured opportunities, and we left them with peace of mind.

We are at Joseph G. Rowland's, who, with his worthy wife, has received us with a hearty welcome and entertained us kindly.

With the addition of my affectionate love and regard to thee, thy dear wife and children, I subscribe thy assured friend,

ELIAS HICKS.

TO JOHN MERRITT, NEW YORK.

DEAR FRIEND, *Byberry*, 12th mo. 27th, 1822.

I have for some time felt warm desires to address thee in this way, but no favourable opportunity has presented ere now. After leaving thee at Newark, we proceeded on our journey, taking meetings on our way to Baltimore, where we arrived in good season to attend the Yearly Meeting.

Our journey was very prosperous, the meetings were generally large and greatly favoured, and the apparent universal unity and kindness of my friends was beyond the expression of words, and caused deep humiliation and grateful acknowledgments to my Heavenly Father, for the unmerited mercy.

The Yearly Meeting of Baltimore I think was a very favoured meeting; the unity and harmony that generally prevailed among the living, active members, through the several sittings, was truly precious; at the close of which we took leave of our friends in much unity and harmony, and left there with sweet peace of mind and with thankful hearts for the favours received.

We proceeded on our journey, attended the meetings of Friends on the Eastern shore of Maryland, and all but one in the State of Delaware, to great satisfaction, and in the feeling of near unity with our friends. Passing on we came to Philadelphia, where a few made some opposition, though mostly behind our backs; yet here our joy was transcendently greater, although it was before as great as we could dare to ask for; but here it was much greater by contrast, for we had not met with any opposition before we came here, and here the Lord, our gracious preserver, openly and obviously defended us against our opposers, and turned the mischief and evil machinations of their designs upon their own heads, and has confounded their evil devices, and caused them to be taken in the snare they had prepared for their friend, who, through the spirit of envy that predominated in them, they were led to consider their enemy, but who nevertheless is still their friend, and prays that they may be delivered from their wretched infatuation.

We left Philadelphia the 25th instant. Our friends in an abundant manner expressed their sorrow for our leaving them so soon, as our time had been so generally taken up in our visits to the families of Green Street meeting and in attending the public meetings, that they could not have so much of our company as they desired, although nearly every evening when we retired to our lodgings, which was seldom earlier than eight o'clock, we found from thirty to fifty, and sometimes near a hundred Friends, young and old, being desirous of our company and conversation, and many of those opportunities were solemn and instructive seasons to those thus assembled. Surely it is the Lord's doing, and marvellous in our eyes. The fourth, fifth, and sixth days of this week we attended meetings at Frankford, Germantown, and Abington, all very large and favoured. We are now at Byberry, with our friend John Comly, who, with his family, is well. We expect to attend the meeting here to-morrow, the next day at Middletown, the next at Bristol, the next at the Falls, the next at Pennsbury, being fifth of the week; after which we shall cross the Delaware to Trenton, and, if the travelling will reasonably permit, attend some more meetings in Jersey, down the Delaware. I should be willing to reach home by the time of our Quarterly Meeting, if way opens for it, but must submit that to higher authority than man.

My companion joins me in love to thee, to dear Phebe, and the children, in which I rest thy affectionate friend.

ELIAS HICKS.

P. S. Please to remember me to dear E. Coggeshall and family, to dear Elizabeth Haydock and family, and let the two Elizabeths see this letter, as I have thought of communing with them in this way, but the urgency of the work I am engaged in, affords me but little time to write to my friends. And should Samuel Titus, of New Rochelle, be in town, please let him see it, and present my love to him; also to John R. Willis and other inquiring friends, in thy freedom; also to thy neighbours, Samuel Willets and wife.—I am as well nearly as when I left home. Farewell.

E. H.

TO WILLIAM POOLE, WILMINGTON.

Jericho, 2d mo. 3d, 1823.

MY DEAR FRIEND,

Thy letters of 12th mo. 30th, and 1st mo. 5th, were duly received, and read with interest and satisfaction. And as thou requests to know how I got on in my journey, I feel willing to give thee a summary thereof; as it has been, take it in all its parts, the most satisfactory and the most peaceful one I have ever taken, from the first step taken therein to my return home.

In my first opening the concern to my friends in the Monthly and Quarterly Meetings, their unity, sympathy, and encouragement were more fully expressed therewith, than I had ever before witnessed on any like occasion, and it seemed as a precursor of what might eventually follow, and tended to establish my faith and dependance in that arm and power that at first opened the prospect and engaged me in the service; and who graciously condescended to be with me and guide me through the journey, and opened a way for me, that neither man, nor all the united powers of darkness, were able to shut. From a grateful sense thereof, my spirit is humbled in deep self-abasement for the unmerited favour; for my peace, through his mercy and power, was preserved unbroken, out of the reach of all opposing spirits. Thanksgiving and praise be rendered to his right worthy name, who is over all, God blessed for ever.

As to what thou observes respecting Jesus not being the Son of God, spiritually, until after the baptism of John and descent of the Holy Spirit upon him, it is a subject that appears to be a very simple one, as all truths are, and does not admit of any speculation, as the whole rests upon matter of fact, as recorded in the Scriptures.* For do they not fully testify, that Jesus was born a real and true Israelitish child, being the offspring

---

* Deut. xviii. 15, 18. Acts ii. 22; iii. 22. Hebrews, ii. 16, 17, 18; iv. 15. Isaiah. ii. 1.

of Abraham and David, and born into the world as was Isaac and John the Baptist, by the special interference of the Divine power, through the medium of the flesh and blood of a woman, and therefore, as Jesus himself testifies, "that which is born of the flesh *is flesh;* and that which is born of the spirit is spirit."

Hence we reasonably suppose this testimony of Jesus might set the matter at rest, with every man endued with a rational understanding. For the miraculous conception in either case, could not constitute a difference of nature in the being produced; especially when we consider that the immortal soul cannot be generated in the flesh of woman, as there is no analogy between matter and spirit; and when we consider further, that the flesh of every child born of a woman, is only animated by the breath and air of this world: take that away, and the animal man dies immediately. That was the case with Jesus on the cross; but his immortal spirit, born of God, returned to God, who gave it, as it stood superior to death, Hell, and the grave.

We likewise find him growing up from a child to the state of manhood, like other children, and no doubt his soul when it entered the body prepared for it, was furnished with such a portion of the Divine spirit, as was most consistent with the will of his Heavenly Father, and by which he was enabled to fulfil all the righteousness of the law and covenant given to Israel by Moses; and therefore, in a certain sense, might be considered a Son of God, as much so as that dispensation would admit of. But if he had been completely so before the baptism of John and the descent of the Holy Ghost, why was that superadded, and why did not his Heavenly Father, previous to that time, declare him his Son in whom he was well pleased?

And when we further consider, that we do not hear any thing of him, after he was grown to man's estate, not even so much as being tempted, until after the Holy Spirit descended upon him, and by which he was then more fully the Son of God, and filled with the Divine nature of his Heavenly Father, and thereby qualified to meet the temptations that assailed him, and when he had vanquished temptation, we then find him entering upon his mission, and not before.

And that must be the experience of every gospel minister; for I cannot conceive that any can arrive to a state for gospel ministry, until they have first fulfilled the substance of the moral law, as Jesus did; and that opens the way for the reception of a further infusion of the Holy Spirit, as a necessary preparation for gospel ministry. For every one who ministers of the things of God, must first be born of the Spirit of God, for none can be the sons of God but those who are born of his Spirit. And nothing but Spirit can be born of the Spirit of God, so as to become his children, and be taught of him, as God is a pure, holy, immortal, invisible, infinite, and unchangeable Spirit, possessed of every virtue and excellence that can be attributed to him, and all his children must really partake of his Divine nature, without any mixture, to qualify them for heaven, and those celestial joys that constitute that happy state.

We arrived safe in New York on 7th day, the 18th of 1st month; attended their fore and afternoon meetings on 1st day. They were large and favoured, as was generally the case with all the meetings we attended after parting with thee.

On 1st day evening as I retired to bed, I was taken with a turn of gravel, which held me through the night, and prevented my getting much rest, but was so much better next day, that I rode home in the afternoon, and found my family all in usual health; which, together with the many favours dispensed to me in the course of my journey, by a Gracious Providence, was cause of deep humility and thankfulness. On 3d day I rested with my family. On 4th day attended our select Quarterly Meeting, in which I had some service. On 5th day, about five in the morning, I was taken with a very severe turn of my old complaint, which held me in much severe pain for about twenty-six hours, but getting relief about seven or eight o'clock on 6th day morning, I ventured to attend the public parting meeting of the quarter, which was large, and I think, a favoured meeting, and held, I trust, to our mutual comfort and rejoicing; my friends generally manifesting much gladness in my being restored to them again. I accounted it as one of the special favours received, my being permitted to get home previous to the severe attack of my old, and in some sort habitual, complaint; that the query arises very fresh at times, what shall I render unto the Lord for all his benefits? for surely his mercy endureth for ever.

I rest thy affectionate and sympathizing friend.

ELIAS HICKS.

AN ADDRESS TO YOUTH.

The following Address to the Youth, was annexed to a letter written by Elias Hicks to two Friends in Philadelphia, in the early part of the year 1823.

Since penning the foregoing, my mind has been drawn into a renewed feeling of near sympathy and gospel affection with the dearly beloved youth, not only those of your Monthly Meeting,* that fell more particularly under my notice in the family visits I made when with you, but all others of your city, whom the Lord in the riches of his mercy, is renewedly visiting with the day-spring from on high, through the immediate manifestation of his love and light in their inner man, as the guardian angel of his presence to guide them and keep them; and as they take heed thereunto, will preserve and keep them from all evil, and will lead them up to the head-spring and fountain of living water, of which, when they drink, they will never thirst again after the muddy waters of tradition and education, that stands in the letter that killeth. But their thirst will be continually satiated with the pure water of life, that makes glad all Zion's dedicated and devoted

* Green Street.

children, and which adds no sorrow with it. And as they give good heed to this holy anointing, which is truth and is no lie, it will lead them off from all dependance on man, whose breath is in his nostrils, for wherein is he to be accounted of; and they will have no need that any man teach them then, but as the same anointing teacheth. It will bring them to see the end of all shadows that stand in outward visible things, let them be ever so great or excellent, and will gather them into itself (the invisible power) to the law of the spirit of life, that sets the soul free from the law of sin and death, and from all condemnation. And may the dear youth dwell near and in this holy principle, in this day of trial and rebuke, for the Lord's hand is stretched out upon the nations, and he "will overturn, overturn, overturn it, and it shall be no more, until he come whose right it is, and I will give it him." The Lord I believe is about to put an end to, and overturn all man's work in religion, and to put an end to all man's forms, creeds, and professions, that stand in man's will and spirit, that *He only*, may come to rule and reign in the hearts of his children, that so all may savingly come to know but one Lord, one faith, and one baptism; one God and Father of all, who is above all, through all, and in you all. May the dearly beloved visited youth press forward toward this blessed and happy state, and come to know an establishment therein, is the sincere and sympathetic desire of their ancient, affectionate, and exercised friend and elder brother.

ELIAS HICKS.

TO J. WILSON MOORE, PHILADELPHIA.

Jericho, 3d mo. 26th, 1823.

DEAR FRIEND,

Thy letter, accompanying one from thy father of the 14th ult., was very acceptable; a feeling sense of the kindness and regard of my friends, manifested in an epistolary way, is truly grateful to my mind. I anticipate with thee, at least in desire, that bigotry and superstition may be banished from the mind of every member of our highly favoured Society. For what reproach and inconsistency must attach to every rational being, who makes the high profession that we do, of being led and guided by an unerring principle of light and truth in the mind, as a sufficient and only rule of faith and practice, when such turn back to the letter, and presume to establish a rule from the writings of men in former ages, and so contradict their profession. And the inconsistency appears the more glaring and reproachful, when the enlightened mind takes a correct view of the records of past ages, wherein it clearly appears, that nothing but a strict adherence to this unerring rule, has ever reconciled man to his Maker, or to his fellow creature. But every man, in all ages, who has attended strictly to this rule, regardless of every external rule, unless first sanctioned by this internal rule, has never failed of being reconciled both to God and man.

I will go no farther back, to prove these assertions, than the introduction of the gospel dispensation by the blessed Jesus; who in his last counsel and command to his immediate followers, turned their attention entirely away from placing any dependance on external evidence, even the best that was ever dispensed to the children of men, in any age of the world; that is, what is contained in his own life and doctrines, that was super-eminent to all external evidence that had ever been dispensed to man before his coming. This was the view, no doubt, his disciples had concerning him, and that he would continue with them and be their preserver and comforter. But he showed them their error and mistake, when he declared to them, that it was expedient for them that he should go away, for if he went not away, he assured them that the comforter would not come unto them. " But if I depart, I will send him unto you, and when he is come, he will reprove the world of sin ;" that is, every rational creature that is in the world at any time. " He will guide you into all truth," consequently out of all error ; and this corroborates the testimony of John, who assured the believers of his day, that they had an unction from the Holy One, and needed not any man to teach them, but as the same anointing taught them, which is truth, and is no lie.*

And while the believers attended to this, they were of one heart and one mind, being all baptized by this one spirit of truth into one body, and all made to drink into this spirit—of that water that whosoever drinks of, will never thirst again after the lo! heres, or lo! theres, that are in the world; and which all have their source and spring from the letter that killeth. And it is of no avail who wrote the letter, whether Paul or Apollos, or Cephas, or George Fox, or Penn, or Barclay, or any other man, still as we turn to it, we turn from that which is a thousand fold better, even the spirit of truth, that is ever nearer to us than it is possible the letter can be, as it dwelleth with and is in every believer, and is the only present helper in every needful time. The letter, or what is composed in writing, can only direct to this spirit of truth, and may be one among the many outward instruments that a gracious God, in his wisdom and goodness, has dispensed to the children of men, to lead them from their unbelief, by pointing and directing their attention to this inward teacher, the spirit of truth, which, as they obey it, will lead them into all truth, without the aid of any other teacher, and will bring about their salvation without any other Saviour. But to know this work fully effected, we must cleave wholly and alone to this inward guide, and leave all outward guides behind; seeing we cannot serve two masters, neither can we follow two guides, the one inward and the other outward, at the same time. But when the outward weaker one, suited to the darkness and carnality of our hearts, has brought us to the inward one, in which is all wisdom, strength, and power, then we ought to quit the weaker one, which never was able, nor ever was intended, to make the comers thereunto perfect, as respects the soul. Hence all those who profess to believe in this internal teacher, the spirit of truth, and turn back to the letter or

* 1 John, ii. 27.

writings of Paul, of Peter, of Fox, or Barclay, or any other outward teacher, and undertake from their writings to form creeds or confessions of faith as a rule of conduct to the believers, clearly indicate that they have fallen away from the faith once delivered to the saints, and turned back to the weak and beggarly elements, and justly incur the severe reprehension of Paul to the Galatians—" Are ye so foolish? having begun in the spirit, are ye now made perfect by the flesh?"

And every enlightened mind, who hath been conversant in the history of the primitive church, may clearly discover that a departure in the believers from this inward perfect guide, and turning their attention to the writings of the primitive saints, was one principal cause of the apostacy that so soon after the apostles' days overspread the Christian Church. And to such an excess did it soon arise, as to turn the professors of Christianity back into a state of greater darkness than they were in while conversant among the Gentile nations; not only denying this inward guide, the spirit of truth, but actually denied all internal immediate revelation, which is going a step below the most ignorant inhabitants of the wilderness. And when George Fox was raised a witness to the truth, his whole errand appears to have been, to turn people from darkness to this inward light, as the only and alone sure rule and infallible way to blessedness; and so long as our primitive Friends kept to this as their only guide, love and unity prevailed. But when they began to set up for one, against another, divisions and disputes arose and broke the unity; one party saying, I am of Penn, others, I am of Mead, &c. Thus the harmony was broken; and this for want of keeping to the inward guide, which is the same in all, and letting the eye wander without to external evidence, which never made the comers thereunto perfect, as pertaining to the conscience, as all external evidence is conveyed to the spirit of man through the medium of the animal senses. And as the spirit of man cannot rise any higher through this medium, than to know the things of man, therefore no external evidence can reveal the things of God, which are only known by the Spirit of God.

As my paper is now nearly full, I will draw to a close, and in much love to thyself, beloved wife, and little daughter, rest thy affectionate friend.

ELIAS HICKS.

TO NATHAN SHOEMAKER, PHILADELPHIA.

Jericho, 3d mo. 31st, 1823.

DEAR FRIEND,

Thy acceptable letter of 1st month last, came duly to hand, but my religious engagements, and other necessary concerns, have prevented my giving it that attention that its contents seem to demand. Thou queries after my views of the suffering of Jesus Christ, the Son of God, and what was the object of the shedding of his blood on the cross, and what benefits resulted to mankind by the shedding of this blood, &c. I shall answer in a very simple way, as I consider the whole subject to be a very simple one, as all truth is simple when we free ourselves from the improper bias of tradition and education, which rests as a burdensome stone on the minds of most of the children of men, and which very much mars the unity and harmony of society.

1st. By what means did Jesus suffer? The answer is plain, by the hands of wicked men, and because his works were righteous and theirs were wicked. Query. Did God send him into the world purposely to suffer death by the hands of wicked men? By no means; but to live a righteous and godly life, (which was the design and end of God's creating man in the beginning,) and thereby be a perfect example to such of mankind as should come to the knowledge of him and of his perfect life. For, if it was the purpose and will of God that he should die by the hands of wicked men, then the Jews, by crucifying him, would have done God's will, and of course would all have stood justified in his sight, which could not be. But it was permitted so to be, as it had been with many of the prophets and wise and good men that were before him, who suffered death by the hands of wicked men for 'righteousness' sake, as ensamples to those that came after, that they should account nothing too dear to give up for the truth's sake, not even their own lives.

But the shedding of his blood by the wicked scribes, pharisees, and people of Israel, had a particular effect on the Jewish nation, as by this, (the topstone and worst of all their crimes,) was filled up the measure of their iniquities, and which put an end to that dispensation, together with its law and covenant. That as John's baptism summed up in one, all the previous water baptisms of that dispensation, and put an end to them, which he sealed with his blood, so this sacrifice of the body of Jesus Christ, summed up in one, all the outward atoning sacrifices of the shadowy dispensation, and put an end to them all, thereby abolishing the law, having previously fulfilled all its righteousness, and, as saith the apostle, "He blotted out the hand-writing of ordinances, nailing them to his cross;" having put an end to the law that commanded them; with all its annexed legal sins, and abolished all its legal penalties, so that all the Israelites that believed on him, after he exclaimed on the cross, "It is finished," might abstain from all the rituals of their law, such as circumcision, water baptisms, outward sacrifices, seventh day sabbaths, and all their other holy days, &c. and be blameless; and the legal sins that any were guilty of, were now remitted and done away by the abolishment of the law that commanded them, for "where there is no law there is no transgression." But those that did not believe on him, many of them were destroyed by the sword, and the rest were scattered abroad in the earth. But, I do not consider that the crucifixion of the outward body of flesh and blood of Jesus on the cross, was an atonement for any sins but the legal sins of the Jews; for as their law was outward, so their legal sins and their penalties were outward, and these could be atoned for by an outward sacrifice; and this last outward sacrifice was a full type of the inward sacrifice that every sinner must make, in giving up that sinful life of his own will, in and by which he hath from time to time, crucified the innocent life of God in his own soul: and which Paul calls "the old man with his deeds," or "the man of sin and son of perdition," who hath taken God's seat in the heart, and there exalteth itself above all that is called God, or is worshipped, sitting as Judge and Supreme. Now all this life, power, and will of man, must be slain and die on the cross spiritually, as Jesus died on the cross outwardly, and this is the true atonement, which that outward atonement was a clear and full type of. This the apostle Paul sets forth in a plain manner, Romans vi. 3, 4. " Know ye not that so many of us as were baptized into Jesus Christ, were baptized into his death? Therefore we are buried with him by baptism into death, that, like as Christ was raised up from the dead" outwardly, "by the glory of the Father, even so we." having by the spiritual baptism witnessed a death to sin, shall know a being raised up spiritually, and so "walk in newness of life."

But the primitive Christian church having soon after the apostles' days, turned away from their true and only sufficient guide, the Spirit of Truth, that Jesus commanded his disciples to wait for, and not attempt to do any thing until they had received it, but assured them that when they had received it, it would be a complete and sufficient rule, *without the addition of any other thing, as it would lead them and guide them into all truth.* And to its sufficiency, John, the beloved apostle, bore this noble and exalted testimony, in full accordance with his Divine Master, in this emphatic language to his fellow believers: " Ye have an unction from the Holy One, and need not that any man teach you, but as the same anointing teacheth you, which is truth, and is no lie."* But the believers, by too much looking to their old traditions, soon lost sight of, or neglected fully to attend, as they ought to have done, to this inward guide, and turned their attention outward to the *letter,* which *always killeth those who lean upon it as a rule.* Hence, the successors of those meek and self-denying followers of the example and commands of Jesus, apostatized

* 1 John, ii. 20, 27.

from the simplicity of the gospel, by which the unity was broken, and they soon became divided into sects and parties, and persecuted each other; and invented and promulgated inconsistent and unsound doctrines, such as original sin, certifying that all Adam's offspring are condemned to eternal punishment for one mis-step of our first parents; for they do not appear to have been guilty of but one failure, and that, it appears, they made satisfaction for at the time of their first arraignment by their benevolent Creator, manifesting sorrow and repentance: which seems to be fairly implied by the sequel of the interview between them; for it is said he clothed them with coats of skins, to hide their nakedness, which is an emblem of durable clothing, *and as their nakedness was not an outward one, but a nakedness of soul*, not being able to conceal their sin from the All-penetrating Eye of Divine Justice, so when he had brought them, through conviction, to see their error and to repent of it, he was reconciled to them, and clothed them again with his Holy Spirit.

And inasmuch as those idle promulgators [of the doctrine] of original sin, believe they are made sinners without their consent or knowledge, which, according to the nature and reason of things, every rational mind must see is impossible; so likewise they are idle and ignorant enough to believe they are made righteous without their consent or knowledge, by the righteousness of one who lived on the earth near two thousand years before they had an existence, and this by the cruel act of wicked men slaying an innocent and righteous one; and these are bold and daring enough to lay this cruel and unholy act to the charge of Divine Justice, as having purposely ordained it to be so. But what an outrage it is against every righteous law of God and man, as the Scriptures abundantly testify. See Exodus, xxiii. 7. " Keep thee far from a false matter, and the innocent and righteous slay thou not, for I will not justify the wicked." Deut. xxvii. 25, " Cursed be he that taketh reward to slay an innocent person;" and much more might be produced to show the wickedness and absurdity of the doctrine, that would accuse the perfectly just, all-wise, and merciful Jehovah, of so barbarous and cruel an act, as that of slaying his innocent and righteous Son, to atone for the sins and iniquities of the ungodly.

Surely, is it possible, that any rational being that has any right sense of justice or mercy, would be willing to accept forgiveness of his sins on such terms ! Would he not rather go forward and offer himself wholly up to suffer all the penalties due to his crimes, rather than the innocent should suffer? Nay, was he so hardy as to acknowledge a willingness to be saved through such a medium, would it not prove that he stood in direct opposition to every principle of justice and honesty, of mercy and love, and show himself to be a poor selfish creature, unworthy of notice !*

---

* George Whitehead, one of the most distinguished and approved early writers in the Society of Friends, when speaking of the doctrine of satisfaction, or justification by imputative righteousness, expresses himself in the following terms, viz. "The Quakers see no need of directing men to the type for the antitype, viz. neither to the outward temple, nor yet to Jerusalem, either to Jesus Christ or his blood ; knowing that neither the righteousness of faith, nor the word of it, doth so direct. (Rom. x.) And is it the Baptists' doctrine to direct men to the material temple, and Jerusalem, the type for the antitype? What nonsense and darkness is this! And where do the Scriptures say the blood was there shed for justification, and that men must be directed to Jerusalem to it ? (Whereas, that blood shed is not in being.) But the true apostle directed them to the light, to walk in the light, for the blood of Jesus Christ to cleanse them from all sin."—*Whitehead's Light and Life of Christ*, p. 34.

" You blasphemously charge Divine justice with punishing your sins to the full in Christ, or punishing him, that was ever innocent, to the full for your sins ; so that you account it against justice to punish your sins again in you, though you live and die in them. And yet you think it an excellent piece of *justice, to punish the innocent to the full, for the guilty.* But your mistake in this is gross, as will further appear, and you will not hereby be acquitted, nor cleared. This will not prove you invested with Christ's everlasting righteousness, nor will this cover your own filthy rags, or hide your shame.

" And while you think that you are secured in your sins, from the stroke of justice, as having been fully executed, and that by way of revenge, upon the innocent Son of God, in punishing your sins to the full upon him ; I say, while you state this as the nature of the satisfaction by Christ's suffering *in your stead*, the whole world may as well acquit itself thereby from punishment as you ; for he died for all, and is ' the propitiation for the sins of the whole world.' And therefore if this must be looked upon as the full punishment of sin, that it was laid upon Christ, and that ' the sin cannot be again punished after such satisfaction,' this may make a merry world in sin—once punished to the full in Christ, never to be punished again upon the offender, which the law directly takes hold of. Oh, soothing doc-

Having given thee a sketch of my views on the subject of thy queries, how far thou may consider them correct, I must leave to thy judgment and consideration; and may now recommend thee to shake off all traditional views that thou hast imbibed from external evidence, and turn thy mind to the light within, as thy only true teacher: wait patiently for its instruction, and it will teach thee more than men or books can do; and lead thee to a clearer sight and sense of what thou desirest to know, than I have words clearly to convey it to thee in. That this may be thy experience, is my sincere desire; and with love to thyself and family, I conclude, thy affectionate friend.

ELIAS HICKS.

TO WILLIAM POOLE, WILMINGTON.

New York, 5th mo. 23d, 1823.

My Dear Friend,

Thy affectionate remembrance of the 24th ult. is now before me, having perused it several times, and not without feeling near sympathy with thee and thy dear companion, under your present bodily affliction. But these seemingly unfavourable tidings, were nevertheless accompanied with a comfortable hope, that through the patient and quiet acquiescence of thy beloved companion to the present dispensation of a wise and gracious providence, as noted in thy letter, and thy intention to copy after such an excellent example, will, I trust, as you continue to persevere therein, bring you to witness the truth of the apostolic declaration, " that all things work together for

---

true to sinners! the plain effect of which is, to make the wicked world rejoice in a sinful state, and say, ' O, admirable Justice, that was pleased thus to revenge thyself upon an innocent man, that never sinned, and to punish our sin to the full upon him! O transcendent mercy! that hast found out this expedient, that we might be fully acquitted, pardoned, and discharged from the penalty that is just and due to us for all our sins, past, present, and to come !' O! what glad tidings are these to the hypocrites and drunkards."—*G. Whitehead, Christian Quaker,* pp. 404, 405.

good, to them that love God." And should you be permitted to finish your course in this toilsome probationary state, a few years sooner than some of your ancient brethren and sisters, whose lot it has been to bear the burden and heat of the day; yet this would be no cause of regret to you, but rather of joy and rejoicing, in the fruition of that sweet peace that this world, with all its best accommodations, can never give, neither can the want of them ever take away, nor the remembrance of them tend, in the least, to sully that joy that is unspeakable and full of glory.

I am quite in sentiment with thee respecting the case of trial, and test of our religious principles, in the late Yearly meeting in Philadelphia;* and had there not been light and strength enough vouchsafed by the head of the church, to condemn and put to silence that mass of incongruous matter, brought forward by a party in the Meeting for sufferings, as a creed, or test of the faith of the members of our Society, it would, I believe, have convinced every sensible enlightened member, that the glory of the Divine presence had entirely departed from us, or at least as much so as from any of the formal professors of Christianity. I think we might as well have gone back and submitted to the Episcopalian, or Presbyterian creed, as to have adopted the one brought forward by that meeting.

Please to remember me affectionately to thy wife and children, and with a large share to thyself, I rest thy assured friend.

ELIAS HICKS.

* An attempt by the opposers of Elias Hicks to obtain the sanction of the Yearly Meeting to a document called, Extracts from the Writings of Primitive Friends, &c., and intended to operate as a creed or test of faith; but which was rejected by the meeting.

TO J. WILSON MOORE, PHILADELPHIA.

Jericho, 6th mo. 22d, 1823.
DEAR FRIEND,

Thy very acceptable letter of 5th month last is now before me, and has received several perusals with additional pleasure, in finding the views and sentiments of a younger brother so coincident with my own. As it leads to the anticipation of a hope, that the Lord has not forsaken his people, but is raising up many from among the younger classes of society to advocate his cause of truth and righteousness in the earth. And as these abide faithful in lowliness and true humility and in an entire abasedness of self, and move forward under the leading and operation of Divine love and light upon their minds, some of these will be qualified and enabled to advance the cause of righteousness, and carry forward the reformation to a greater state of purity and perfection, than has ever been experienced since the fall of man. And my mind, while penning these lines, is inspired with gratitude and thanksgiving to the God and Father of all our sure mercies, in that he hath been graciously pleased to lengthen out my days, to see and behold the approach of that blessed day. Blessed to those who are prepared to receive it, a day in which the Lord is arising to shake terribly the earth; but to those who oppose him in the way of his coming, a day of darkness and distress, of burning and fuel of fire. Wherein a birth is bringing and will be brought forth in many minds; not an outward one, not located to any particular place, people, or person, but an inward and spiritual one; a birth begotten of God in every rational soul that is willing and prepared to receive *it,* in likeness and operation to the little stone that Nebuchadnezzar saw cut out without hands, or the aid of any thing that is mortal, and which that outward birth of Jesus of the Virgin Mary, was a figure of, he being located and limited in his outward manifestation to the people of Israel. But this birth of God, brought forth in the immortal soul of man, God being its father, and the willing, devoted soul of man its mother: this brings us, and nothing short of this can bring us, to understand the prophecy, "For unto us a child is born, unto us a son is given;" or in other words, this new birth of the spirit every soul of man must witness brought forth within, or he cannot enter the Kingdom of Heaven. This is fully illustrated by the apostle Paul, when he says, "For as many as are led by the Spirit of God, are the Sons of God, and if sons, then heirs, heirs of God and joint heirs with Christ." This is the birth and Son that none know but the Father, and this is the Father that none know but the Son, or new birth, that is, as above described, begotten by him. And this comprehends that mystery of Godliness that is hid from the wise and prudent in this world's wisdom, but which is revealed by the Father to all his innocent and obedient children, who, as babes and sucklings, draw all their life and support from the breast of divine consolation. And although those who have been as princes among the people, may "set themselves, and the rulers take counsel together," in their traditional zeal, "against the Lord, and against his anointed:" Yet "he that sitteth in the Heavens shall laugh: and the Lord shall have them in derision; and vex them in his sore displeasure;" and will cast up a way for all his faithful and devoted children to walk in; a highway of holiness, wherein none shall be able to make them afraid. May the Lord hasten it, in his own time and will.

As thou observes, I have been favoured with a full statement of particulars that transpired in the course of your Yearly meeting. And it was cause of much joy to my mind, to find that truth bore away the victory and triumphed over delusion and error.

I shall repay thy namesake's kindness in his own coin; therefore tell him from me, that my heart would be truly gladdened to see him come forth more boldly and firmly in preaching the gospel of the grace of God, and directing the minds of the people, as the blessed Jesus and the worthy G. Fox did, to the spirit of truth or light within, as the only true and essential teacher and way of salvation, unembarrassed and separated from all the entanglements of Jewish and heathenish traditions and superstitions; as also from all and every dependance upon any external evidence, whether it be the testimony of men or of angels; for even outward miracles are not sufficient evidence to any but those who are present at the time of their manifestation, and even then they often are too weak to gain the full assent of a rational mind; of course, no evidence of the gospel. For what a sad predicament would the professors of Christianity be in, if they had no evidence of its truth but outward miracles, seeing when they were accomplished in the view of the bystanders, the magicians of Egypt could render the evidence of some of them doubtful. Therefore the written or verbal testimony of an outward miracle, is no certain evidence of the thing spoken of, hence not essential to us under the gospel, as that wholly depends upon much higher evidence. For had Moses told Pharaoh and the Israelites, that the Lord had sent him to deliver Israel from their bondage, and for proof of his mission, told them, that when he was in the wilderness, where the Lord spoke to him, in order to confirm them in the truth of his message, he cast his rod on the ground, and it became a frightful serpent; and when he was commanded to take it up again, it became a rod in his hand: had Moses come down with this story, would they not have been unwise to have believed him, had he not wrought the same miracle in their sight. Hence we learn that the hear-tell of an outward miracle is no miracle to us, and of course is no sufficient evidence to the real truth of any proposition unless supported by some better evidence.

As to what thou observes respecting the crucifixion of Jesus on the outward wooden cross, &c.; I meant no other than what thou observest, as applying only to the believing Jews, and I supposed that what I wrote to N. S.* implied the same. Be that as it may, that was the idea I intended to convey; for although that offering would have been sufficient for the

* See letter to Nathan Shoemaker.

whole nation, yet those who did not believe on him rendered it abortive, as to themselves, and therefore they lay under the penalties annexed to any breach of their law.

As to what thou observest about my using smoother instruments in order to render my work more pleasing and still as useful, if thou shouldst ever be brought to the trial from experience, the answer would then be plain; for the servant has no right to reason from consequences, nor to use any management, but when he is commanded to smite the rock, to do so, and when to speak calmly to it, to do so, let the consequence be what it may. And if a Moses could not be permitted to vary in the least degree, from the simple and plain word of command, without incurring a severe censure and a great loss to himself, what can such as I expect, if we undertake to indite for Jehovah? And I believe many precious gifts have been greatly marred and some lost, by endeavouring to please man.

Thou wilt not impute to neglect my not answering thy letter sooner, when I tell thee, that such is the number of letters received from many of my dear friends, that a dozen or more still remain unanswered, and some of considerably older date than thine; although I have industriously filled up all my time to clear myself of debt, when not employed in other pressing engagements.

Please present my dear love to thy wife and other of my dear friends, as the way opens, and with a large share for thyself, I rest thy assured friend.

ELIAS HICKS.

TO ABRAHAM LOWER, PHILADELPHIA.

Jericho, 7th mo. 26th, 1823.

My Dear Friend,

Although considerable time has elapsed since I last saw thee, yet the length of time and distance of way that have separated us, have not, in the least, diminished that cordial friendship and uniting love, that, I trust, was mutually witnessed between us, in the course of my last visit to your city: in the fresh feelings of which I affectionately salute thee, attended with desires that grace, mercy and peace may be with thee and abound. And this no doubt will be experienced, as we are unceasingly engaged to dwell deep with the immortal seed of eternal life in our own minds, whereby we shall be enabled to hold fast the profession of our faith without wavering, regardless of the frowns or favours of mortals. And as we persevere herein, through all the bustles and tumults that are in the world, and in its spirit, unshaken and immovable, in and through this day of trial and rebuke, for such it is, in which the Lord is arising to shake terribly the earth, and not only the earth, but the heavens also, that is, every false rest and self-created place of refuge, that man, in his own devising, hath set up, together with all man's earthly dependance, upon the work of his own hands,—those who thus persevere without wavering, being willing to endure hardness for the truth's sake, will, no doubt, in the close, obtain the end of their faith, even the salvation of their souls.

My lot and service since my return, have mostly been in and about home, in the compass of our own monthly meeting. I have likened my present situation to that of Mordecai of old, sitting quietly and patiently, in nothingness of self, at the waiting gate; a situation truly grateful.

I understand by letters from your city, our valued friend, Priscilla Hunt, met with much the same treatment, while among you, as fell to my lot: a few opposers, but many friends; that truth through her labours reigned triumphant, and clothed her mind with peace in the end, which is cause of grateful acknowledgment to Him, from whom all our rich blessings flow.

What will be the fate of these opposers? Have they become so exalted as to consider themselves only, the people, and that wisdom will die with them, that they thus withstand the truth? If they were wise of heart, would they not have learned submission to the truth, and to their friends, by the

things they have suffered, and no longer, by their adverse
proceedings, break the unity and disturb the peace of society.
I sorrow for them, lest they put off repentance to too late an
hour, and be led into such a dilemma as to become fighters
against God and his truth. Surely they stand in great need
of the sympathy and prayers of the faithful.

My bodily health is much the same, in general, as when I
was with you, and my peace of mind and confidence in the
Divine sufficiency steady and unshaken. To the Lord be
the praise of his own works, whose power is over all in the
truly obedient and humbly devoted soul.

My love flows to all my friends, particularly to those united
with me in the arduous labour of visiting families, Samuel
Noble, Joseph Warner, and George Woolley; and now, with
a large share to thyself, dear wife and family, I subscribe thy
sincere friend.

ELIAS HICKS.

TO WILLIAM POOLE, WILMINGTON.

Jericho, 9th mo. 12th, 1823.

My Dear Friend,

Thy letter of 6th mo. last, is now before me, and which I
have perused a number of times, with interest and satisfaction;
and although nearly three months have elapsed since its
reception, without an answer, yet believe me, my dear friend,
it is not owing to any abatement of love, and sincere regard
for thee and thine, that I have thus procrastinated. Being
circumstanced like other dependant mortals, who have not
times and seasons at their command, I have found it expedient
to wait, not only to know the right time, but also to feel, if
possible, some right qualification.

And although I cannot, at this time, lay much claim to
those requisites, yet, having thee in lively remembrance, with
thy dear companion, this morning, and feeling renewed sympathy with you, I was induced to put pen to paper, although

I might not be furnished with more than to acknowledge the continuance of my brotherly love, and sympathy with and for you; accompanied with desires for your steady progress in the path of duty, which is the path to life and peace; and I may add, that as a considerable time has elapsed since I have had any particular account from you, I feel desirous to hear how you fare.

I am quite of the mind with thee, that the limiting power, given to, or taken by our meetings for sufferings in this country, is inconsistent with the true liberty of the gospel state, and repugnant to the liberty exercised by our primitive Friends. It is sorrowful to observe, that almost every right step of reformation has gone down to the grave with the first instruments of such reform, or soon after. Their successors, instead of coming up in the same life and power that qualified the first instruments to set on foot the work of right reform, have set down at ease in their labours, as though the work was now completed. Hence they dwindled into a state of lifeless formality, contenting themselves with a form of godliness, while, in their lives and conduct, they manifestly denied the power thereof; which only can redeem the soul from sin and death. Then in come creeds and confessions of faith in lieu thereof, formed out of materials made ready to their hands, like as is represented by the brick and mortar made use of by the sons of Noah, that is, they are endeavouring to get to heaven through other men's experience, without coming to know and witness in themselves the heart-rending power of Divine love and light, by which the man of sin and son of perdition in them, might have been fully revealed; and by their willing obedience to the operation thereof, and their co-working with it, they might have come to witness, as their faithful predecessors had done, the man of sin cast out, and know a deliverance from the power of darkness, and a being translated into the kingdom of God. But, alas! instead thereof, "how is the gold become dim! how is the most fine gold changed!" The beautiful sons of the morning of our day, viz. our faithful and worthy predecessors, comparable to fine gold, how are too many of their successors changed and become as earthen pitchers.

The records and testimonies of past ages, amongst all nations, show the short existence and continuance of every right reformation, even from the days of Noah up to the present time. The family of Noah, although so awfully warned, how soon they returned to their old courses. The reformation, through Moses and Joshua, and the elders of Israel, lasted no longer than to the time of their death; and the several reforms after the death of these, by prophets and such as the Lord raised up for that end, were of short duration. So likewise, the reform produced by Jesus and his disciples, lasted very little longer than the life of John, the beloved apostle; and with what mighty power did Anti-christ reign from the beginning of the third century until Luther's small reform, which was soon lost in his successors. It so fared with Calvin and some others, up to the time of George Fox; and, although his reform very far exceeded all others since the fall of primitive Christianity, yet alas! how is life, how is power, how is faithfulness wanting among a very great portion of his successors? Many of whom, nevertheless, are very zealous to set up forms and confessions of faith, instead of coming to and submitting themselves to the real life and power of Godliness: which, if it is abode in, renders all creeds and confessions of faith nugatory and of no avail.

In answer to thy request respecting my age, &c., I may reply, that according to the record of my birth, as found in an ancient Bible in my father's possession, I was born the 19th day of 3d month, 1748. My father was considered a member among Friends at the time of my birth, which in that day gave me the privilege of taking a wife in the order of Society, and that established my membership. My mother was never in strict fellowship with any religious society, but was a woman of strict morality, and generally beloved and respected by her neighbours and acquaintance of every profession. She died with the consumption, when I was about ten years of age.

I was born in Queens County, Long Island, on the north

side of the great plains, generally known by the name of Hempstead Plains, about three miles west of the meetinghouse at Westbury; but in my eighth year, my father removed to the sea shore, on the south side of the island, where I continued to reside until married: I then settled at Jericho, my present residence.

As to thy inquiry, whether I have any settled intention respecting leaving a journal of my life, &c., I am at present not prepared to answer. For, although I have made some notes of my journeys, and of some things that have transpired in the course of my pilgrimage, yet I have doubts, of latter time, whether there is a propriety and a utility in so much written testimony, or whether it does not tend to clog and shut up the avenue to better instruction, and whether, what is revealed to one generation, is as likely to be profitable to a succeeding one, as to that to which it was particularly directed and opened, and therefore, to intrude that upon a succeeding generation, which was particularly adapted and suited to the state of a previous one, may it not have a tendency to cause the succeeding generation to look back to the letter, instead of keeping a single eye to the spirit, which can only furnish us with knowledge and ability to make progress in reformation? For nothing short of an advancement in light can enable us to advance reformation. Therefore every generation must have more light than the preceding one, otherwise they must sit down at ease, in the labour and works of their predecessors, and hence, of such it might be said, ye have done nothing at all, ye have only lived in a state of idleness on the labour of your fathers.

Just like such young men, who have a very large temporal property left them by their fathers, and therefore think they have enough without labour. And although it may bring them through tolerably well, yet, as they bring their children up in idleness, we find the third or fourth generation are often reduced to a state of abject poverty; and it is the same, I believe, in religion. And this accounts for the falling away of every right reformation, the successors of the reformers sitting down in a state of idleness in the labour of their predecessors. And is it not reasonable to suppose, that what was revealed to our predecessors was most peculiarly adapted to them and to their states, and not to ours of a succeeding generation.

Jesus says, "I have yet many things to say unto you, but ye cannot bear them now. Howbeit when he, the Spirit of Truth, is come, he will guide you into all truth." This certainly is better than the journals and epistles of men's writing, in a previous age, although written by Divine inspiration.

I must now conclude, with just observing, that since I began this letter, I have been informed that our friend Isaac Stephenson, from old England, has appointed a meeting to-morrow at this place. I have not yet seen him, but reports speak well of him, as a plain, simple, worthy Friend, and a good minister. He proposes taking some meetings this way.

In much love to thee and thine, in which my wife and daughter Elizabeth unite, I subscribe thy affectionate friend.

ELIAS HICKS.

TO SAMUEL COMFORT, BUCKS COUNTY, PA.

Flushing, 10*th* mo. 23*d*, 1823.

My Dear Friend,

Thine of last month was duly received, and was very acceptable, for although as to any outward acquaintance, thou art to me an entire stranger, yet in the feeling of that love that is stronger than death, and which binds together all the living children of the Heavenly Father's family, I feel thee near in the unity of the one spirit, and in the fresh feelings thereof I greet thee, accompanied with desires that grace, mercy, and peace may be with thee and abound.

I am here attending our Quarterly meeting, and have with me a minute of concurrence from our Monthly meeting, with a concern I have some time felt, to perform a small tour of religious duty to some of the adjacent quarters of our Yearly meeting, and look up some of the publicans and sinners, who, or many of them, as Jesus said, are likely, I think, to enter into the kingdom sooner than many of our high professing scribes and Pharisees, who are not only not willing to enter themselves, but are endeavouring to hinder those that would.

As my time is limited I shall not write much at present, but may just add, that I unite with thee, that the views generally held by the professors of Christianity, as to what it is and who it is, that bruises the serpent's head, are very incorrect, as they consider it all effected by the man Christ Jesus. But he only did his own part; for the woman here is spoken of by way of allegory, as representing the true church, the King of Heaven's true spouse, whose seed comprehends all the faithful devoted children of our Heavenly Father, all of whom have their part in bruising the serpent's head, by slaying the enmity in themselves; by getting a complete conquest, through the aid of Divine grace, over the serpentine wisdom of the creature, that leads the mind into reasoning against the Divine commands, aided by the natural propensities of the earthly or fleshly part; from which all our temptations arise. Hence there is always enmity between the flesh and the spirit, until one or the other overcomes; for the flesh warreth against the spirit, and the spirit against the flesh: hence the creature hath no true peace until the spirit overcomes and subjects and silences all the motions of the flesh. Then the creature can rejoice and say with one formerly, "There is therefore now no condemnation to them which are in Christ Jesus," that is, those who through Divine grace have come up into his likeness, into his righteousness, into his image, "who walk not after the flesh, but after the spirit. For the law of the spirit of life in Christ Jesus," or the same law that ruled and governed in Jesus Christ, "hath made me free from the law of sin and death." Even so let it be in all the Lord's children, even Amen for ever.

In much love to thee and thine, I rest thy sincere friend.

ELIAS HICKS.

P. S. Please to remember me affectionately to all my friends in thy neighbourhood, as way opens in thy freedom, not forgetting thy brother John. E. H.

TO WILLIAM POOLE, WILMINGTON.

Jericho, 12th mo. 7th, 1823.

MY DEAR FRIEND,

Thy letters of 9th month 18th, 10th month 24th, and 11th month 26th, that remain unanswered, are now before me. And although I could give several reasons for not answering them, yet I will mention but one, and that is, way has not opened for it until now: and notwithstanding a near sympathy with thee in thy tribulations has been witnessed, yet it may be that Infinite Wisdom, in the riches of his love, is leading thee off from all outward dependances, that so thy hope and trust may be more fully and firmly fixed on him alone, who is the everlasting and inexhaustible source of strength and consolation. And although the severing of those who have been bound together in the strong bands of conjugal love, is like the parting of bone from bone, yet, as all our rich blessings are but the goods of our kind and gracious benefactor, and are only loaned to us during his good pleasure, so when he calls for them, as they are his just right, we ought cheerfully to surrender them, with due acknowledgments and gratitude for the unmerited favour, in suffering us to enjoy them so long as we have. To which I may add for thy increased comfort, that I have not the least doubt, that, although the absence of thy dear companion may seem to thee at the first view, a great loss, it is to her an eternal gain, and may eventually also, as thou acquiesces in the Divine will, bring thee to realize, in contemplation, a portion of that celestial joy that encircles her mansion.

As relates to a memoir of my life, &c., it appears that my reasons for objecting to such a publication, are not satisfactory to thee. What those reasons were I do not remember, as I have no copy of that letter, and I seldom keep a copy of my letters, unless they are of a controversial kind. But may now further observe, that I agree with thee, that the abuse of a blessing is no argument against its being dispensed; but it must be first proved that the thing is a blessing, and was intentionally dispensed as such, by the great Dispenser of all real good. I have no doubt when the apostle, under the influence of Divine love, addressed an epistle to the Corinthians, that he was rightly directed therein, and as he knew and was led into a right knowledge of their states, so he could administer to their needs and to their instruction. But I do not apprehend that he had the most distant idea that he was writing to nations yet unborn, and of whose state and condition he could have no knowledge. Nor do I believe that Divine Wisdom, when he influenced the mind of the apostle to write his several epistles to the Corinthians, &c., intended them for a rule to after ages; for had that been the case, he would have made them as plain and clear as he did the law to Israel, so that every one should understand them alike. And although the law to Israel does not concern us in the present day, yet every one that sees it reads it alike—it admits of no controversy. But not so with the writings of the apostles; for the best and wisest of men disagree respecting them. And the Scriptures of the primitive Christians, from the early ages of Christianity, have been made a principal cause of the division, the controversy, the war, and the persecution and cruelty, that have convulsed and drenched Christendom in blood ever since it has been called Christendom. And does it not impeach the wisdom and goodness of our great Benefactor, to suppose he ever intended those writings as a rule, when the best of men cannot understand them alike?

But the reason is obvious. The gospel law is inward and spiritual, and cannot be comprehended in outward characters, but must be written in every heart distinctly, as our states and conditions are all different and distinct; and it is always suited to the state and condition of every heart, and of course must act diversely in each mind, according to the diversity of their several dispositions, propensities and passions. Therefore no literal law, or creed, can take place under the gospel, except in moral or outward things; for no outward law can bind the soul, as the government of the soul is exclusively the prerogative of God and not of man.

Thou sayest, the same arguments would operate against preaching the gospel; but I say nay, not in the least degree; for if the minister is under the right influence, he will be led more or less into the very state and condition of the hearers, and his words will carry their own evidence, being clothed with power. But it cannot be so with epistles written to certain states a thousand years ago. And I make no doubt but thou sees clearly, that should we now go to make up a rule, or creed, from the writings of primitive Friends, what breach of harmony, nay what confusion it would make in Society. And although preaching the gospel with the Holy Ghost sent down from heaven, is the best and most excellent of all outward means, and it was all that Jesus directed his disciples to practise, yet I will also admit that epistles may be written suited to the time in which they are written. Nevertheless, if the right improvement was made by every generation, truths would be so opened in every age as to supersede the use of what had gone before. Thus an advancement in reformation would be experienced, old things would be left behind, and new things, in the wisdom of truth, would be opened on the minds of honest travellers Zion-ward.

But, alas! instead of pressing forward toward the mark for the prize of the high calling of God in Christ Jesus, how many are looking back to the weak and beggarly elements, to which they seem willing to be in bondage.

Had the successors of the apostles attended, as they ought to have done, to the command given by Jesus to his disciples, to wait for the promise of the Holy Spirit, as no doubt they were directed to do by the disciples, that being the only necessary and sufficient qualification to preach the gospel, as the disciples had done, with the Holy Ghost sent down from heaven accompanying their words, and so in succession from generation to generation, the apostacy never could have entered. But instead thereof, they turned their attention to the letter, one crying I am of Paul, another I am of Apollos, &c., and neglected the spirit; hence divisions and contentions originated in the church, and destroyed the peace and unity thereof, and, in process of time, plunged it into a desperate state of total darkness. The same fate from the same cause has befallen, in a great degree, our poor Society. But had Friends kept to the light and spirit of truth, as recommended in the preaching of George Fox and our primitive worthies, and waited for its clear manifestation, and moved only under the operation of its power, no apostacy could have entered; but the Society ere now would have made great advancement on the labours and experience of those early worthies. Many things would have been opened in succession on the minds of the faithful, by the same light of truth, that George Fox and the people of that day could not have borne. But instead thereof, Friends turned their attention back to the letter of the Scriptures and the writings of our primitive Friends, which were particularly useful in the day and time in which they were written; but in after time, when the light was leading, or would have led, all who were faithful to its manifestations, to an advancement to greater and brighter experience in divine things, they have blocked up their own way by an undue attention to the letter.

But when the light is calling away from these weak and beggarly elements, those old writings are no more nor less than the letter that killeth, and, if rested in, will have the same effect as the reading of the law of Moses had upon the primitive disciples; it will and does bring a veil upon the heart, and turns backward to a former dispensation, instead of leading forward in the new and living way, which only can add fresh life and vigour to the soul, and enable it to go forward on its heavenly journey, without fainting by the way.

Could I pen down something that might be useful to the present and succeeding generation, and then be obliterated, it might not be amiss; but as I am looking forward in the faith, that greater and brighter things will be opened to a succeeding generation, than I and the people of this generation can bear, this makes me unwilling to leave any thing of my experience, that might tend to hinder the reception of those new and advanced revelations. For thou seest clearly, I trust, that the writings called the Scriptures, and those of our primitive Friends, are the strongest bulwark made use of by the carnally-minded, to put to silence new openings of truth, on the minds of the faithful in the present day.

I might add, but must draw to a close for want of room; and in renewed feeling of brotherly love to thee and thine, bid farewell.

ELIAS HICKS.

N. B. Please to excuse the incorrectness of my letter, as I have not time to copy it, nor room for much alteration, but hope thou wilt be able to come at the substance.

E. H.

TO ABRAHAM LOWER, PHILADELPHIA.

Jericho, 1st m.o. 26th, 1821.

My truly beloved Friend,

Thy very acceptable letter of the 15th ult. came duly to hand, and its salutary contents revived afresh, that near sympathy, fellow feeling and unity, I trust mutually witnessed, when favoured with each other's company for a short season, and at which time was verified that saying, "As iron sharpeneth iron, so doth a man's countenance that of his friend."

I often look back with pleasure on the time I spent with my dear friends at Philadelphia, and, in a particular manner, the near unity and fellowship witnessed with those of Green Street monthly meeting, whom I visited in the Gospel of Christ. And although the enemy of all good seemed busy in endeavouring to stir up opposition, yet, through the condescending goodness of Israel's Shepherd, the truth was raised so above him, and so bruised his head, that he had no power to bruise the heel, but was cast out into the earth, the habitation of beasts. And, dear friend, seeing the Lord, by his own right hand of power, hath been with us, and preserved us thus far, and hath enabled us to set up our Ebenezer, let us thank him and take courage, standing fast in the faith, without wavering or turning aside in the least degree, although all men may rise up against us; ever remembering, however we may be buffeted within or without, his grace is sufficient for us in the midst of all our tribulations; and as we continue faithful, without turning aside, to the right hand or to the left, through the fear or favour of man, he will carry us through and over all to his praise who is calling us to glory and virtue.

I find by thy letter that some of your elders, &c. are still proceeding in the same disorderly manner, as when I was with you. How presuming, for a quarterly meeting of ministers and elders, to intermeddle with the local concerns of a monthly meeting. I should not think it necessary for the monthly meeting to pay any attention to them, nor be turned aside from proceeding in the regular line of discipline, with any of their members, whether ministers or elders, who act disorderly by breaking the unity of the meeting. We have a small number in our quarterly meeting who seem to have been led away somewhat in a manner similar to those in your city, who opposed us when I was with you; but they are more mild, and some of them seem as though they might again come into unity with Friends.

I have been engaged of late around the suburbs of our quarter in searching out, in the highways and hedges, the halt, the maimed, and the blind, among Episcopalians, Presbyterians, Baptists, Methodists, and Nothing-arians, and I perceive, among the ministers of the various sects, my communications have made the Methodists the most uneasy; they talk pretty loud, and finding no better way to vent their malice, they have been endeavouring to prove that I am no Quaker, and, Herod and Pontius Pilate like, the Presbyterian minister and Methodist have made friends, in order to persecute me; but their arrows are all blunted like those in your city; they dont hurt, they fall to the ground before they reach me. I was out in this little tour about eleven days, and attended seventeen meetings, and previous thereto, in the latter part of the fall, I visited three of the adjacent quarterly meetings, next above our quarter, and have great cause of humble gratitude and thankfulness to the great and blessed Author of all our rich mercies and blessings, who continued to be near, a present helper in every needful time: blessed be his great and excellent name, for his mercy endureth for ever.

I have circulated the proposals thou sent me, on behalf of Joseph Rakestraw, for printing the Christian Quaker, by William Penn and George Whitehead.

I apprehend, with the present prospect, he may go on with the work, and strike off a pretty large edition. And I am like-minded with thee, that there has not been a time, previous to the present, that these writings could be read to more advantage and profit than at this time; for such was the bias of tradition and superstition that covered with darkness the minds of the people when they were first published, that none but a few of the most enlightened, could then bear them. The people's minds in general were so bound down by the prejudice of a corrupt education, and by the teachings of their blind leaders, that they were offended at every advancement of reformation. For traditional religion, as the records of past time assure us, cannot admit of any advancement, hence we see that traditional religion is always a persecuting one, and always stands in opposition to reform.

To conclude: may grace, mercy, and peace be with thee and abound, and may the Lord Almighty be thy stay and thy staff in every proving season, and carry thee through and over all, to the praise of his great and excellent name, who is over all, blessed for ever.

In near and dear love to thee and thine, I rest thy friend.

ELIAS HICKS.

N. B. Please to present my love to inquiring friends, especially those who were united with me in the work of the Gospel, as also in the fellowship of the suffering and joy dispensed to us in the visit to the families in your monthly meeting, not forgetting our ancient friend George Justice.

E. H.

TO WILLIAM POOLE, WILMINGTON.

Jericho, 3d mo. 26th, 1824.

DEAR FRIEND,

Thy kind letter of the 3d instant came duly to hand and fully confirmed my suspicion concerning thee, that something had transpired which led to so long silence, and I had become very anxious to hear from thee, before the reception of the letter above alluded to; the contents of which, if possible, have increased my sympathy with and for thee in thy present afflicted state; accompanied with a hope, that thou mayest be favoured yet, to see good days and be enabled to join thy rightly exercised brethren in the arduous labour, in pulling down error and exalting the standard of truth upon its own sure foundation.

The following Essay was written some time past by a correspondent of mine, in answer to a small pamphlet entitled, "A False Position Exposed." The author, to show what he considered a false position, observes, that "some persons dogmatically asserted that we are under no obligation to believe what we do not understand."

The tract entitled, "A False Position Exposed," has fallen short of its design, so far as it relates to me, in rendering a reason for rejecting a doctrine, founded in reason and substantiated by experience.

From the tenor of the arguments adduced to expose the unsoundness of the position, I am convinced the writer has mistaken its nature and legitimate meaning. If he had quoted the writers in the affirmative of the question, we should have been able to judge more accurately of the motive which caused them to adopt and promulgate the sentiment. For my own part I am willing to be considered a friend to the proposition.

and fearlessly assert, that we *cannot*, and therefore *are not*, bound to believe what we cannot comprehend. I observed the position is founded in *reason*, because it is the essential property of reason to analyze every subject which challenges belief, and decide according to the greater measure of evidence; and if the subject brought before its view is too mighty for its limited powers, it must remain in darkness; for it is an undoubted truth, that secret things belong to God, but things revealed, to us and our children. It therefore follows that things which are secret cannot be believed, because they cannot be comprehended: the admission of this theory limits the mind to the acknowledgment of truths revealed, and effectually prevents our professing to know and understand things or subjects which have been kept secret from the foundation of the world. It would bring to pass what the author of the expose says; "It is extremely desirable that every man should use his own understanding, and not implicitly take any thing for granted, as being wise and true, merely because another person may dogmatically and roundly assert it to be so." And it would present insuperable difficulties to the conscientious sectarian when required to acknowledge creeds and systems, which their warmest advocates admit are contradictory.

No matter how true a proposition or thing may be, or is in itself, if the witness does not know it to be so, his testification is false. The application of this rule to religious opinions would enable us to distinguish between those who have a faith according to knowledge, and those who have a faith according to tradition. The admission of such a principle would not destroy our belief in the Scriptures, but rather establish it, because it would induce an honest inquiry after truth, and make us extremely cautious how we became witnesses, one way or the other. We may understand and believe the Scriptures to be divinely inspired writings, without being able to unravel all their mysteries. We may comprehend the truth of Paul's declaration, that all scripture was given by inspiration of God, (that was so given,) although we may not comprehend his meaning when he wrote things hard to be understood, which no man can say he believes until he has been learned the interpretation thereof, by the same Spirit that searcheth all things. If Paul did not comprehend what he believed and taught, he was certainly like those he reproved, who had a zeal for God, but not according to knowledge; and all those who pretend they believe what they do not understand, certainly confess they know not what they say, nor whereof they affirm. The Essay before mentioned is as follows:—

"'Comprehension is that act of the mind, whereby it apprehends any object that is presented to it, on all the sides whereon it is capable of being apprehended or known.' If the above definition be true, we will at once perceive that the proposition does not embrace the idea that we must reject things we positively know to exist, because the manner or reason of their existence is a mystery. It is not necessary for us to know the motives of a writer, or to believe all his assertions, to enable us to understand that such a book was written, or that the author was in existence. We need not know why A gives his bond to B in order to ascertain the amount of the bond, or to establish its reality. No man pretends to comprehend the *manner* in which God exists, and yet by things which are made, he can comprehend and believe that such a being made the worlds, and all that in them is.

"We can comprehend that the world exists without being able to conceive the necessary relation that exists between the act by which God decreed that the world should exist in time, and its actual existence. It is not necessary for us to know how, or in what manner, the Creator made the sun, moon and stars, and appointed their several stations, to enable us to comprehend their use and actual existence. We are not obliged to analyze the beams of the sun, which warm and enlighten us, or to decompose the air we breathe, in order to comprehend the benign influence of the one, or the absolute certainty of the other.

"I can comprehend this drop of water, this grain of sand, and this slender herb, without a knowledge of their intrinsic properties or nature; and although I cannot comprehend how matter and mind are united, nor explain how the nourishment taken into the stomach, is converted into blood or bones, yet I know and comprehend the fact : 'I think therefore I exist.' To know certainly what we believe, we must certainly understand what we know. We read of some in old time, who, when they knew God, refused to worship him as God ; and others. who knew their master's will, yet did it not. I would ask the objector to the position, whether these persons comprehended the object and subjects, the Scriptures declare they knew. If we refer to the experience of the apostles, we find they could not believe, until they were made to understand what was required of them : that which they knew, and had seen, they testified of; they were substantial witnesses, because they were enabled to comprehend the mystery. And they strove 'by the foolishness of preaching' to enlighten the understanding of their hearers; and all those who thought the evidence strong enough, believed.

"When the eunuch read Isaiah, without comprehending his meaning, he was an unbeliever; but when his understanding was opened, he believed. 'Ye do err, not knowing the Scriptures,' said Jesus to his unbelieving neighbours. Did he intend to say they did not believe in the book? No. They believed the Scriptures to be the words of God ; but pretending to give an interpretation to them, before they comprehended their meaning, they became blind : but when the medium of comprehension was opened, and the light of truth rendered them intelligible, they made a proper application of the prophecies. Hence we see a belief without knowledge, was like faith without works, a perfect nonentity. Knowledge must precede belief, conviction must precede conversion, and truth must be understood before it can be loved. Ignorance is no longer held to be the mother of devotion. A blind adherence to any doctrines, whether true or false, generates darkness; and the adoption of unintelligible dogmas gives a doubtful character to truth itself.

"If the writers against the proposition mean to say, that faith enables us to comprehend all things which reason cannot unfold, I am ready to unite with the sentiment, because it establishes the truth of our position, by admitting the absolute necessity of that light which makes all things manifest, and introduces evidence into the mind, and proves to a demonstration, that we can *believe* only in proportion as we are enabled to *comprehend*. And as it is the special province of the spirit of truth, to lead into all truth, it follows as a certain consequence, that we shall never be able to comprehend all truth, until we are led into the knowledge of it."

Some of my friends at Wilmington have recently furnished me with the first number of a new periodical work, called "The Berean," in which I perceived an attempt to prove the same plain truth, which was the design of the author of the foregoing essay, viz. that we are not *bound*, and because we *cannot* believe what we do not understand. And although it would seem that there is scarcely any axiom in Euclid more self-evident than the above position, yet how astonishing it is to consider, that there are many among the professors of Christianity, so blind and so bewildered by the force of tradition and superstition, as to oppose such a self-evident proposition. As to the hireling clergy opposing it, it is not so strange; as this, like many other truths of real Christianity, touches them in such a very tender place, to wit, the purse, that we are not to wonder; as its tendency, if generally acknowledged, would take from them their fat benefices, and spoil the trade of priestcraft. Therefore, when the people's eyes are likely to be opened, as were the Ephesians,'by Paul, they cry out, (Demetrius-like, when they have called together the workmen of the same craft,) saying, "Sirs, ye know that by this craft we have our wealth;" for Paul had convinced them, "that they be no Gods, which are made with hands;" and surely the Trinitarians' Gods are less so, as they are neither visible to the external nor internal senses, of course they are, as to their personality, a nonentity, the mere creatures of the imagination. But, inasmuch as there are many led away with the delusion, that we must believe some things that we neither know nor understand, one of the most inconsistent and hurtful of which is, the absurd doctrine of the Trinity; therefore, I hope, the individual who has taken his pen in "The Berean," to confute it, will not lay it down again, until he has razed it to its very foundation, and will not leave a single vestige of it to interrupt the minds of any of the children of men in future.

I was likewise favoured, by some of my friends of Wilmington, with a copy of Brownlee's book, entitled "A careful and free Inquiry into the true Nature and Tendency of the Religious Principles of the Society of Friends." Had he said he had carefully examined and searched in all the envious, slanderous books, of the old persecuting enemies of the Society of Friends, and had carefully culled the falsehood and gross misrepresentations they contained, or that the most inveterate opposers could invent, to scandalize the Society, and had added to it not a little of his own, his book would then have answered better to its title. My friend aforesaid, suggests a thought, that should I think proper to communicate any matter concerning said book, it would be acceptable to his friends at Wilmington.

But I am ready almost to conclude, whether entirely to neglect it, would not be the best answer; for really it does not appear to be worthy of a serious answer, as its contents are generally made up of irrelevant, contradictory, and heterogeneous matter, that I think he answers and confutes himself, as he goes along. But as some person has made some correct remarks on said book, in the first number of the Berean, I shall not cast any discouragement in his way; for such is the influence that many of the hirelings have over the credulous, that let them say what they will, some are ready to receive it as truth. How such are to be pitied!

I shall now draw to a close, and in near affection and sympathy rest, as ever, thy friend.

ELIAS HICKS.

TO SAMUEL COMFORT, BUCKS COUNTY, PA.

Jericho, 4th mo. 4th, 1824.

Dear Friend,

Thine of the 15th ult. was duly received, and read with satisfaction, tending to excite renewed feelings of that love and true Christian fellowship, that binds together in the indissoluble bond all the living children of our Heavenly Father's family.

The young Friends, who were the bearers of it, have been agreeably with us for several days past; and my engagements have been such since they came, that I rather despaired of writing by them, agreeably to thy request. But having a little leisure this afternoon, after my friends had retired, I concluded I would attempt to indite a few lines, without expecting to satisfy thy request in regard to church government, for want of ability, although I consider it a very simple thing to the truly enlightened mind.

The root and ground of all right church government, is laid down by the great Christian lawgiver, as it respects moral order. "If thy brother shall trespass against thee, go and tell him his fault between thee and him alone; if he shall hear thee, thou hast gained thy brother.

"But if he will not hear thee, then take with thee one or two more, that in the mouth of two or three witnesses every word may be established.

"And if he shall neglect to hear them, tell it unto the church: but if he neglect to hear the church, let him be unto thee as an heathen man and a publican." Matthew xviii. 15, 16, 17.

"All things whatsoever ye would that men should do to you, do ye even so unto them: for this is the law and the prophets." Matthew vii. 12.

These doctrines, I conceive, comprehend the substance of all church order. If any part of our discipline does not stand in accordance with these doctrines, such part ought to be considered spurious. But I have often thought that much more harm arises to Society from a wrong execution of the discipline, than from the letter itself. For, as many undertake to be active in the execution of the discipline, who have never passed under the baptizing operation of the spirit of truth, that can only prepare for the work, these darken counsel by words without knowledge, and bring death over a meeting, and stop the progress of right order. These are "sensual, having not the spirit, having men's persons in admiration, because of advantage."

To free the Society from such officious innovators, requires the united exertions of all the faithful, and which can only be done by a firm and faithful administration of right gospel order, without partiality.

Did each monthly meeting attend closely to the order comprehended in the foregoing doctrines, we should soon get rid of many unworthy members, who are destroying the peace of the Society. That when any member should report any thing publicly against a brother or sister, without first going privately to see them, let the matter be true or false, they ought to be dealt with, and unless they make satisfaction to the party aggrieved by such tale-bearing, they ought to be disowned. For as the wise Solomon saith, "The words of a tale-bearer are as wounds, and he that repeateth a matter separateth very friends."

There is another evil increasing of late in Society, that of publicly opposing a Friend, who may apprehend it is his or her duty to speak by way of exhortation in a meeting. If the person so opposed be a member, and the monthly meeting, to which he belongs, have not declared their disunity with him, such person, so opposing, ought to be dealt with without fail.

If our monthly meetings were, in general, as faithful and firm as one of late has been in your parts, it would soon restore peace and tranquillity; for nothing, I believe, but disorderly conduct of that kind, has been the occasion of the present uneasiness and disturbance in the Society.

Many persons from mere envy, I believe, have been induced

to spread evil reports, in direct violation of the discipline, and some of them have led others to join them in the same disorderly practice; and these kind of disorders seem increasing among us by some from whom we might have expected better things,—among the rest, that of not rising from their seats in times of public supplication. The preservation of peace in Society, depends much upon monthly meetings and individuals keeping close to the order of our discipline; and if circumstances have altered, so as to make it necessary for some alteration in the discipline, let that be done as way opens for it.

But as the law outward is only made for transgressors, so it will never be sufficient for a righteous man to square his conduct by; for every man who attends to the inward Divine law, rises above the control of all outward law; and it is such that are only qualified to make and execute discipline, consistent with the order of the gospel.

In much love and Christian affection, I subscribe thy sincere friend.

ELIAS HICKS.

TO WILLIAM POOLE, WILMINGTON.

New York, 5*th* mo. 25*th*, 1824.

My Dear Friend,

Thy very acceptable letter, finished on thy way home from Philadelphia, and the one by the bearer of these, was duly received, and their contents were very grateful and encouraging, tending to strengthen the bond and brighten the chain of that mutual love and friendship, that has existed between us ever since our first acquaintance, and which, I trust, will live beyond the grave. I find that thou still feels thyself as dwelling in Mesheck, or in the low valley; a situation that gives us a better estimate of our dependant and real character, than when we are permitted to ride the king's horse, and, for a short time, to be clothed in his royal apparel; as the former places us in a state of safety, if we patiently acquiesce therein, as when we are at the bottom we can fall no lower. And I never feel myself safer and better situated than when I am at the King's gate, waiting and watching that none might be permitted to destroy the King's life, not even his chamberlains, or principal servants, nor intrude upon his power, but that he may quietly and peaceably sit upon his throne, and all the earth keep silence before Him; then continued peace will reign, and the earth and its inhabitants, as they quietly submit and resign to His holy will, are permitted to rejoice before him, in every diverse allotment or dispensation, of his loving kindness, wisdom and power. Therefore, I hope my dear friend, thou wilt not dwell too much upon the dark side of things, but endeavour to dwell in that cheerful state of mind recommended by our great pattern, when he mentioned that great truth to his disciples, and which we all know and experience as such; viz. "In the world ye shall have tribulation; but be of good cheer; I have overcome the world,"—and doubt not but that we, by the same power that enabled him to overcome, may also overcome: therefore, my dear friend, let us, in every dispensation of his love and power, cheerfully resign and thank God, and take courage.

We have proceeded but a little way in the business of our yearly meeting as yet, nevertheless, one subject has brought us to a pretty close trial of our faith and patience. A proposition was brought forward, previous to reading the epistles, to omit noticing or reading the London printed epistle, and although it appeared very clear, that much the greater part of the meeting were ready, and even desirous of adopting the measure, yet a few were so opposed thereto, that it was thought best, for the present, to condescend to them and suffer it to be read; which, I hope, will be the last time such epistles will be read in our yearly meeting.

We have heard much said in Society of late, concerning new doctrines, but in the course of this yearly meeting we have already had more novel and strange doctrines held forth among us, than I have ever heard before; such as these, that our victory over sin is not to be known on this side the grave; that the humanity of Jesus Christ prays to his own divinity; that not to believe, that the crucifixion of the body of Jesus without the gates of old Jerusalem, was a sufficient atonement for the sins of the whole world, unchristians us, and renders us criminal, &c. Our yearly meeting for discipline was conducted in a good degree of harmony and condescension, but our select meeting was the most trying I ever experienced. A. B. took such a high stand in our public meetings, as to leave scarcely any time for others to exercise their gifts, greatly to the wounding of many exercised minds, that I fear, instead of promoting the noble cause we are called to promote, weakness and suffering have been increased, greatly to the grief of the honest-hearted.

28th. Our yearly meeting of discipline closed this afternoon, but the select meeting stands adjourned until to-morrow morning.

In much love to thee and thine, in which my wife joins, I subscribe thy affectionate friend.

ELIAS HICKS.

TO WILLIAM POOLE, WILMINGTON.

Baltimore, 10th mo. 26th, 1824.

My Dear Friend,

Thy letter of the 22d instant was duly received, and its contents were very acceptable, excepting the part announcing thy late affliction, and present weak state of body; which information has excited afresh near sympathy with thee, yet not without a hope, that in the end all these bodily afflictions, which for the present are not joyous, but rather grievous; as the mind is raised to look beyond the present to the future, and thereby becomes strengthened to acquiesce in all the varied dispensations allotted us by a wise and gracious providence, while passing through this vale of probation, so necessary in order for our advancement in the pathway to virtue and glory; will work together for good in the accomplishment of the noble end and glorious designs of the heavenly Father, in the creation and restoration of his children. As to the time, if health is continued, of our seeing our friends at Wilmington and its vicinity, as I feel myself as a poor dependant day labourer, I cannot at present ascertain when it will be; but from my present prospect, believe I shall call upon you in my way home, and it may be within the compass of ten or twelve days from the present time.

Friends here seem progressing in their yearly meeting concerns, as far as they have advanced, cheerfully, and with apparent unanimity.

The meeting of ministers and elders got through the business of that meeting in one day, and closed for this year at five o'clock last seventh day evening, in apparent harmony and concord.

The yearly meeting has several subjects of considerable moment now before it, which have been committed to the consideration of committees.

29th. One of the subjects mentioned was a proposition to omit reading the London printed epistle, on which the committee thereon unanimously reported as their sense, that the reading of it be discontinued; which report the meeting confirmed, and it was laid by without further notice.

A proposal came up from Baltimore quarter, for altering the discipline in such manner, that when any member goes out in marriage it may be considered a voluntary relinquishment of his or her right in Society, and to be disowned without any further notice; but this proposition was not agreed to. And as we shall likely, in a few days, be favoured to speak together face to face, I will now come to a close, with just observing, that I feel very thankful that it has been my lot to attend this yearly meeting; as I do not remember that I ever sat a yearly meeting with greater satisfaction. Friends having passed through their business in much harmony and brotherly condescension, the meeting closed last evening.

Meetings are laid out for us in our way to your place as

follows; to-morrow evening at six o'clock, at Bush, first day at Deer Creek, second day at Little Britain, third day at Eastland, fourth day at West Nottingham, fifth day at East Nottingham; after which, we shall direct our course towards Wilmington, without any present prospect of stopping much on the way. In much love to thee and thine, in which my wife unites, I subscribe thy affectionate friend.

ELIAS HICKS.

TO WILLIAM POOLE, WILMINGTON.

Philadelphia, 12mo. 4th, 1824.

MY DEAR FRIEND,

Thine of the 28th ult. excited afresh in my mind deep sympathy and fellow feeling with thee, in thy present state of complicated bodily affliction; and although, as thou observes, it is undoubtedly all under right direction, and which is altogether in accordance with my views, nevertheless, no affliction for the present seems joyous; yet they tend to create a hope in the minds of those who continue in the way of well doing and are rightly exercised thereby, in full acquiescence with every dispensation of a gracious providence, that they will all work together for our good, and produce, to those who hold out to the end, a more exceeding and eternal weight of glory. And having this hope as an anchor to the soul, amidst every conflicting and trying scene, let us, my dear friend, thank God, and take courage, in a full belief that he will never leave nor forsake the upright in heart.

I have so far recovered my usual state of health, that I ventured out and attended three meetings this week, on third, fourth, and fifth days, viz. the North, Twelfth Street, and Green Street, to the peace of my own mind, and, I believe, to the general satisfaction, comfort and encouragement of my friends; but some cavilled, viz. an hireling priest and two or three of those who style themselves orthodox; and there is no doubt in my mind, that should the purest departed saints be permitted to return and preach among these, the pure unsullied doctrines of the Gospel, they would make a much greater uproar among the people. Such, I conceive, is the deplorable state of the professed churches in Christendom.

We expect to leave town this afternoon and ride to Germantown, to be at meeting there to-morrow; on second day at Abington, and on fourth day at Byberry. So far meetings are laid out for us. On fifth day will be the monthly meeting of Newtown, on sixth day at Middletown, on seventh day at Falls; should we find it in our way to attend those meetings, and be able to go forward, we shall likely attend the meeting at Trenton to-morrow week; after which, if health is permitted, we shall bend our course homewards.

In that love that many waters cannot quench, I subscribe, thy affectionate friend.

ELIAS HICKS.

TO SAMUEL R. FISHER, PHILADELPHIA.

Jericho, 12*th mo.* 26*th,* 1824.

DEAR FRIEND,

Although it has rested on my mind most of the time since I returned home, to address a few lines to thee in this way, not only to acknowledge, with grateful sensations, the many especial favours and abundant kindness received from thee and thy dear children, by myself, my wife and daughter, grand-daughter, and other companions in travel, while I was confined by bodily indisposition under thy hospitable roof, but also to inform thee a little of our fare while progressing on the way to our own habitation,— yet such has been the weak state of my body, and trembling of my hands, that I have not attempted to put pen to paper to write a letter, until the present time; and I very much doubted when I commenced, whether I should succeed. But I do much better than I anticipated.

After taking an affectionate farewell of our friends in the city, we proceeded, agreeably to our previous conclusion, taking meetings at Germantown, Abington, and Byberry. These three meetings were to me favoured and encouraging opportunities, though pretty trying to my weak body. And after the close of the meeting at Byberry, the concern to attend the three monthly meetings of Newtown, Middletown, and Falls, the three successive days, was renewed and so fixed on my mind, that I found my peace consisted in submitting thereto, which I cheerfully did when I clearly saw it was my Heavenly Father's good pleasure, and I found abundant peace in so doing. The meetings were very large; and, I trust, through the gracious condescending goodness of our never-failing Helper, many were instructed, comforted, and edified.

On first day we attended the morning and afternoon meetings at Trenton, and as thy children Thomas and Sarah, and divers other Friends from Philadelphia, were there, thou no doubt hast heard all that is needful in relation to them. On second day we proceeded to Stonybrook. On the way my wife was taken ill, insomuch as not to be able to sit up any after our arrival at the widow Clark's. After meeting, we returned back to the widow's and lodged. The next day, my wife being better, we proceeded on our journey, through mud and mire, the roads being very heavy, and arrived, near evening, at our friend Samuel Pound's, about six miles short of Plainfield, who, with his worthy wife, received us with tokens of sincere friendship.

The next day we attended a monthly meeting at Plainfield, held for Rahway and Plainfield, and the day after had an appointed meeting at Rahway. Both these meetings were satisfactory and encouraging seasons; and we left them the next day in the fresh feelings of mutual love and affection. and rode to New York, where we arrived, a little before sunset, on sixth day evening. We tarried here until first day, and attended the two meetings in the city, both of which were crowded and overrunning full, like some of the large meetings in Philadelphia.

On second day we returned home, and, to our mutual comfort and satisfaction, found our children and friends in usual health, except Phebe, our grand-daughter, who had some return of her fever, and was not so well as when she first got home, but is now in a favourable way of recovery.

The second day after getting home, I was favoured to get clear of the gravel, that had occasioned me such a long season of pain. I feel now pretty free from pain, and my strength is daily increasing.

In much love to thyself and dear children, I subscribe thy affectionate friend.

ELIAS HICKS.

TO WILLIAM POOLE, WILMINGTON.

Jericho, 1st mo. 5th, 1825.

MY BELOVED FRIEND,

Not having heard any thing from thee since I wrote thee from Philadelphia, I feel very anxious to hear how thou art getting along under the pressure of thy bodily afflictions, as by thy last letter, thou informedst me that they had become complex. Hence, in the near sympathy that impresses my mind on thy behalf, I feel very desirous of hearing from thee, as soon as is reasonably convenient.

After leaving Philadelphia, we proceeded, taking meetings at Germantown, Abington, Byberry, and the three monthly meetings at Newtown, Middletown, and Falls. These were all large, and, I think, favoured meetings, through the condescending goodness and unmerited mercy of the Shepherd of Israel. The day after the monthly meeting at the Falls, being the first of the week, we attended fore and afternoon meetings at Trenton, in Jersey. In the morning, several hundreds assembled more than the house could contain; and in the afternoon also, many went away for want of room. They were, I trust, both solemn and profitable meetings. The Governor and many of the members of the Legislature being in town, they made us an offer of the state house for our accom modation; but as the two meetings of our Friends came in course on that day, I felt most easy to attend them as they came, and my bodily infirmity was such, that I did not think it prudent to attempt a third meeting in the evening; therefore way did not open to accept the offer. On second day we proceeded on our way homeward, taking meetings at Stonybrook, Plainfield, Rahway, and New York, and got safe home on the following second day, and found our children and friends generally well; which, together with the attendant peace of mind, was cause of thankfulness and gratitude to the blessed Author of all our manifold blessings and favours dispensed from his bountiful hand. I have not fully recovered my usual state of health, but am able to keep about and attend meetings.

I subscribe thy affectionate friend.

ELIAS HICKS.

TO THOMAS M'CLINTOCK, PHILADELPHIA.

Jericho, 1st mo. 24th, 1825.

My Dear Friend,

Thy very acceptable letter of the 10th instant was duly received, and I have taken my pen in order, as way may open, to answer the queries it contained.

Query 1. "What dost thou mean by the terms, 'outward legal sins'?" I mean the breach of those outward legal rites and ceremonies, such as circumcision, &c., contained in the law of Moses, the non-observance whereof was accounted a transgression of that law, and rendered the animal bodies of the Israelites legally unclean and unholy; but which was not any breach of that universal moral law given by God to mankind from the beginning, and which is manifested to every man by the two witnesses which God has placed in every rational creature, as the only sufficient rule and guide, to wit, reason and truth. And as man is a two-fold creature, so his gracious Creator has given him a two-fold revelation, viz. the light of the outward sun to reveal to him, through the medium of his external senses, the things of a man, and the internal sun, which is the truth, or light and spirit of God, to reveal to him, through the medium of his internal senses, the things of God: and through the medium of these two witnesses, when rightly adhered to, every rational being is clearly and self-evidently instructed in his duty both to God and man.

But sorrowful to relate, the professors of Christianity have, generally, slain these two witnesses, and they are now lying dead in the streets of Sodom and Egypt, as the apostle John saw was the case in his day; that is, in the defiled hearts of the formal professors in Christendom. By renouncing and turning from the leading and guidance of these two witnesses, and adopting in lieu thereof the letter of the Scriptures, and a belief in mysteries they do not understand, both of which in themselves are dead things, and cannot communicate any life to the soul of man, they have brought over themselves a state of death and darkness, and thereby slain these two witnesses, or "pressed them down as a cart with sheaves," by which they have rendered them entirely useless to them in the things of God and true religion. But to return. As the observance of these rituals did not cleanse nor redeem the soul from moral evil, so, by a parity of reason, the non-observance of them did not pollute the soul, but only prevented the Israelites from freely and fully partaking of the outward blessings of their good land, which was their only promised reward for their obedience and faithful adherence to these outward rituals, and moral precepts contained in their outward law.

Secondly. It was not the sufferings and death of Jesus on the cross merely, that abolished the law, and did away those legal transgressions: that was only the finishing work. The abrogation of the law, and the cancelling the breaches of its legal precepts, were principally effected by Christ's declarations in his sermon on the mount, and his offering himself up to the will of his Heavenly Father, when, in his fervent prayer in the garden, a little before his crucifixion, he earnestly besought him, if it was possible, he would let that cup pass from him; but in his usual submission, as a dutiful son to the will of his Father, he exclaims, "Not my will, but thine be done." He never offered himself up to his cruel persecutors, but they came upon him in a malicious manner, and took him by force, in his quiet retreat in a public garden.

Having, by his sermon on the mount, publicly abolished the "law of carnal commandments contained in ordinances," and introduced a "better testament," in direct opposition to it, and thereby cancelled the obligations of it, his disciples were no longer bound to observe its requirings; which is manifested by his justifying them for a breach of their seventh-day sabbath, assuring them that he was "Lord of the sabbath day." And as Moses was authorized, by divine command, to give them that law and covenant, with all its legal rites and ceremonies, so likewise he, as paramount to Moses, was authorized by his Heavenly Father to do it away, and abolish the whole; agreeably to the declaration of the apostle Paul, Colos. ii. 14. And he finished his mission when on the cross he said, "It is finished! and bowing his head he gave up the ghost:" at which time the vail of the temple was rent in twain, from the top to the bottom, in confirmation of the consummation and total end of that dispensation.

This vail was fixed by Moses to prevent the Israelites from coming into the immediate presence of the Lord, in the inner court, where none but the priests were permitted to enter during that dispensation. This vail represented Moses and that outward law. But this vail was done away by Jesus on the cross, he having previously, as aforesaid, abolished the law, with all its rituals and ceremonies, and introduced the new covenant. And the vail being now done away, the people, all that believed on him, were now permitted to appear before the Lord without a mediator, as a mediator makes a vail between God and the soul. Hence the apostle exhorts the believers to come boldly to the throne of grace, that they may obtain mercy, and find grace to help in the needful time. See *Heb.* iv. 16.

Apprehending that what I have said may furnish the means

to thee by which thy first four queries may be resolved, I now turn to the fifth, and may observe, that the abrogation of the law and the introduction of the gospel, or new covenant dispensation, to that people, as declared by the prophet, was the principal end of the mission of Jesus, and which was verified by his so exactly fulfilling the declaration of his Heavenly Father to Moses, so long before his coming. Hear Jehovah declare his intentions. "I will raise them up a prophet from amongst their brethren, like unto thee. I will put my words into his mouth, and he shall speak unto them whatsoever I shall command him." This was just the case with Moses, for he spake nothing to the people but what the Lord commanded him. Hence their likeness to each other. By comparing this with his sermon on the mount, we shall clearly discover a full abrogation of the law, as also a clear introduction of the gospel or new covenant, as promised to that people, so long before, by the prophet Jeremiah.

And in reply to the latter part, where thou queries—Were any of the Jews who came into the spirituality of religion, previous to his coming, at liberty to decline the observance of the external rituals? I answer, by no means. For as the Israelites had refused to come into the presence of the Lord, or to hear his commands immediately from him, and chose rather that he would speak to them through the medium of a man, so he gave them Moses and the prophets as mediators, who received the word at his mouth, and conveyed it to the people. And although these had immediate access to the Divine presence, yet they were not permitted to omit any obligation of that law while that covenant stood unrepealed, as their principal business was to teach it to the people during its continuance. Hence a failure in them would have been as great, if not a greater crime, than in the common people.

Now, these mediators formed a vail between them and their God, for the Israelites could not look beyond them for the knowledge of him, and of what he should require at their hands, while this vail continued. For they chose to be instructed by external evidence, and thereby disavowed all inward and spiritual evidence. Hence arose the occasion and necessity for external miracles. For had all the Israelites been prepared, and as willing as Moses was, to receive God's word and will immediately from his own mouth, there never would have been any reason or use for outward miracles; as it does not appear that he has dispensed any to other nations, and as is manifest by the prophet Jeremiah's testimony concerning the new covenant dispensation to that people, (which was only new to the house of Israel, but was the same old covenant to the rest of the nations, that he made with man in the beginning,) when the Lord would speak immediately to every individual of them, by his own spirit and word in their hearts. So that none now, who come into this new or inward covenant, need go to a Moses or a prophet, or any other fellow creature, to know the Lord, or his will concerning them; for all, through the inward law and light of this covenant, are made to know him, from the least to the greatest.

This vail that was fixed by God between him and his people, at their own request, was figured out by the vail which Moses, by God's command, set up in the tabernacle to keep the people from approaching the inner court, where none were to enter but the Lord's priests, whom he had consecrated by his own spirit; and, while this tabernacle and vail continued, the people received the commands of the Lord from the priests' lips. But this vail was done away in and by Jesus, as saith the apostle, when he concluded his mission on the cross, as before cited. And all the Israelites that believed on him, and submitted to his doctrines and commands, by which he abrogated the law and introduced the gospel, and confirmed the latter by his holy example, way was made for them to come freely to the throne of grace, in the inner temple of their hearts, where the Lord makes himself known to his children, and they receive his word immediately from his own mouth, every vail and mediator being removed from between them.

Jesus had nothing outward to offer but his bodily life, as saith the Psalmist, speaking in his name, "A body hast thou prepared me," and that he was under the necessity of surrendering up, as there was no other way to save it but by conforming to the will of the Scribes and Pharisees, which he could not do without losing his spiritual life; agreeably to his own doctrine, "He that saveth his life shall lose it: but he that loseth his life, for my sake and the gospel, the same shall save it." Thus he set an example to all his followers, that, in order to be saved, they must surrender themselves, as he had done, a willing offering to God. And we must suffer the fire of his divine word in us, to burn as an oven, (which is what John the Baptist called the baptism of the Holy Ghost and fire,) until all the chaff, and every thing in us and of us that the controversy of God is against, is burned up and consumed, and the soul made pure and clean, a fit receptacle for his holiness to dwell in; and even our natural lives must likewise be surrendered to his holy will. This comprehends the true atonement, which all the external atonements under the law were but a type and figure of.

As to the advantage the reviewers have taken, or pretend to take, on what they construe as a concession on my part, in my letter to Dr. Shoemaker, that the death of Christ, merely of itself, was an atonement at all, I had no such idea; for I believe I rested it principally on *the effects of his mission and death*. As is very clear, not only from the apostle's testimony, where he asserts that Jesus had abolished the law and "blotted out the hand-writing of ordinances, nailing them to his cross," &c., but also by the facts which followed, some of which were manifest while he was with his disciples, in justifying them for a breach of their shadowy sabbath, and divers other things in their conduct which made a breach upon the letter of their law. By which the design of his mission is proved, and that it was purposely to put an end to that law and covenant, and to introduce a better: not another outward one, but an inward one, agreeably to the prophecy of Jeremiah. And this he clearly and amply did in his sermon on the mount, as is before shown, but was finished by his last act of surrender on the cross, when he bowed his head and said, "It is finished." At which time "the vail of the temple was rent in twain from the top to the bottom."

Here the Divine power interfered, and set its seal to the complete abrogation of the law; and at that very time, all the legal transgressions that any of the Israelites lay under the censure of, by a breach of their ceremonial law, were done away and abrogated with the law of carnal commandments that instituted them. So that every Israelite, that believed in Jesus as their Messiah, was now at liberty to abstain from all the rituals of the law and be blameless. That, strictly speaking, it was not the persecutions he suffered, nor the cruel death by which he finished his mission, that atoned for any sins; but it was his godly life, his commands and doctrines, that abolished the law and introduced the gospel, and put an end to these legal sins and transgressions, and in the room thereof brought in everlasting righteousness.

As to what may be the fate and condition of the unbelieving Jews, I am not at present prepared to give a full answer, not having considered it a subject requisite for me to enter into any particular investigation of. But apprehend, if they are rightly engaged to live a virtuous and upright life, according to knowledge received, and the doctrine of their prophets,—"to do justly, to love mercy, and to walk humbly with their God,"—they will be accepted, when thousands of professed Christians may fall short thereof.

In much love to thee and thine, in which my wife and children are united, I subscribe thy affectionate friend.

ELIAS HICKS.

TO MOSES BROWN, PROVIDENCE, R. I.

Jericho, 3d mo. 30th, 1825.

BELOVED FRIEND,

It is with some reluctance that I take my pen to reply to thy letter of the 11th month last; and had it not been for the long unbroken friendship,—at least so on my part,—that has subsisted between us from our first acquaintance, I should not now have done it. For if I hate any thing, it is contention;

as I am fully in unison with the advice of the wise Solomon, when he recommended to "leave off contention before it be meddled with." I mostly answer false accusations with silence, after the example of our great Pattern, when he was falsely accused before the Roman governor. And had I not apprehended that T. H.'s letter savoured more of accusation, founded upon flying and false reports, than it did of that philanthropic Christian charity, that would rather cover than expose the supposed or real faults of a fellow creature, I might have answered it as readily as I did S. F. H.'s. But I consider S. F. H.'s letter very different from that of T. H.; for the latter roundly asserted that D. Slack was a deist, and almost. an atheist, without accompanying his assertions with the least shadow of proof. And I have always considered it a full and clear evidence of the weakness and futility of a cause, when it requires defamation and detraction to support it. And as thou alludest principally to Slack's first essay, as savouring of deism and infidelity, I am willing to acknowledge that I have not been able to discover the least symptom of that kind in that essay, any more than in the general writings of our primitive Friends. They were accused of the same, by the ignorant and superstitious of their day, because they did not acknowledge the Scriptures to be the only rule of faith and practice. And they have, that is, the hirelings and their abettors of the present day, the same view at this time concerning the members of our Society, who are faithful in the support of our ancient foundation, the light and spirit of truth within. But alas! the number of these I fear is too few. But as experience has taught our persecutors to see that the time is past for them to use force, persecution, and detraction, to bring us to submit to their cruel wills; they are now using the cunning of the serpent, by flattery and deceit: and in this way they are much more successful in drawing many away from the simplicity of truth, so as to join with them in their many and various ways and associations, set up in the will and foolish wisdom of man, under the show of doing God service. by which they are robbing widows and orphans, and for a pretence are making long prayers. But to return to the subject of Slack's book, would it not have been more honourable and neighbourly, to say nothing of the Christian, as he considered the youth very erroneous in his views, to have taken the pen and showed him his errors,—as surely it must have been an easy task, if he was so much out of the way, as he asserts him to be—rather than to bear him down with hard names and unfriendly epithets? As he could then have given the public an opportunity to judge for themselves, without trusting to his bare assertions, which carry no evidence at all with them.

I trust I have now given sufficient reasons for not answering the letter alluded to, and I hope they will prove satisfactory; but if not, I am done with the subject.

Thou seems to accuse me of prevarication, but upon what ground, I am unable to conceive; unless it is on what thou afterwards mentions in respect to a message I sent, as thou sayest, to the author of that pamphlet, by a respectable Friend of our city. I have no remembrance of sending any message to that author, by any Friend of our city; but I remember meeting a Friend of Providence in New York, and we had some conversation respecting that individual; and, I think, I manifested to that Friend my regret for the publication of Slack's two last numbers; as I apprehended he was too young in experience to enter so largely into the discussion of matters of such importance, and that if I had the opportunity of speaking with him, I should recommend stillness to him, as the safest in his present child-like state; not doubting but a divine visitation had been extended to him, that enabled him not only to see the bigoted and corrupt state of the hireling clergy and their abettors, but likewise to bear a full and decided testimony to our foundation principle, the light within: and he supported it by as full and conclusive arguments, as I had met with in any Friend's writings. But I knew he must lack, what is entirely necessary in our Christian progress, a train of solid experience, which would require time to effect.

As to the encouraging message thou speakest of, I have no remembrance of it; and it may be among the many false reports, that were circulated by some envious individuals, such as that "I had a continual intercourse with David Slack, while he was writing those essays, and that I had a hand in forming them;" and a great deal more of such lying stuff: when the truth is, I had never heard of the existence of such a person, until some acquaintance of mine in New York sent me the first essay. This was the first time I had ever heard of such a man; and I came to the knowledge of the other essay in the same way.

As to what thou observest in regard to my desiring S. F. H. to show my letter to T. H., it is a mistake; but as I considered, from what I had heard, that D. Slack was considered as confederate with them that dissented from Friends, I apprehended my letter to S. F. H. would be a sufficient answer in both respects; and as S. F. H. would receive my letter at the time of the yearly meeting, I wished him to show it to such Friends as he thought necessary. I had no allusion in particular to T. H., as I had previously concluded not to answer his letter, and for the reason I have now given, and which is only effected by thy importunity; as I should much rather they should have remained in the inclosure of my own thoughts, as it is very unpleasant to impeach a fellow creature of faults, unless it appears absolutely necessary. And as it regards what thou sayest respecting the interview between A. Braithwaite and myself, thou appearest, on account as thou sayest, of my prevarication, incorrectness, &c., to be induced rather to believe the two females, than my statement. Well, let it be so. I know I have spoken the truth; and there I am willing to leave it, let others think as they may. As to what thou sayest of my letter to Dr. Shoemaker, I may observe that it contained my simple sentiments at that time, and I penned it in the sincerity of my heart, and innocency of my hands; and I do not in the least regret that I have written it. But I stand always open to conviction; and if any person, even a child, should convince me of any error it contains, I shall cheerfully yield it up, and acknowledge myself wiser than when I wrote it.

As to what thou sayest of my contradicting myself, by saying at one time, that the Scriptures were the best book, and at another time, that it does more hurt than good; if this is to thee a paradox, it is one, I conceive, thy own common sense and every day's observation would easily solve. For it is my candid belief, that those that hold and believe the Scriptures to be the only rule of faith and practice, to those it does much more hurt than good. And has any thing tended more to divide Christendom into sects and parties, than the Scriptures? and by which so many cruel and bloody wars have been promulgated [promoted.] And yet, at the same time, may it not be one of the best books, if rightly used under the guidance of the Holy Spirit? But, if abused, like every other blessing it becomes a curse. Therefore, to these it always does more hurt than good; and thou knowest that these comprehend far the greatest part of Christendom. As to what thou sayest, of "Once in grace, always in grace," needs no reply.

There is one subject more to be noticed, and which creates a degree of admiration in my mind, that is, thy supposition of my being out of the unity of my friends; when nothing is more notoriously evident than my full unity, and which is so obvious, by its being tested almost from year to year for forty years or more, and never more so than in the past season, in which I have twice been called upon to surrender all, and go forth in my great and good Master's service. The first was a journey to the northward, in our own yearly meeting; the latter, to attend Baltimore yearly meeting, and some other services in Maryland, Pennsylvania, and the Jerseys; both which services I accomplished in the summer and fall of last year, with the full unity of my friends expressed on minute, and was furnished with returning minutes expressive of the full unity of my friends where I visited. And what should induce thee to mention a wish for my returning into the unity of my friends, when I have not been out of it? unless it be in [the case of] some few individuals, who have been led away from the truth, and on their parts have broken the unity towards me, without any cause given by me: therefore I have nothing to do in the concern, but to wait patiently for them to return to me. Which I trust they will all have to do, before they can witness true peace of mind.

In love I conclude, and subscribe myself, as ever, thy sincere and affectionate friend.

ELIAS HICKS.

TO SAMUEL COMFORT, BUCKS COUNTY, PA.

Jericho, 4th mo. 28th, 1825.

MY DEAR FRIEND,

Thine of 2d month last came duly to hand, and its contents were very salutary, tending to revive afresh that near sympathy and fellow-feeling affection, witnessed when favoured with each other's company. What thou remarkest relative to the sufferings of the faithful in the present day, is very correct; we look for no other in the present bewildered state of the people, both within and without the pale of Society. For even some of our members, who think much of themselves, and who, in time past, have been thought something of by their friends, have so far turned away from first principles, as to unite with hireling priests in defaming and gainsaying their fellow members; even some, whom in time past, they at least pretended great respect and regard for; but not abiding in the principle, they lost their first love, and grew indifferent and careless, and became dead and formal, and could not endure sound doctrine. Hence a cavilling spirit got up, which led them to find fault with their brethren, to cover their own nakedness, and jealousy crept in and greatly destroyed love and unity, and a contentious spirit entering filled the vacuum. And it will never be good day to the Society again, until individuals, each one for one, rally back to the standard, and recur to and unite in the first principle, and leave every thing behind that genders to contention, or that has a tendency to lead to different views and opinions.

Things with us, on the Island, remain in a good degree of quiet; but I do not know that those in the opposition have in

any degree mended; but their number is so small they can do
but little. But in New York it is a pretty trying and disturbed time. I know not when it will end, or be better with
us. I apprehend our case is such, that the fire and hammer
will be needful some time longer, to do away the dross and
tin, and reprobate silver. We shall all have need to let patience have its perfect work, that so in the end of the conflict,
we may be entirely refined, wanting nothing.

My wife has been quite ill for two weeks past, but is now on
the mend, and we are in hopes the disorder has pretty much
subsided. The rest of our family and children around us are
in usual health, as are our friends generally here away.

With much love to thee and thy dear wife and children, I
subscribe thy affectionate friend.

ELIAS HICKS.

TO WILLIAM POOLE, WILMINGTON.

New York, 5*th* mo. 4*th*, 1825.
DEAR FRIEND,

I take my pen to write, in answer to thine of the 19th ult.
more particularly as it respects the historical account of the
miraculous conception and birth of Jesus of Nazareth, the son
of the Virgin Mary, as stated in the account of his life by
Matthew and Luke, in their evangelical histories. I shall, in
the first place, state to thee my answer to the first and only person that ever put the question to me, on this wise, Dost thou
believe in the miraculous conception of Jesus in the womb of
his mother Mary? and, although I consider it an impertinent
question, yet, as it was put by a particular friend and neighbour of mine, Thomas Willis, I condescended to answer it,
which was in these words;—That I had believed it from
my youth up to the present time, as far as history and tradition
could give belief, and, I apprehended, no person had any
other, or could have any higher belief, as we did not find that
any nation or people, however highly favoured, had other
knowledge or belief thereof, but those who had the history:

therefore a belief therein was not an essential to salvation. For that which is essential to the salvation of the souls of the children of men, is certainly dispensed by our common Creator, to every rational creature under heaven; for he is unchangeably perfect, equal in all his ways and righteous in all his works, and will do equal justice to all, so that all who disobey his manifested will, are left without excuse. For should he manifest any certain thing essential to salvation, to a small portion of mankind, and keep it secret from the greater part, would it not be partial, seeing he is all-wise and all-powerful, and could as easily manifest it to all as to one? and not only the Scriptures, but the very reason and nature of things prove it. We read that the spirit of the Lord strove in, or with, the people before the flood, no doubt with every individual of them, as it did with Adam, as it did with Eve, as it did with Cain; his call is extended to all as saith the prophet, "Look unto me and be ye saved, all the ends of the earth;" the weakest, the poorest, the farthest off, the least obedient, &c. "He hath showed thee, O man," every man, "what is good; and what doth the Lord require of thee." Not to believe in the hear-tell of outward miracles, outward sacrifices, outward oblations, outward baptisms, outward sacraments of bread and wine, all which only nourish the body and are cast out with the draught, but, "to do justly, and to love mercy, and to walk humbly with thy God?" loving God above all and our neighbour as ourselves, doing always unto others as we would they should do unto us, always attentive to that gospel that the Scripture tells us is preached in every creature, —not out of them, but in them,—by the light and Spirit of God, and is the power of God unto salvation. A belief in, and obedience to this inward gospel and power of God, is all that is essential to our salvation; for this, and this only, can bring us to love God above all, and our neighbours as ourselves, and to love our enemies, and to pray to God for them, and to beat our swords into ploughshares, and spears into pruning hooks, and no more learn war, but be at peace with God, and with all men.

I may further observe, in answer to thy question, that I am in sentiment with thee, as to the subject of the miraculous conception; as it is reasonable to suppose, that when the Great Prophet of the Jews should come, or be manifested to Israel, as spoken of by the former prophets, as that dispensation *with all its parts* had been confirmed by outward miracles, and as that people would not believe any thing of moment without such interference of divine power, hence their Messiah must be ushered in through that medium, or they would not have believed on him. And it was essential to that people to believe on him when he came, or he could be of no use to them. Therefore, I observed to T. Willis, that although there appeared to me as much, or more, letter testimony in the account of the four Evangelists, against as for the support of that miracle, yet it had not altered my belief therein, as stated in my letter to him, which no doubt thou hast read. But my enemies will not believe my positive assertion, expressed in my own words, but will have it according to their own minds. Well, so let it be; if they can live upon their own false construction of my words, let them have it so, till they can feel the weight of their own error, and then they will, I hope, learn better, whilst I enjoy peace through it all. With love as usual, thy affectionate friend.

ELIAS HICKS.

TO ABRAHAM LOWER, PHILADELPHIA.

Jericho, 6th mo. 1st, 1825.

MY DEAR FRIEND,

I trust thou wilt not impute my not answering thy very acceptable letter of 4th month last, to forgetfulness or inattention, but to the real cause, viz. the many and varied avocations that continually press upon my mind, together with the want of qualification to indite any thing worthy thy attention; and I feel but little more at present, than to inform that we are enjoying a usual portion of health, and feel grateful for the favour, and to give thee a little account of our late yearly meeting. We got pretty quietly through the first sitting of the select meeting, excepting that two females, one from the east and another from the west, advanced some heavy charges against us for indulging and supporting a spurious ministry among us; which, at the time, was passed by in silence, but was promptly met in a succeeding meeting. But my mind was so released from that meeting, at the close of the first sitting, as it appeared to me, that nothing further could be done to profit in our meeting again, except closing the minutes, and signing a returning certificate for Isaac Stephenson. And as that meeting coming together again, added a third sitting in a day, it was more than I felt able to bear, therefore, I did not attend the two last sittings; and all that was done, or attempted to be done in them, except what is above noticed, evidently tended to do much more harm than good.

The first sitting of the yearly meeting of discipline, which held about three hours, was principally taken up in settling the point respecting the reading of the London printed epistle; which resulted in not reading it. The subject brought up from Westbury quarter, proposing that all appointments be made for a limited time, &c. and that above mentioned, introduced considerable altercation: the latter finally issued in being referred back to the quarterly meeting from whence it came, to be further explained, although it was thought by most, that it was already sufficiently explicit to all that were willing to see it so. But it is a true saying, "None are so blind as those who will not see." But I believe, on the whole, it was a profitable meeting, in which light was spread on various subjects; and our parting sitting was solemn and edifying. I discover, by letters recently received, that the old accuser of the brethren is still vaunting about, giant-like, and is disturbing Israel's camp, which makes it necessary for all our little Davids to throw off Saul's armour, and betake themselves to their sling and smooth stones, and patiently wait the directions and leave the event to the Lord of battles, who will, in his own time, bring forth judgment unto victory, as the little isles patiently wait for his law.

Time necessarily leads me to a close. My wife and daughter E. join me in much love to you all, and to all our friends of the city, as way opens in thy freedom to communicate it; for I love all, who in sincerity and truth love God the Father, and Jesus Christ his son. In which I subscribe thy affectionate friend.

ELIAS HICKS.

TO WILLIAM POOLE, WILMINGTON.

My Dear Friend,
Jericho, 6th mo. 30th, 1825.

Thy acceptable letter of the 16th instant was duly received, and its contents were comfortable and encouraging in its various views; and as this acknowledgment, in unison with thy sentiments, is all I feel furnished with at present to communicate, to fill up my paper, I will add for thy amusement, when thou can find nothing better, the perusal of a transcript from a letter of a correspondent: take it as follows:—

"It was grateful and encouraging to find, that my ancient beloved friend was still in the keeping of Him who sleepeth not by day, nor slumbereth by night, and who by his hand of power is making strong, even in old age, 'the arms of the hands,' of all his faithful and rightly devoted servants, enabling them to go forth valiantly for the promotion of his dignified and noble cause of truth and righteousness in the earth, to the pulling down of the strong holds of Anti-christ's kingdom, or the man of sin and son of perdition, or in more simple and plain terms, self and self-will in man ; who'hath taken the seat of God in the heart, and exalteth himself above all that is called God, or that is worshipped.* And hence arise all the false worships that now are, or ever have been, in the world, with all the spurious, hireling, and man-made ministry, created and formed in schools, colleges, and seminaries of

* Thess. ii. 3, 4.

human and heatnenish science, out of which have grown all those new and self-conceived institutions and associations, such as Bible societies, missionary societies, and societies for the propogation of the gospel in foreign parts, &c., while at the same time very few of their number understand what the gospel is, judging them by their fruits, with the mind clothed with the best of charity. For their whole superstructure, from the foundation to the cap stone, is of a pecuniary kind, viz. money. Take away that, and they are all at a stand; for what sturdy and successful beggars are all these societies and their agents, whom they are sending forth, in all parts of the country and among various nations, to hoard together these pecuniary means, their only source of strength.

Are not these, like those the apostle speaks of, who have a form of Godliness, but deny the power thereof? From such, he says, turn away.* For of this sort are they which creep into houses and lead captive silly women, under a pretence of religion, when their chief design is to get their money. If this is not the case, from whence arise those associations, such as cent societies, mite societies, &c., that are formed, and which are draining money from poor widows and orphan children, under the show of religion, by which they prove to demonstration, that gain with them is Godliness?"†

Can we, consistently with reason and truth, suppose that those mighty combinations of men of all descriptions, from the highest to the lowest, professors and profane, which go to make up those institutions alluded to, many of whom do not appear to have any more correct ideas of real Christianity, nor do their works carry any more semblance of it, than the works of the untutored Gentile in the uncultivated wilds of America—I say can any rational man, whose mind is free from the bias of a corrupt and superstitious tradition, suppose that the infinite and all-wise Jehovah, hath any part or lot in those institutions, carried on in the very spirit, power, and contrivance of fallen man, and which abundantly less resemble the work

* 2 Tim. iii. 5, 6.   † 1 Tim. vi. 5.

of God than they do the work of Anti-christ, as set forth by John in his revelation: When Satan was loosed from his prison, and went forth to deceive the nations which are in the four quarters of the earth, Gog and Magog, which comprehend all the worldly-minded hypocritical professors of religion and unstable inhabitants of the earth, to gather them together to battle, the number of whom are as the sand of the sea.* What a clear description is this of the unstable multitude that make up these associations, and their abettors.

Therefore, the Lord's call is extended to all his enlightened and truly devoted children, "Come out from among them and be ye separate, saith the Lord, and touch not the unclean thing; and I will receive you, and be a father unto you, and ye shall be my sons and daughters, saith the Lord Almighty."

Are not the fore-named institutions and associations, the principal strongholds of sin and Satan in the present day? for it is in and through these, by fair pretences to do much good, the deceiving spirit transforms himself into an angel of light, and would, if it were possible, deceive the very elect. And who are those elect, that will be instructed and enabled to escape all his snares, and the cunning and creaturely devices of his agents, whom he hath captivated by means of his subtle transformations, joining with them and encouraging them, to go forward in their own wills and according to their own contrivance, furnished, like the Babel builders of old, with the best materials that man hath at his own command, viz. the Scriptures; comparable, when men make use of them to effect their own purposes, by direction of their own wisdom and science, to the brick and slime mortar, that the sons of Noah made use of in days of yore, to build their tower, whose top they, in their presumption, intended should reach to heaven, that they might get to themselves a name. But their language was confounded, and their work ceased. And this, no doubt, will be the case with our modern Babel builders; for the heterogeneous multitude, that form the present group of builders, are very similar to those in former days, and their aim appears

* Rev. xx. 7, 8.

to be the same, to wit, by their own power and wisdom, and in their own way and time, to build a tower, or a something whose top shall reach to heaven, by which to get to themselves a name.

I will now answer the query, Who are those elect, whose eyes are so enlightened by Divine truth, and made so piercing as to penetrate through all the subtle transformations of the enemy of their souls, and strengthened to escape all his snares? They are those, and those only, who, in the day of God's merciful visitation, have surrendered themselves to his government; for he has in his unbounded goodness, visited by his grace or good spirit, the souls of all his rational creation; in which time he has given them the offer of salvation, by setting life and death before them, and enduing them with a capacity to choose. But none are the elect, but those who choose the good and refuse the evil; who in the day of his grace, while it continues to strive with them, choose and elect the Lord for their portion, and the God of Jacob for the lot of their inheritance; and who persevere in the way of welldoing, until they experience a full birth of the spirit, and are born of God, and are established in the truth, and do not sin; because they are born of God, and his seed remaineth in them. These are they, in whom the wicked transforming spirit hath no place, and are passed beyond the possibility of being deceived, being founded and established on that unshaken rock, the revelation of the spirit of God in their own souls, the only true teacher, and sure rule of faith and practice, against which the gates of hell can never prevail.

What thou mentions in regard to my being from home in consequence of an appointment by our yearly meeting, to attend, with some others, the opening of a new quarterly meeting at Scipio, is incorrect; as the time of opening that quarter does not come on until the beginning of 10th month next, previous to which time I have to perform a considerable tour of duty, having obtained the unity and concurrence of our monthly meeting to pay a religious visit to the inhabitants of our island, more particularly the eastern part. I am now engaged near home, and shall not go far to the east until after our quarterly meeting, which comes the latter end of next month. It would be pleasant to see thee here at that time.

I was out five days last week, and attended eight meetings; and I was made thankful in believing, from very apparent evidences, in those opportunities, that the Lord had not left himself without a witness in any of his rational creation; and when his word goeth forth, this witness is raised and the power is manifested. This is the Lord's doing, and is marvellous in mine eyes. For although these opportunities were mostly among such, as the high professing Scribes and Pharisees would deem publicans and sinners, such as dare not lift up their eyes to heaven, but when convicted, and in a degree quickened by his grace, could do no more than smite upon their breasts and cry out, "God be merciful to me a sinner." This was evidently the case in most of these opportunities, as much brokenness and contrition was manifested. Truly the harvest may be said to be great, but the rightly qualified labourers are very few: too many of those who seem to be willing to take a part, are mere traditionalists, who, like the man, prefer carrying a stone in one end of their wallet, to balance their meat and drink, and give as a reason for so doing, that their fathers and grandfathers did so before them, and think it a crime to know more than they did; so instead of advancing go backwards.

My love to thee and thine, and to the rest of our friends in thy neighbourhood and elsewhere, as opportunity offers in thy freedom, for I feel that I love all men, and in that I have peace with all; and in this I subscribe thy affectionate friend.

ELIAS HICKS.

TO SAMUEL COMFORT, BUCKS COUNTY, PA.

Jericho, 7th mo. 19th, 1825.

My Dear Friend,

Thy letter of the 5th mo. last is now before me. I have oft perused it; as its contents tend to revive afresh the feeling of that brotherly love that binds together in one all the truly begotten children of the heavenly family. And did all the members of our highly favoured and highly professing Society, abide in this love, it would drive out and banish from the Society all tale-bearing, detraction, discord, envy, and every evil work, and in lieu thereof peace would reign within our walls, and prosperity within our palaces.

But, alas! it is otherwise. The wild boar of the forest has made an inroad in our pleasant places; the lion, that in times past was made to lie down with the lamb, is now prowling about, seeking to devour and destroy the innocent life, and the subtle fox is endeavouring to deceive and bring within the reach of his power the innocent lambs, insomuch that wasting and desolation are within our borders, and the ways of Zion do mourn, for her solemn assemblies have, in some instances, become places of discord.

Hence the necessity of every individual rallying to the standard, the light within; for in that only can we, as a people, unite our strength; that being our only standard principle from the beginning; and if we desert that, or add any thing to it, as essential, besides good works, we shall become a broken and divided people, and must remain so until all recur to this first principle as our only rule of faith and practice; and prove by our fruits that we are led and guided by it; that is, by our just and righteous works, doing unto all others as we would that others should do unto us. We are then as perfect as Jesus and the gospel require, being perfect as our Father in heaven is perfect; and, if any man requires more than this of any of his fellow creatures, he requires more than God and his prophets, and his son Jesus Christ require, and therefore proves himself to be a proud man, and if a proud man, then a fool, and knows not what he says nor whereof he affirms. And this is the sad and dreadful lot of every man and woman who say they believe what they do not understand, which no man can do; as no rational creature can believe any thing without evidence, and that which we do not understand cannot be evidence:—for instance, a

Greek may be brought forward as an evidence in case of theft, before a judge who did not understand his language, and although he was an eye and an ear witness in the case, and might express before the judge the truth, the whole truth, and nothing but the truth, yet the judge could not believe, and that *because he could not understand;* and so it must be with every thing we do not understand.

By information from Philadelphia I find that the case respecting the Green Street monthly meeting, improperly taken up by the quarterly meeting, remains yet undecided. Surely, when will the Philadelphians learn wisdom, and be willing to submit to right order. May it not be right for some plain simple countrymen, under right direction, to step in and lend them a hand of help, that they may not die in their sins.

I subscribe myself thy affectionate friend.

ELIAS HICKS.

TO WILLIAM POOLE, WILMINGTON.

Jericho, 1st mo. 21st, 1826.

My Dear Friend,

Thy very acceptable letter of the 14th instant came duly to hand, and its contents excited renewed feelings of near sympathy with thee, in thy present trials and bodily afflictions, and my desire and prayer is, that the Lord Almighty, in whom is our life, and the length of our days, may so strengthen thee with might in thy inner man, and endue thy mind with everlasting patience, that thou mayest not repine nor be discouraged, but be enabled to put thy whole trust and dependance in the Lord, for in the Lord Jehovah is everlasting strength.

My long silence in regard to communing with thee in this way, as noted in thy letter, I can assure thee has not arisen from any diminution of that near love and regard, that has subsisted between us from our first acquaintance, and which knows no abatement; but from the continued exercises and avocations of various kinds that press upon me and swallow up my time, not allowing me to spend any in idleness, and this agrees with my best wishes, for none of the moments of time allotted to me, have been so burdensome as those I have spent in idleness.

Anna Braithwaite and husband have been with us this week, she attended Westbury monthly meeting last 4th day, and ours the day following; I attended them both. I had not seen her, until now, since her return to this country, and have not spoken to her as yet, saving at the close of the first meeting, on fifth day last, as I sat next to her. When I arose to close the partition, I offered her my hand, which she faintly received. We have interchanged a letter or two. She informed me by a short note, that if I had any wish to have any communication with her she was entirely willing; to which I replied, that I had no desire to have any communication with her, either directly or indirectly, until she had made an acknowledgment for her breach of friendship, and of the salutary discipline of our Society; and as she has not yet complied, the way is closed between us, and will continue so until she does comply. But I informed her that, as it regarded myself, I freely forgave her, but I could not as it respected the breach made on the wholesome order of the Society, as that was not in my power to do. Her services with us were not acceptable to the meeting, her certificates were read and minuted, without any expression respecting her company and service, and alike in both the men's and women's meetings, and in the same way in the men's meeting at Westbury.

I have made some remarks on Joseph John Gurney's letter to his friend, on the doctrine of redemption, and have thought of sending them to thee, if a suitable opportunity offered.

I will note one passage of his letter, pages 31, 32,[*] viz. "Here I would remark, that while the inspired writers bear the most ample and decisive testimony to the unity of the Supreme Being; while the great principle, that God is one, lies at the very foundation of their scheme of religion and

[*] J. J. Gurney's letter has been published by the American Tract Society, and the passage here quoted is to be found on page 13, Tract No. 33.

pervades it in every part; we nevertheless learn, from many of their declarations, that in that great scheme of mercy which he has ordained for our salvation, the one God has manifested himself to mankind (with reverence be it stated) as the Father, the Son, and the Holy Spirit."* Why should he feel more reverence or fear in mentioning the Father, Son, and Holy Spirit, than in mentioning the Supreme God? The reason is very obvious, it is because God has manifested himself to every rational being under heaven by the immediate impression of his own life, light, and power, and has manifested himself self-evidently, so that all must know him, and his will concerning them; but man cannot know him self-evidently when, in his own foolish wisdom, he divides him into three *distinct parts*, by which he lowers down and degrades the divine character, not knowing what he says nor whereof he affirms. He cannot possibly prove it to be true; that is the reason, I apprehend, the friend, when he wished to give an idea of three in the Divine nature, was made fearful, even more so abundantly, than when he mentioned the one Supreme God; and had he attended to that fear when he was about to divide God, to support a superstitious dogma, he would have been preserved from this absurdity. This doctrine has grown out of the apostacy, and has no evidence for its support in Scripture, reason, or truth, for the Scripture they mostly adduce, is, no doubt, an interpolation.† Another reason why our author felt such reverence, or fear, I apprehend, is what every man witnesses when he is about to assert something to justify himself in a wrong act, knowing he cannot bring any evidence to prove the truth of the assertion, and that it may as likely be false as true, he trembles at the attempt, and this will be the case until custom has confirmed him in it. And this fear, I

* Elias Hicks was a firm believer in the Father, Son, and Holy Spirit, "*and these three are one;*" it is not therefore, to the terms that he objects, but to the manner in which they are here used, as implying a distinction in the Divine nature—this distinction is clearly expressed in the paragraph immediately following that quoted by Elias Hicks.

† 1 John v. 7. The authenticity of this text appears to have been doubted by Richard Claridge, a learned and highly esteemed writer among early Friends, and it is now admitted to be an interpolation, even by many Trinitarians.

have no doubt, has attended, more or less, all who have asserted the trinity of *persons* in God, unless they were educated in the belief of it from their childhood. For it greatly derogates from the unity and majesty of God, as it divides him into three separate substances, and of course must destroy his unity, and lessen in the mind the idea of his self-existing power, for if each of these substances is equal in power, then God the Father has but one third of the power that he possessed when the fulness of the divine unity comprehended, in his undivided essence, all power in heaven, and in earth. And as every subsistence must have its own proper substance, independent of any other, hence, if the Father is God, and the Son is God, and the Spirit is God, and each of these a distinct person, or being, then certainly three Gods, instead of one God, the absurdity of which must appear to every man of common sense.

Thy affectionate friend.

ELIAS HICKS.

TO WILLIAM POOLE, WILMINGTON.

New York, 6th mo. 1st, 1826.

DEAR FRIEND,

Since my arrival in this city, I have received two letters from thee—the first dated 5th month 12th, 1826; the other, the 18th. They were both very acceptable, especially the latter. In the course of the sittings of our select yearly meeting at this time, every portion of the wisdom of the creature has been exerted, to get a committee appointed to visit our quarterly meeting of ministers and elders. The whole design, no doubt, is to find some way to criminate me; but all these efforts have been fully defeated thus far. The subject sent up from our quarterly meeting to the yearly meeting, proposing the appointment of elders to be for a limited time, and their appointments also to be exclusively the business of the monthly meeting, is thrown into the hands of a large committee for consideration, and to report their views upon the subject to a future sitting of the meeting.

There was rather an uncommon circumstance transpired yesterday in our meeting for worship. A few minutes after the meeting assembled, one of our English Friends, E. R., took the floor, and stood so long that the assembly appeared to be wearied, and as soon as she sat down, A. B. kneeled, and almost as soon as she had resumed her seat, R. J., E. R., and A. B. attempted to break up the meeting by shaking hands; and a number in the next raised seat also shook hands; but the whole assembly sat still as though riveted to their seats. As the Friend who sat next to E. Bates, believing the motion to be premature and not in order, refused to give him his hand, they could not effect their object. And as he and T. Wetherald sat still and did not unite with the motion, not an individual left their seats, but appeared more composed. In a few minutes Thomas stood up, and had a very favoured opportunity with the people, to the rejoicing of every heart, I believe, except those who might have let in prejudice and envy.*

* The stenographer who took in short hand the communications delivered at the meeting here referred to, made the following note, which was published with the sermons:

"As the circumstances of this meeting were peculiar, and have been variously represented, it becomes the duty of the stenographer to give a statement of facts as they appeared to him at the time.

"At an early period of the meeting Mrs. Robson rose, and continued to speak for more than an hour. She was very soon succeeded by Mrs. Braithwaite in the foregoing prayer; immediately after which, Richard Jordan and Elisha Bates, who sat at the head of the meeting, shook hands as the customary signal for a separation: but contrary to any thing ever before witnessed by the stenographer, or by any other person with whom he has conversed, not a solitary individual, among more than two thousand, was seen to move!

"In the course of about a minute, there was another and a similar attempt made to close the meeting, by R. Jordan, E. Robson, A. Braithwaite, and some persons occupying the second galleries, but it was with the same effect! A profound silence now pervaded the whole of this large assembly, and, in breathless expectation, every eye seemed riveted with intense interest upon the galleries. The whole meeting, simultaneously breaking through the rules of the Society, remained fixed and immovable, as if controlled by some invisible power. Such was the effect, that the beholder might have easily conceived himself surrounded by a congregation of statues, instead of animate beings. During this interval, Mr. Wetherald rose and delivered the following discourse, which being succeeded by a few remarks from Elias Hicks, a short pause ensued—when Mr. Hicks and Mr. Wetherald shook hands, and the meeting quietly dispersed."

With much love to thee, with every branch of thy family and inquiring friends, I rest thy sympathizing and very affectionate friend.

ELIAS HICKS.

TO WILLIAM POOLE, WILMINGTON.

Jericho, 8th mo. 9th, 1826.

My Dear Friend,

Thy two letters of 6th mo. and thy last of 7th mo. 31st, are now before me. I have perused them several times with much satisfaction, as they contained nothing to induce regret, except the account thou givest of thy continued bodily infirmity, and the burdens of thy temporal business, which tends to excite renewed and continued sympathy with thee amidst thy various trials. But let us, dear friend, through and over all, gratefully remember that He whose mercy is over all his works, and who careth for the sparrows, will in his own time cause all things to work together for good, to those who truly love him.

I fully accord with thy views as it respects the several subjects treated upon in thy letters, and especially as it regards our English visitors, now supposed to be on their passage to this land, as experience teacheth, it is not good to lay hands suddenly on strangers, but much safer to be reserved and cautious both on the right hand and the left.

I feel for them as they are coming among us in rather an evil time; a time, I conceive, in which they will be closely watched, and in which they will have need to attend steadily to the advice given by Jesus to his disciples, "be ye therefore wise as serpents and harmless as doves," for should they happen to tread in the steps of their forerunners, some of whom have lately departed our coast, they may have cause to rue the day they landed on our shore, which I fear is the case of those who lately left us.

We had the company, last first day week, of J. W. and com

panion from the district of Maine, and A. B. from your yearly meeting.

J. W. appears to be an innocent and well intentioned person, but of small experience, and not sufficiently established on the one only unshaken foundation, to travel abroad in the work of the gospel, in the present time of commotion in the Society; for I fear that in his late journey he has not only suffered loss himself, but, in some instances, has rather wounded than promoted the cause he professed to advocate.

Things, as they relate to the discordant sentiments of some among us, are at present somewhat at a stand, but I don't know that the professed orthodox, have, as yet, become so convinced of the weakness and inconsistency of their traditional views, as willingly to barter them away for those that are better. But this is no strange thing, for it is as Paul says, blindness in part has happened to Israel, and that not only in Paul's time, but in every age and dispensation of God to his creature man; for children are so apt to place implicit confidence in their parents and tutors, whose seeming pious conduct they are led to venerate, that often, for want of due consideration, they set up the standard their parents left them, insomuch that the reproof of the martyr Stephen will, more or less, apply to some in every succeeding generation, "As your fathers did so do ye." This has been very apparent in our Society, as well as in every other, both in a moral and religious point of view. See how hard it has been for Friends in Pennsylvania, to give up the part they took in the coercive governments of this world, and what a struggle Friends had to bring their members from holding their fellow men in slavery. An old man, an elder and leader in Society, and one whom I truly loved, chose rather to be separated from society than to set his slaves free, and was disowned, as were several others of my acquaintance. And we need only examine the history of the past, and it will appear that in all ages, since the fall of man, tradition and popularity have been in general the governing principle among the children of men, in preference to strict justice and truth, and never more so than in our day,—if we are to judge professors by their works and fruits.

Thy affectionate friend.

ELIAS HICKS.

TO THOMAS M'CLINTOCK, PHILADELPHIA.

Jericho, 8th mo. 14th, 1826.

My Dear Friend,

Thy letter of 3d month last, by W. B. I., was duly received, and very acceptable, as its contents were corroborative of my own sentiments and feelings, on the several subjects of which it treated, particularly as respects the agitation in Society. For no real and perfect birth, either in a moral or religious sense, is brought forth without pain and labour. And this was the prophet's view formerly, which led him to exclaim, " When Zion travailed, she brought forth children." And I have no doubt but that the present stir and agitation in our Society, has been productive of many living and substantial births.

Had the same state of supineness and ease continued, that had for a long time been prevalent among us, many, I believe, who are now quickened, and alive in concern for truth's prosperity, might still have remained easy and secure amidst their worldly enjoyments. But the conflicting views and discordant opinions, that have for a few years past agitated the minds of the people, have naturally led the minds of our Friends, especially those in younger life, into an investigation, to think and search for themselves, and no longer pin their faith on the sleeves of their predecessors, but to know the foundation that is immovable, and that cannot be shaken, for themselves. And many, I believe, have profited greatly by their own right labour and exercise. But all who may seem to take part in the commotion and exercise, may not, for want of faithfulness and stability, prove good and wholesome fish, but as is represented by the parable of a draw-net, many may be enclosed therein that the head fisherman, when he comes to make his selection, will cast back into the sea again, while he will sav all the good. And some may be like the seed that fell on the highway; the light chaffy spirit may devour it. And some like the seed on stony ground, that springs up quickly, but for want of depth, when trials and tribulations attend, they are scorched by the heat, or give back and are offended. And some may be like the seed in thorny ground, which, although it springs up and seems to take root for a time, yet through the admission of the cares of this world, and the deceitfulness of riches, it is choked, and brings forth no fruit, to the honour of the husbandman. But those who, out of a good heart, receive the seed in the love of it, and give all their strength and ability to its support and growth, in these it will produce "some thirty, some sixty, and some an hundred fold," to the honour of the Great Seedsman.

Our transatlantic friends, I. and A. B., have, I think, by keeping their design so much behind the curtain, made rather an inglorious exit, especially the latter, not giving their friends generally an opportunity of a parting kiss, and the accompaniment of their good desires for a prosperous and pleasant passage to their native shore. However, they are gone; and I apprehend if they have made any right move while among us, this latter stands paramount to all the rest: so that they have left nothing else for us to do relative to them, but to pray for their safe arrival to their native land, and the gladdening embraces of their family and friends, and an increase of light and knowledge in wisdom's ways; which the upright in heart know to be ways of pleasantness, and all her paths to be paths of peace.

We will now take leave of those that are gone, and reflect a little on their anticipated successors, for whose preservation and safe-keeping while among us, should they be permitted to land on our shore, I feel considerable solicitude. For unless they attend carefully to the advice given by our great Pattern and perfect Way-mark, to his primitive disciples, to be " wise as serpents, and harmless as doves,"—that is, unless through deep suffering and temptation, they have so learned in the school of experience, as to become real adepts in the mysteries of iniquity, and fully so in the mysteries of godliness, both which I conceive are comprehended in the above declaration of Jesus, they may have cause rather to curse than bless the day they landed on the American shore. And it is my sincere desire, that Friends here may lay fast hold of the same advice. For if good to the visiters, it is surely as necessary for the visited, in order that we may be mutually improved, and harmoniously build together the waste places, by each carefully building against his own house.

We have recently, in our family circle, met with a very close trial, in the decease of our grand-daughter, Mary Hicks, second daughter of Valentine and Abigail Hicks. A very great trial to her parents and their surviving children, and to all of us indeed, as she was a very sensible and promising young woman, and bid fair to be a great comfort and strength to her parents. But she has gone, I trust, to her peaceful home, " where the wicked cease from troubling, and the weary are at rest," beyond the reach and noise of archers. And all we have on our part now to do, is quietly to acquiesce in the Divine will, and passively and cheerfully submit to the disposings of a gracious Providence, who, in his infinite wisdom and mercy, does all things well. She departed last evening, about 11 o'clock, in great quiet, without any struggle or bodily emotion.

In near love to thyself, wife, and children, in which mine unite, I subscribe thy affectionate friend.

ELIAS HICKS.

TO WILLIAM POOLE, WILMINGTON.

Jericho, 2d mo. 10th, 1827.
DEAR FRIEND,

Thy two letters received since my return home, have been very acceptable ; and although I have not wrote, yet the omission has not arisen from any abatement of love and regard, but from the press of many avocations, both of a moral and religious nature, that absorb my time, so that my correspondence with my friends in this way, is generally much in arrear.

I observe that thou hast a hope, that amidst all the agitation and intemperance that is manifested by the intolerant party in Philadelphia, called Orthodox, that the truth is making its way. But, I apprehend, it is possible that through the supineness of those who see the incorrectness of those who are opposing the truth,—by their keeping silence, and not standing forth to show themselves to be on the Lord's side,—they will greatly strengthen the hands of those opposers of right order, as they will consider all who sit silent, while they are pressing forward their proposals, are on their side; for, I apprehend, in this time of trial, none ought to be neutral, but stand forth openly and boldly for the promotion of truth's cause; for otherwise, they will strengthen the hands of their opposers. Since my return home, I have been considerably afflicted with a cold and cough, and am now keeping house on that account.

On my return, at our last monthly meeting, the only one I have attended since I came home, I found a necessity of laying before my friends a concern that had been for some time impressive on my mind, to pay a religious visit to the families of Friends in the two monthly meetings of Westbury and Jericho, which, after consideration, was fully united with by the meeting. I made a little beginning last week, but have been prevented from going on this week through indisposition.

The case of the three Friends under the notice of our monthly meeting for a breach of unity, is still under care, as the committee in the case have not made any report thereon, but probably may at our next monthly meeting. Except these, our monthly meeting is generally united, and in harmony one with another. Our late quarterly meeting united in establishing a meeting for worship in the village of Jerusalem, about seven miles from this place, in a southern direction.

Thy friends and acquaintance hereaway are generally in usual health, colds excepted, which are pretty prevalent. Abraham Hicks is still very ill, and we are ready to conclude he can continue but a little longer, without some essential amendment. His has been a very long and trying scene of affliction, which he has borne with patience.

Thy affectionate friend. ELIAS HICKS.

TO SAMUEL COMFORT, BUCKS COUNTY, PA.

Jericho, 3th mo. 29th, 1827.

My Dear Friend,

Thy kind and very acceptable letter of 1st mo. last was duly received, but through the intervention of various exercises of different kinds, which have taken me from home a considerable part of the time since its reception, way has not opened to answer it till now.

As to thy proposition for writing an essay on the various subjects therein mentioned, I feel myself entirely inadequate for the purpose at present; although I have often had very clear presentations on some of those subjects, but I was circumstanced as one formerly, who was commanded to seal up the vision and not write it for the present, as it is likely most of the people could not bear it at the present time, even some of the members of our favoured Society.

But the time is hastening apace when those things that are opened or spoken in secret, will be published on the house top, and no power on earth can let or hinder truth's spreading, and it will prosper and prevail, and overturn all those Antichristian structures that the man of sin and son of perdition has reared, during the long and dark night of apostacy, that has overspread all Christendom for more than fifteen hundred years, a darkness like that of Egypt, a darkness that all the Lord's living children can feel and are at times baptized therein for the dead.

Thou hast, no doubt, been informed of the Protests that two of the monthly meetings of Philadelphia, viz. that of Pine Street and Twelfth Street, have sent forward against me to our monthly meeting; they were brought by two Friends.

that from Pine Street by Isaac W. Morris, and that from
Twelfth Street by Jasper Cope; they attended our monthly
meeting on the occasion, came in rather late, and after the
meeting had proceeded a little in the business before them,
I. W. Morris arose and informed the meeting that he was the
bearer of a communication from their monthly meeting to
ours, and handed it to the clerk, and the other Friend made
the like observation and handed forward his paper; they then
took their seats, and neither of them opened their mouths
again during the meeting. A month before this I handed in
my certificate, which had been granted me to perform my late
visit in your parts, with an indorsement of unity from the
southern quarterly meeting, and one of the same tenor from
Darby monthly meeting. I also opened a prospect of a
visit to the families of Friends of the two monthly meetings of
Westbury and Jericho, at that meeting, and received the full
unity of my friends therein, all which was entered on minute,
and these minutes were read at the present meeting, in the
hearing of these two Philadelphia Friends, as also three other
certificates from the monthly meetings of Green Street, Abing
ton, and Byberry, all expressive of their unity and satisfaction
with me in my late visit among them. We likewise conducted
all the business that came before us in harmony and concord.
I omitted in the right place to mention, that when the Friends
handed in their communications to the clerk, he informed the
meeting what they were, and proposed that a few Friends should
be verbally appointed to examine them and report to next meeting, whether they were suitable to be read in the meeting, the
proposition was united in without a dissenting voice; when
the meeting closed, I spoke with the Friends, and pressingly
invited them to go home with me and take dinner, as did
several others of my particular friends, but they excused themselves by informing us they were under a pre-engagement to
dine elsewhere. At the next monthly meeting the committee
nominated, proposed the reading of those communications;
they were accordingly read and unitedly reprobated by the
meeting, as comprehending little besides falsehood and

calumny, and were judged to be unworthy of a place on our minutes, and were accordingly rejected and no further notice taken of them. Thus ended a monstrous deal of useless labour and toil of a part of a monthly meeting, in the city of brotherly love, which, it is to be feared, is degenerated into a city of brotherly hatred and envy. Alas, for the day! Would not the blessed Jesus, if he were now to visit her, wail over her as he did over Jerusalem formerly, and say, O, Philadelphia! Philadelphia! thou that wouldst kill the prophets, and stone them that are sent unto thee, how oft would I have gathered thee, as a hen gathereth her brood under her wings, but ye would not, therefore some of your houses are left unto you desolate.

I am just about closing my family visit, above alluded to, and feel peace in my labours of love among my friends, all whose houses and hearts appeared to be open kindly and cheerfully to receive me in this arduous exercise, and, to all appearances, we were mutually comforted in each other, as fully so as could reasonably be expected in the present weak state of the Society.

I am now about retiring to the king's gate, like Mordecai formerly, there to wait for fresh orders and whether it may be to retire from the field of labour and rest for a while, and put my house in order, and be prepared to go hence and be seen of men no more on this stage of action; or, whether I may be called to some small chores of farther labour in the vineyard of the heavenly husbandman, suited to my declining years, I know not, but cheerfully submit to His heavenly disposal, who doeth all things well, and endeavour to be continually prepared to say, in whatever way he may be pleased to turn his hand upon me, "Thy will be done, O Lord."

My family and friends hereaway, of thy acquaintance, are in usual health. Abraham Hicks, who has been for a long time very ill, is at present a little better, but very weak.

With near love to thyself and family, and other friends of our acquaintance in thy neighbourhood, I subscribe thy affectionate friend.   ELIAS HICKS.

TO ISAAC T. HOPPER, PHILADELPHIA.

Jericho, 6th mo. 8th, 1827.

MY DEAR FRIEND,

Thy very acceptable letter of 29th ult. was duly received, bearing information of the steps some of my dear friends have been driven to take, in order to maintain their just rights and that Christian liberty that the gospel has entailed as a perpetual legacy on all its devoted and faithful children. And although the present state of things among us, a once highly favoured Society, may look dark and gloomy, nevertheless, I anticipate a hope, that the Lord Almighty, in the riches of his love, and in the majesty of his power, will, in his own time, which only is the best time, arise for the redemption of the oppressed seed, and will open a way for their deliverance, and cause them to tread upon the necks of all their enemies and those who rise up against them, and cause them to sing on the banks of deliverance; while that Egyptian spirit, that delights in oppression, will be swallowed up in the Red Sea of their own unstable thoughts and vain imaginations, while it goes stalking about with its chariots and horsemen, to wit, the arm of flesh, in order to bring back again into Egyptian bondage the wrestling seed of Jacob. For the Lord from his holy hill, will look down upon them and cause confusion in their camp, and confound all their counsels, and cause them to fall a prey to their own deceivings; and they will not be able to rise any more. May the Lord hasten it in his own time and will.

Our yearly meeting has been the most distressing and trying we have ever known; and although those who would be rulers have taken counsel together, and imagined vain things, nevertheless it has all been turned backward, and made to rest on their own heads.

As the bearer of this, Phineas Janney, is about taking his leave to proceed homeward, I must now draw to a close; and with much love to self, wife, and children, in which mine unite, I subscribe thy affectionate friend.

ELIAS HICKS.

TO MOSES PENNOCK, CHESTER COUNTY, PA.

Jericho, 7th mo. 22, 1827.

ESTEEMED FRIEND,

Thine of the sixth month last was duly received, and its contents have been examined, and I was made to marvel, why any in this enlightened age, who have the opportunity of reading and examining the Scriptures, should be at a loss for answers to the queries therein contained—especially such who profess being led by an unerring guide, the light within, or spirit of truth, or law written in the hearts of the children of men, by which all may know God for themselves; as saith the Lord by his prophet, " All shall know me from the least to the greatest;" and therefore have no need to inquire or to say to a neighbour or brother, know the Lord. And when we come truly to know God, all such queries will be answered.

The first query necessary then to be considered is, what is God? To which the answer is plain; as is testified through the whole scope of Scripture, and the general consent of mankind,—" God is a spirit." And he is one spirit and not two— a complete unity in himself, entirely independent of all other causes, being the only self-existing great first cause, to whom all other causes owe their existence, and from whom they have derived their being. And as God is but one spirit, so of necessity there is but one sole good; for which truth we have the absolute testimony of his Son, for he saith, " There is none good but one, and that is God." Hence, of course, there is but one self-existing divinity, and that is God alone, who filleth all things, and by whom all things consist, and in whom all things that have life, live and move, and have their being, from the most exalted inhabitant of the highest heaven, to the smallest insect in earth or sea. And each must possess a fulness of his power, according to their nature and being, as every effect must rest upon its cause, or it would fall into a state of annihilation. Even the vegetable tribes depend upon his power for being and life, as does every other part of his creation.

As to the divinity of Jesus Christ, the son of the virgin,—when he had arrived to a full state of sonship in the spiritual generation, he was wholly swallowed up into the divinity of his heavenly Father,* and was one with his Father, with only this difference ; his Father's divinity was underived, being self-existent, but the son's divinity was altogether derived from the Father ; for otherwise he could not be the son of God, as in the moral relation to be a son of man, the son must be begotten by one father, and he must be in the same nature, spirit, and likeness of his father, so as to say, I and my father are one in all those respects. But this was not the case with Jesus in the spiritual relation, until he had gone through the last institute of the law dispensation, viz. John's watery baptism, and had received additional power† from on high, by the descending of the holy ghost upon him as he came up out of the water.‡ He then witnessed the fulness of the second birth, being now born into the nature, spirit, and likeness of the heavenly Father, and God gave witness of it to John, saying, " 'This is my beloved son, in whom I am well pleased." And this agrees with Paul's testimony, where he assures us that as many as are led by the spirit of God, do become the sons of God.§ So Jesus, by being faithful to the leading of the spirit of God, fulfilled all the righteousness of the Jewish law,‖ and was then prepared to receive additional power from on high, by which he was qualified to enter upon his gospel mission, and introduce the new covenant, prophesied of long before by Jeremy the prophet, and by which he went far beyond all the former prophets,¶ and witnessed in spirit the substance of all the shadows of their law and covenant, being the son of God with power, according to the spirit of holiness by the resurrection from the dead."** And all who come rightly into the new covenant, and are led by the spirit that Jesus commanded his disciples to wait for,†† become the sons of God, and joint heirs with Jesus Christ,‡‡ and are made kings and priests unto God,§§

---

* 2 Pet. i. 4.   † Luke ii. 52.   ‡ Matt. iii. 16.   § Rom. viii. 14.   ‖ Matt. iii. 15.
¶ Acts, iii. 22.   Heb. i. 6, 9.   ** Rom. i. 4.   †† Luke, xxiv. 49.   ‡‡ Rom. viii. 17.
§§ Rev. i. 6, and v. 10.

having overcome the world as Jesus did, and are preachers of righteousness both in word and deed.

Thy next query respecting the miraculous conception, &c. is to me a very plain, simple thing. All the external miracles of the Jewish covenant, had but one aim and end: and the miraculous conception of Jesus, and of Isaac and John the Baptist, were among the greatest; all of which were intended to prove to that dark and ignorant people, debased by their bondage, that there was a living and invisible God; for such was their degraded state, that no other means seemed calculated to awaken them, and raise in them a belief in that invisible power, that made and governed the world, but an external manifestation thereof, through the medium of outward miracles. And as Moses and the prophets had foretold of the coming of their last great prophet, it was of singular importance to that people, that they should know and believe in him when he came; and as they depended on outward miracles as the highest evidence under that dispensation, so it is not only reasonable, but even natural to suppose, that he would be ushered in by some miraculous display of divine power. Hence the reason, likewise, of the many miracles that Jesus was empowered to work among them, as they were too outward and carnal to receive evidence through any other medium. And we likewise see, that none but those who believed on him as their promised Messiah, were prepared to receive and obey his last counsel and command, to turn from outward and external evidence, to that which is inward and spiritual;[*] the latter being as much above the former, as the gospel state is above the law state, or the spirit above the letter. For where Moses is read, or the law state with its outward miracles, there is a veil upon the heart, and it leads back to the letter, or external evidence, which killeth;[†] but this veil is taken way in Christ or the gospel state, wherein all have free access to the throne of grace, without priest or book.

Thou further queries, why was he permitted to suffer death? Is not the reason obvious. Why were the Lord's prophets and

[*] John, xiv. 16, 17, and xvi. 7.   [†] 2 Cor. iii. 6.

faithful servants, in the various ages of the world, permitted to suffer death? Was it not always the same thing, because there was no other alternative; for they must either give up their lives for the testimony of truth, and a good conscience towards God, or they must deny the truth, and disobey God, by conforming to their opposers and persecutors. But they chose rather to obey God than man; therefore they had rather suffer death, than to balk their testimony to the truth, which every wise and honest man would likewise prefer. And it was the same case with Jesus; he had rather suffer death, and seal his testimony to the truth with his blood, than to turn aside from the truth to please his wicked persecutors, as he told Pilate the Roman governor, " To this end was I born, and for this cause came I into the world, that I should bear witness unto the truth."

And as to his resurrection from the dead, it is simple and plain, as all the ways of an infinitely wise and gracious God are, and must be so to his rational creature man, whom he hath created for the purpose of his own glory, and therefore his whole duty must be comprehended in plain simple truth, that every individual endued with common understanding may know and comprehend. Even the wayfaring man, though a fool to the wisdom and science of this world, cannot err therein. And for any reasonable creature to judge otherwise, I conceive is casting a great indignity on the Divine character.

When we consider the outward law and covenant made with the people of Israel, with all its parts and appendages, from its first institution to the ascension of Christ, we shall perceive that it is to be regarded as a mere shadow or figure of good things to come. And all those shadows were manifested externally to the outward senses of man, and all comprehended in and by external objects; but the good things pointed to by them, are internal, in the soul, and only known by the inward and spiritual senses; and this last shadow of the resurrection of the outward body of Jesus, and of some few others in the course of that dispensation, is the highest and most valuable, as it had in its design and tendency the awakening of the unbeliever, the Sadducee, to a belief of the sufficiency of an invisible power, that was able to do any thing and every thing, that is consistent with justice, mercy, and truth, and that would conduce to the exaltation and good of his creature man. Therefore the resurrection of the dead body of Jesus, that could not possibly, of itself, create in itself a power to loose the bonds of death, and which must consequently have been the work of an invisible power, points to, and is a shadow of, the resurrection of the soul, that is dead in trespasses and sins, and that hath no capacity to quicken itself, but depends wholly on the renewed influence and quickening power of the spirit of God. For a soul dead in trespasses and sins, can no more raise a desire of itself for a renewed quickening of the divine life in itself, than a dead body can raise a desire of itself for a renewal of natural life; but both equally depend on the omnipotent presiding power of the spirit of God, as is clearly set forth by the prophet under the similitude of the resurrection of dry bones: Ezekiel, xxxvii. 1.

Hence, the resurrection of the outward fleshly body of Jesus, and some few others, under the law dispensation, as manifested to the external senses of man, gives full evidence as a shadow, pointing to the sufficiency of the divine invisible power of God, to raise the soul from a state of spiritual death into newness of life, and into the enjoyment of the spiritual substance of all the previous shadows of the law state. And by the arising of this Sun of Righteousness in the soul, all shadows flee away and come to an end; and the soul presses forward, under its divine influence, into that, that is within the veil, where our forerunner, even Jesus, has entered for us, showing us the way into the holiest of holies: as is typed forth by Moses in the tabernacle he set up in the wilderness, as commanded by the Lord, into which holy place, none were to enter, but the Lord's priests. But that is taken away in Christ or the gospel state, with the veil that separated the people from the inner court, where the Lord manifests himself to his children face to face by his spirit, which is the dispensation of sonship, and fulness of the gospel state.

Thus far I have felt a liberty to give thee my views in answer to the queries proposed by thee; and in that love that breathes peace on earth and good will to all men, I subscribe thy sincere friend.

ELIAS HICKS.

TO WILLIAM POOLE, WILMINGTON.

Jericho, 8th mo. 2d, 1827.

MY DEAR FRIEND,

I feel myself indebted to thee for two very acceptable letters, which I have not answered, and although I have now taken my pen with a view to attempt a reply, yet, I feel so little to communicate that will, in any wise, be interesting to thee, that I am almost ready to despair of going forward. But considering the particular satisfaction I take in the reception of letters from my friends, I am encouraged to make the attempt, although I should find but little to communicate.

I unite with thy views in relation to the doctrines of Christianity, and the abuse of them, as also in relation to the doctrines, precepts and example of Christ, who hath laid down a rule for his friends to follow in his example of perfect righteousness. But it is indeed sorrowful to reflect that the general body of Christendom, who profess to be his followers, have so far deviated and gone counter to his precepts and example, that we can discover but very little of it in their lives and conduct, very many of them having verged back to the law state, and, instead of worshipping God in spirit and in truth, they have instituted a worship to mental shadows and forms, by erecting in their minds the appearance of the fleshly body of Jesus, and are falling down to it and worshipping it, as though it was God, calling it by that exalted title. And what makes it the more grievously affecting is, that many of the leading characters of our favoured Society, have gone back into the same error, until darkness has clouded their minds.

In regard to the movements of my friends in Philadelphia and adjacent parts, I feel nothing but peace and quietness when I look towards them, for, I trust, I feel them in that love that casts out all fear, but I have not, as yet, found it my place actively to put a hand to it. As nothing but the internal evidence and power of divine truth, inwardly revealed, will be sufficient to carry on and effect the arduous undertaking, let all dwell low in the life and in the light that makes all things manifest: for in the life and light, which is one, there is power to effect all its own purposes. And, my dear Friends who have been driven, from necessity, to adopt means for the preservation and peace of Society, I conceive have nothing to fear, as they keep low in the principle of divine love and light, that has ever been the rock and foundation of the righteous in all the preceding ages, and will ever continue the same through all the succeeding ages, as they move forward when it opens the way, and stand still, when it stands still, in the all-conquering patience of our blessed pattern. In this state they will be brought to experience the salvation of God, and have cause to rejoice on the banks of deliverance.

Thy affectionate friend and brother in the fellowship of the gospel.

ELIAS HICKS.

TO WILLIAM WHARTON, PHILADELPHIA.

Jericho, 10th mo. 12th, 1827.

MY DEAR FRIEND,

Although I feel but little to communicate, yet as I have so convenient an opportunity to convey a few lines to thee, by my son in law V. H., who is about setting out this morning for your city, I was not willing to let it pass without improving it, so far as just to inform thee I am still in the body, and in the enjoyment of a full share of health and peace of mind; which favour I ascribe to the unmerited mercy of our gracious and benevolent Creator and Preserver, whose mercy is over all his works, and who is dealing out to all, severally as he will, in his infinite wisdom and justice, with an equal hand. And although my health of body, and ability to move about, are beyond what is common with men in such an advanced state of life, yet I feel a steady decay in both respects, which I account as a favour from my gracious Lord, who is paving the way, by daily slight or moderate pains of body, to make the passage through the valley of the shadow of death so tolerable, as not to interrupt the mind in its progress heaven-ward, and it makes death to the body as a mere shadow indeed to the upright in heart; which often inspires the grateful mind with this acclamation : What shall we render unto the Lord for all his benefits ! for his mercies are new every morning and his faithfulness every night; as he guards his devoted children by the angel of his presence through darkness and the shadow of death, to the glory and praise of his ever blessed name.

I was pleased to find, by thy letter, that you were getting along in your religious engagements so favourably, and that you had in your meetings frequent evidences of the Divine approbation. And I have no doubt but, as Friends steadily endeavour to dwell low in the innocent life, keeping a single eye to the Divine Monitor, that grace, mercy, and peace, will be with them, and no weapon formed against them will be permitted to prosper. But the spirit of opposition, that is sowing discord and contention, will be confounded in its own work of darkness.

Please present my love to thy dear Deborah and children ; to thy father Fisher and family, and to all inquiring friends in thy freedom, as though named ; and with a large share to thyself, in which my wife and children present unite.

I subscribe thy affectionate friend.

ELIAS HICKS.

TO WILLIAM POOLE, WILMINGTON.

Jericho, 2mo. 29th, 1828.

MY DEAR FRIEND,

In looking over my letters I found I was indebted to thee for two very acceptable ones, the latter of which was dated 12th mo. 24th, since when I have been, the greater part of the time, disqualified for writing by the accidental bite of a cat. But within three or four days past I have ventured to set pen to paper, to answer some of my friends' letters, having received a number during my illness. And although I feel but little ability, either of body or mind, to write any thing that will be very interesting to my friends, yet as thou hast heard of my being hurt, and as many reports have been spread abroad respecting it, and some pretty much exaggerated, I apprehended thou wouldst be willing to hear the present state of the case. And although my hand, that was hurt, is still lame and almost useless as to any manual exercise, yet, the inflammation and swelling is pretty much subsided, and is free from pain, so as to let me rest pretty well through the night, and is in a good way of recovery, although it progresses but slowly. And although the dispensation has been afflictive to the body, yet it has been a season of instruction and real profit to the mind, by which it is inspired with humility to thank God for all his wonderful works to the children of men, and to take courage to persevere in the way of well doing.

I rest thy affectionate friend.

ELIAS HICKS.

TO JOHN C. SANDERS, OHIO.

Jericho, 3d mo. 28th, 1828.

DEAR FRIEND,

Thy letter of the 10th instant was duly received, and its contents have been considered. I very often have letters of the same import, and I am as often led to marvel why any rational being should be at a loss about the right way of salvation, as it is the plainest and easiest way ever cast up for reasonable beings to walk in; even so plain, that the wayfaring man, though a fool, as to the wisdom and science of this world, cannot err in it. For the truth of which I dare appeal to the whole race of mankind that dwell on the face of the earth. Did thou ever meet with a man that was rational, however wicked and ungodly, but who had a consciousness of what was good and what was evil, without going to men or books for a solution? Is not this a plain way, a sure way, and the only way worthy of the Divine character, who is an omnipotent, omniscient, and omnipresent Being. And none know this plain way, but those who know this Being for themselves, without priest or book. For not all the books ever written, nor all the external miracles recorded in the Scriptures, nor all other external evidence of what kind soever, has ever revealed God, who is an eternal invisible Spirit, to any one of the children of men.

This truth is fully established by his son Jesus Christ, when he interrogated his disciples on this wise: "Whom say ye that I the son of man am?" Peter answered, "Thou art Christ, the son of the living God." And what was his answer to Peter? It was on this wise: "Blessed art thou Simon bar-Jonah, for flesh and blood hath not revealed it unto thee, but my Father which is in heaven. And upon this rock," that is, this revelation of my Father, "I will build my church, and the gates of hell shall not prevail against it." And how does God reveal himself to men? Not by Jesus Christ whom the Jews crucified; for had Jesus been able to reveal God he certainly would have done it. But it required the immediate revelation of the Spirit of God to reveal Jesus to them as being their promised Messiah. By this it appears, that nothing but God's omnipresence can, or ever did, reveal him, savingly, to any man.

The Scriptures bear full testimony to this truth, that "in him we live, move, and have our being." But people, in their natural estate, do not love this intimate knowledge of God, as it requires our dying to self, and all our selfish inclinations. I will appeal to thy own experience, did thou ever do a bad act, knowing it to be so, without feeling immediate conviction and reproof? and did thou ever do a good act without feeling thyself justified, and at peace? Hereby God's omnipresence is established, as there is no other principle, in heaven or earth, that would act such a part toward man; as "there is none good but one, and that is God."

As to the paragraph thou hast transcribed from one of my public communications, published by the stenographer, which created a difficulty in thy mind in regard to its correctness, and which some of my opposers make a handle of to vilify my character, if rightly considered, it would be plain and clear to every rational mind. For the infinitely wise and perfect God, in creation, has seen fit to make man a rational being, hence all his communications and revelations to him, must and will be rational, and in a way to be rationally understood. And as we are all made for the same glorious end and purpose, to glorify and enjoy him, and as we come into the world free from all pollution, innocent, but without knowledge, yet endued with a capacity and propensity to seek and obtain it, so the way is made plain by which only true knowledge can be obtained, which is by obedience to the manifested will of the Creator. But he did not see fit to fix man in that state of innocence, as it would have been a state of bondage, therefore he placed him in a state of freedom, and gave him the power of choosing his own way, but not without informing him of the danger of a wrong choice. But man, through the excitement of a desire after knowledge, turned aside from the divine command, and lost his standing in the favour of the Creator by rebelling against his will. And this has been the lot of every transgressor; and as all know by what means they have fallen, so they likewise know the way of return. For, as by disobedience to divine command, sin entered into the world, and death by sin, so by our obedience to divine command, life and immortality are brought to light by the Gospel.

Hence, the just and holy God deals out and dispenses to his rational children with an equal hand, to every one according to their several abilities; to one he gives five talents, to another two, and to another one. And where much is given much is required, and where less is given less is required; but always in a perfect and equal way, without respect of persons. And although Jesus, the great prophet and messiah of Israel, went far before the former prophets, and had a greater power given him, as he had a greater work to perform, yet it must have been just and equal in proportion to what was dispensed to others; for if otherwise he could be no example to them that follow after: for if the one talented servant had been as faithful in the improvement of his talent as the five talented one, his example would have been equally as good.

As to original sin, according to the acceptation of some professors of Christianity, that we are under the curse for the transgression of our first parents, I abhor the idea, as it casts a great indignity on the divine character, to think that a gracious and merciful God should condemn us for an act that was wholly out of our power to avoid! I consider it very little short, if any, of blasphemy against God. For I have never felt myself under condemnation for any sin but my own, neither have I felt any justification for any righteousness but what has been wrought in me by the grace of God; believing with the apostle that "by grace we are saved, through faith, and that not of ourselves, it is the gift of God; not of works lest any man should boast;" that is, not any works of our own; "for we are his workmanship created in Christ Jesus unto good works, which God hath before ordained that we should walk in them." Hereby we discover, as also from the very reason and nature of things, the incorrectness and absurdity of the doctrine of unconditional and personal election and reprobation, as held by some professors of Christianity, by which they exceedingly derogate from the excellence and perfection of the divine character, and accuse God of being a partial Being, a respecter of persons.

But it is perfectly consistent with truth, and the reason and nature of things, that as God is the only good, so he never does nor can, according to his own unchangeable nature and essence, command or ordain any other than good works, for his rational children to walk in. He has set them at liberty to make their own election, to good or evil works, as is self-evidently manifested by the acts and doings of all the children of men. And this is the rule Jesus gave to his disciples: "By their works or fruits ye shall know them." And it is only those who choose the good and refuse the evil, that God accepts as his children, and these only he qualifies as his messengers to mankind, as saith the Psalmist concerning the great Prophet and Messiah of Israel. For he had to make his choice, like the rest of mankind, being tried and proved as we are; therefore David says, and gives this reason for his exaltation, "Thou hast loved righteousness, and hated wickedness, therefore God, even thy God, hath anointed thee with the oil of gladness above thy fellows." Hence it appears, that all his exaltation emanated from his obedience and faithfulness to the manifested will of his Heavenly Father. This he learned by the sufferings that fell to his lot, like other men, as the Scriptures declare, Hebrews v. 8, "Though he were a son, yet learned he obedience by the things which he suffered." Hence we see, that the ways of God to man are all equal: which is also declared by the prophet Ezekiel, chap. xviii. in a full and clear manner. And abundance more plain Scripture testimonies might be produced, to show the correctness of the paragraph thou hast quoted; but what are already noted may be sufficient for thy satisfaction, and that of all others who are honestly disposed to seek after truth, freed from the prejudice of tradition and education, those fetters of the human mind.

I will now conclude, having wrote much more than I anticipated when I first took my pen; and if what is written does not satisfy thee, it may be, if we are favoured to live, and have our health a few months longer, we may be permitted to speak face to face, to our mutual satisfaction. In which view I subscribe thy sincere friend. ELIAS HICKS.

TO CHARLES STOKES, RANCOCAS, N. J.

New York, 4th mo. 3d, 1829.

DEAR FRIEND,

Thy acceptable letter of 2d month last was duly received, and its contents have been considered; and although I apprehend there is enough already in print of my own clear testimony, and spread before the public throughout most parts of the United States, in my communications and letters, some published by my consent and some by my opposers, to answer and confute all those several matters and charges specified by thee; yet inasmuch as thou desirest to have a clear statement in relation to those subjects noted in thy letter, take it as follows :—

First. As to the Scriptures of truth, as recorded in the book called the Bible, I have ever believed that all parts of them, that could not be known but by revelation, were written by holy men as they were inspired by the Holy Ghost, and could not be known through any other medium; and they are profitable for our encouragement, comfort, and instruction, in the very way that the apostle Paul testifies; and I have always accounted them, when rightly understood, as the best of books extant. I have always delighted in reading them, in my serious moments, in preference to any other book, from my youth up, and have made more use of their contents to confirm and establish my ministerial labours in the gospel, than most other ministers that I am acquainted with. But at the same time, I prize that from whence they have derived their origin, much higher than I do them; as "that for which a thing is such, the thing itself is more such." And no man, I conceive, can know or rightly profit by them, but by the opening of the same inspiring spirit, by which they were written, and, I apprehend, I have read them as much as most other men, and few, I believe, have derived more profit from them than I have.

Secondly. I have always believed, since I have been a man

and reflected on the subject, in the miraculous conception of Jesus, as far as history can give belief; and no man, I conceive, is possessed of a higher belief. And, as to his divinity, I am fully convinced that he was truly the son of God, and that he could not be so, unless he fully partook of the very nature, spirit, likeness, and divinity of his heavenly Father. As in the moral relation none can be a proper son of man unless he fully partake of the very nature, spirit, image, and likeness of his Father. That his mission, as the last and greatest prophet of the law state, was, first to fulfil the righteousness of that shadowy covenant, and thereby abolish it and all its outward ordinances, and by which he was prepared to receive additional power from on high; as the Scriptures assure us, that when he came up out of John's watery baptism, the last institute of that dispensation, the Holy Ghost descended upon him, and a voice from heaven was heard to say, "This is my beloved son, in whom I am well pleased." He now witnessed the fulness of the spiritual birth, and was thereby qualified to enter upon his gospel mission, and usher in the new covenant, prophesied of long before by the prophet Jeremy, being the son of God, with power according to the spirit of holiness; by which he went far before all the former prophets.

As to the disposition of his body of flesh, I consider it a secret that infinite wisdom hath seen fit to hide from man, as he did the bodies of Moses and Elijah, lest some of their admiring followers should idolize them. One thing the Scriptures assure us, and which I fully believe, that "flesh and blood cannot enter the kingdom of God." And Jesus fully confirms this view when he told Nicodemus, "that which is born of the flesh is flesh, and that which is born of the spirit is spirit." As to heaven and hell, and the devil, I am astonished to think that any, even though of small experience, should not have a real knowledge of them. Does not heaven signify a joyful state to the soul, and hell a state of torment? And does not the presence of God by his spirit, either by justifying or condemning us, always produce one of these two states, according to our obedience or disobedience to the divine requirings? I am fully persuaded I was a witness to these things before I was twelve years of age, and, therefore, I consider that the torment of a soul separated from God, by sin and transgression, far exceeds what the Scriptures make use of as a figure thereof, under the similitude of a body cast into a lake of fire and brimstone. But we cannot suppose that external fire and brimstone can have any effect on an immortal spirit; and the Psalmist clearly justifies this view in his appeal to the Almighty. "If," says he, "I ascend up into heaven, thou art there; if I make my bed in hell, behold thou art there," &c. Here we see that his presence constitutes the state and condition of every immortal soul, according to their obedience or disobedience to the requirings of his holy spirit, a manifestation whereof is given to every rational, accountable being to profit withal; by which all are made to know his will concerning them, unless they are wilfully blind.

And as to what is called a devil or Satan, it is something within us, that tempts us to go counter to the commands of God, and our duty to him and our fellow creatures; and the Scriptures tell us there are many of them, and that Jesus cast seven out of one woman. And I remember hearing, in my young years, a very able and fully approved minister, among Friends, give his explanation of that portion of Scripture. He said that the evils she had fallen into were caused by an unlawful indulgence of the propensities of our common nature, as probationary creatures; which, although necessary and useful in their place, when indulged beyond the bounds of reason and truth, produce sin. And I should suppose that every man of common understanding, by a proper introversion into himself, would immediately discover, that he was never tempted to any evil, but through one or other of the propensities and desires of his common nature, as an accountable being, and that those propensities and desires, while kept under the discipline of the cross of Christ, which is God's law written, as the Scriptures declare, on the tablets of our hearts, were all ministers of good to man, and qualified him rightly to answer the end of his creation. For without these propensities and desires, man would be a dormant, inactive creature; as he would have nothing to excite him to action, to procure those things necessary to preserve his life, or to seek after an attainment in true knowledge, sufficient to introduce him into the knowledge of his Creator, and prepare him to be a communicant with him in the realms of blessedness, when done with time here on earth.

Can it be possibly necessary for me to add any thing further, to manifest my full and entire belief of the immortality of the soul of man? Surely, what an ignorant creature must that man be, that hath not come to the clear and full knowledge of that in himself. Does not every man feel a desire fixed in his very nature after happiness, that urges him on in a steady pursuit after something to satisfy this desire, and does he not find, that all the riches, and honour, and glory of this world, together with every thing that is mortal, falls infinitely short of satisfying this desire; which proves it to be immortal: and can any thing, or being, that is not immortal in itself, receive the impress of an immortal desire upon it? Surely not. Therefore, this immortal desire of the soul of man, never can be fully satisfied, until it comes to be established in a state of immortality and eternal life, beyond the grave.

On my return to the bosom of my dear family and friends at home; although under the severe operation of the cold I took in Jersey, that confined me to the house for several weeks; nevertheless, such was the unsullied joy and peace of mind I witnessed, in a retrospective view of my late journey to the west among my friends, and the unmerited favours dispensed to me through the whole arduous labour, for the promotion of the noble cause of truth and righteousness in the earth, that a view of it inspires my whole man with humility, thanksgiving and gratitude, to the blessed Author of all our sure mercies, who is over all worthy for ever. Add to that the sweet communion with my much beloved wife and children, I humbly considered a comfort and felicity far beyond my deserts. But, alas! how fleeting and uncertain are all our joys that rest on terrestrial objects; for as soon, almost, as I had pretty well recovered from my bodily indisposition, and in the full enjoyment of the endeared embraces of my beloved companion, she was taken from me.*

And as nothing further has transpired of late worthy of particular notice I will now draw to a close.

I subscribe thy sincere friend.

ELIAS HICKS.

TO WILLIAM POOLE, WILMINGTON.

Shrewsbury, 5th mo. 19th, 1829.

My Dear Friend,

The long interruption of our mutual and friendly correspondence has not arisen on my part from any diminution of that sincere love and regard that has subsisted between us from the time of our first acquaintance, but from causes over which I had no control. For when I returned from my arduous western journey, and was initiated again in the bosom of my dear family, I was under the pressure of a severe cold, which laid me up, and for a number of weeks, disqualified me for writing.

Soon after I had in some degree recovered my usual state of bodily ability, my dear and much beloved wife was taken down with a cold, and although for a number of days we had no anticipation of danger from her complaint, thinking it most likely in a few days, she would again be restored to her usual health, which she had been favoured with during my absence, yet, about five days after she was taken, the disorder appeared to settle on her lungs, and brought on an inflammation which terminated in a dissolution of her precious life, on the ninth day from the time she was first taken ill. She had but little

---

* The remaining part of this letter gives an account of the last sickness and death of his wife, but as a narrative of this event is contained in the letter immediately following, to William Poole, it is here omitted.

bodily pain, yet, as she weakened down, she suffered through shortness of breath; but before her close, she became perfectly tranquil and easy, and passed away like a lamb, as though entering into a sweet sleep, without sigh or groan, or the least possible bodily emotion, and her precious spirit, I trust and believe, has landed safely on the angelic shore, "where the wicked" and all opposing spirits "cease from troubling, and where the weary are at rest."

To myself and family, in the relation she stood to us as a faithful and truly loving wife, and a tender and affectionate mother to our children, instructing them in the path of virtue, by precept and example, endeavouring to guard them and keep them out of harm's way, this is a great and irreparable loss, and nothing is left to console us on that behalf, but a confident belief and an unshaken hope that our great loss is her still greater gain.

And although the loss and the trial as to all my external blessings, are the greatest I have ever met with, or I ever shall have to endure, yet I have a hope, that through Divine aid, I may be preserved from murmuring or complaining, and that I may continually keep in view the unmerited favour, dispensed to us, by being preserved together fifty-eight years, in an unbroken bond of endeared affection, which seemed, if possible, to increase with time to the last moment of her life, and which neither time nor distance can lessen or dissolve; but in the spiritual relation I trust it will endure for ever, where all the Lord's redeemed children are one in him, who is God over all, in all, and through all, blessed for ever.

I am now here attending the quarterly meeting of Shrewsbury and Rahway, which closes to-day, and we propose to return to New York to-morrow. My daughter Elizabeth is here, and unites with me in love to you all, which is the same as ever, and in which I conclude and subscribe thy affectionate friend.

ELIAS HICKS.

TO BENJAMIN FERRIS, WILMINGTON.

Jericho, 6th mo. 17th, 1829.

My Dear Friend,

Thy very acceptable letter of 5th month last was duly received, and the very comfortable and interesting account it contained of the life and death of our very dear and mutual friend, William Poole, was truly grateful. His departure will cause a real chasm in my most interesting correspondence; for although I have a large circle of friends with whom I occasionally correspond, yet with none, for a great number of years, have I so often corresponded, as with my dear friend, William Poole. Our social intercourse was such, that it was almost like near neighbours; and I shall sensibly feel a loss in our separation. But I have this to console me,—that however great the loss may seem, it can be but for a short season,* as I confidently believe it will redound to his eternal gain, and that his precious spirit is safely landed on the angelic shore, where the wicked, and every opposing spirit, will cease from troubling, and the weary are at rest, with a crown of everlasting joy upon their heads.

It was cause of gladness to me, when I heard the decease of dear William announced, that I had written him just previous thereto; as there had been a longer space of silence between us, when I last wrote, than usual, occasioned on his part, I apprehend, by his indisposition; and on my part, by the transpiring of certain events, which tended to shut up the way very much from writing to my friends. But I felt the impression so strong on my mind, when I wrote the last, that I could not be easy to delay any longer.

We have John Comly with us, visiting our meetings, and appointing some among those not in membership with us. He is on his way to visit the meetings of Friends in Purchase

---

* It will be seen by a reference to the note accompanying the last letter of E. H., which closes this volume, that the aged and venerable writer closed his earthly pilgrimage in about eight months from this period.

quarter. He had made a beginning there about two weeks past, but was called home on account of the indisposition of his wife. She being much restored, he came on here again last seventh day, and expects to be in New York next first day. My family and friends hereaway are in usual health, except a little grand-daughter, that was taken yesterday with a chill, followed with considerable fever.

Please to present my love to thy dear wife and children, and to all inquiring friends, particularly to the children of my dear departed friend, William Poole, and say to them on my behalf, that strong and fervent are my desires, that they may walk in his footsteps, and follow his virtuous example; that so it may be said, instead of the father there is the children; for I confidently believe, that nothing could have given their dear father greater joy, than to have seen his children walking in the truth.

Thou wilt excuse the imperfections of the above, as I write in haste, and have no time to copy—my time being steadily employed in making preparations for my northern journey, in order to finish the remaining part of my religious concern in our own yearly meeting, as expressed in my certificate of last year; expecting to leave home on that account a few days hence.

And with a large share of love to thee, I subscribe thy affectionate friend.

ELIAS HICKS.

TO ELIAS WILBUR, SARATOGA, N. Y.

Jericho, 1*st mo.* 1*st*, 1830.

DEAR YOUNG FRIEND,

Having thee in remembrance for several days past, I was induced to take my pen and commune with thee a little in the letter line, and give thee a little sketch of our progress homeward. After we took leave of thy father's hospitable roof, and since we parted with him at Pittstown, though we then separated as to the body, yet in mind I often feel him as though present, with grateful sensations for his kindness in accompanying us in our journey from place to place, through rough and smooth, with such cheerfulness and good will as tended to smooth the way before us and made our journey more pleasant.

After parting with thy father at Pittstown, we took leave of our friends there and proceeded directly to Troy, where we arrived in good season. Here we rested the next day, and the day following we rode down to Thomas Wright's; and the day after being very stormy and my head pretty much out of order, we tarried there over first day and attended Hudson meeting. On second day we proceeded to Ninepartners, and after attending the quarterly meeting there, and that at Stanford, both of which, I think, were favoured seasons, in which the canopy of love was spread over the assemblies to the comfort and rejoicing of the honest-hearted, and to their edification; we parted with them in true peace of mind and with thankful hearts, and proceeded directly to Cornwall, where we arrived in season to attend their meeting the following first day. This was a large and favoured opportunity, the people came together freely, and appeared to go away well satisfied. On second and third days we had appointed meetings at the lower and upper Clove. At the latter place, Friends and those called orthodox, continued to meet together on first days, and word was sent forward to a Friend of that meeting to spread the notice at the close of their first day meeting, of our appointment on third day, which was accordingly done by our Friend Wait Pearsall, which raised the resentment of the orthodox; and one of their principal leaders, as soon as the meeting was closed, fell upon the Friend who gave the notice and asked him how he dare give out notice for me who was a Deist, &c., and had been regularly disowned, and that he likewise had been disowned. And two or three of the orthodox got about him and assured him, that we should not have the privilege of going into the house; but the Friend assured them that he would have the house opened. However, they appeared determined that we should not have it; and to prevent Friends getting in, they sent the key away two miles off; but before the time of our meeting came about, they took wit in their anger, and their chief man went and got the key and opened the house without giving Friends any farther trouble, and we had a large favoured meeting, without any interruption. After which, the next day, we rode to New York. Here we tarried until after first day, and attended Friends' meetings as they came in course; at Hester Street on fifth day, and Rose Street on first day morning, and at Hester Street again in the afternoon. These meetings were large, especially the two last, the latter of which Friends thought contained more people than ever had been in that house before, as there had been a new arrangement of some of the seats which had made room for a number of seats to be added. These were all favoured seasons, worthy of our grateful remembrance. On second day evening we had a large favoured meeting in the town of Brooklyn, which closed my concern and crowned my labours in the gospel among my friends the two preceding seasons, with true peace of mind; a sense of which unmerited favours, inspires my heart with thanksgiving and gratitude to the blessed author of all our sure mercies, and who remains to be God over all, blessed for ever. The next day we proceeded homeward, where we arrived safe on fourth day afternoon, and found my family and friends in usual health, which I considered an additional favour, and we were made to rejoice together under a feeling of that love that unites and makes glad the whole heritage of God.

And what shall I say to thee, my dear young friend, for thy encouragement in the way of well doing and path of true and real virtue. Thou hast pious parents, who, no doubt, feel anxious for thy preservation, and who can have no greater joy than to see their children walking in the truth. Can I do better than to remind thee of the counsel of that good man David to his son Solomon, on this wise: " And thou Solomon my son, know thou the God of thy Father, and serve him with a perfect heart and a willing mind, for if thou seek him, he will be found of thee, but if thou forsake him, he will cast thee off for ever." And I will add in confirmation of this counsel of David, that most excellent and perfect lesson of our great and holy pattern Jesus Christ. " Seek first the kingdom of God and his righteousness, and all other things shall be added ;" because, every thing that can be a blessing and real comfort to rational beings is comprehended in this kingdom. And this kingdom, Jesus tells us truly, is within us; and God is ever in his kingdom, and none but he has a right to hand out his blessings to man. And as we have no true wisdom at our command, therefore the apostle tells us where to find it, " If any lack wisdom let him ask it of God, who giveth liberally, and upbraideth not ;" for indeed, "blessed is the man that trusteth in the Lord, and whose hope the Lord is."

Please present my love affectionately to thy dear parents, and to all inquiring friends, as way opens in thy freedom; and tell thy father that a line from him, giving some account of your fare since I left you, will be very acceptable. And may grace, mercy, and peace, be with thee and abound, and then thou wilt be neither barren nor unfruitful in those things that belong to thy everlasting peace. In love I conclude thy friend.

ELIAS HICKS.

SIX QUERIES
PROPOSED TO ELIAS HICKS,
WITH HIS ANSWERS.

TO THOMAS LEGGETT, JR. NEW YORK.

Jericho, 11th mo. 16th, 1829.

DEAR FRIEND,

Thy affectionate letter I have duly received, and its contents were grateful to my best feelings, as they appear to be the result of sincere friendship. But I may acknowledge it was really marvellous to my mind to think how it could be possible, that thou, my friend, should find any inducement to propose to me such questions, as are comprehended in thy first four queries, as I should suppose that no person who has had the opportunity thou hast had, of seeing and of hearing me, in public and in private, and who has known my manner of life for more than twenty years, would have given the least possible credit to any of those irrational and false reports to which these queries allude; and although I consider them as unworthy of my notice, yet friendship induces me, as thou hast requested it, to make a brief reply to them severally.

First Query.—Dost thou wish to be understood, by any thing thou may have said, publicly or privately, that thou denies the miraculous conception of the fleshly body of Jesus Christ, or dost thou believe that Joseph was his father?

Answer.—I have ever believed and asserted, from my youth up, that I had as full a belief in the miraculous conception of the fleshly body of Jesus Christ, as it was possible for the history to give belief. And I may now assure thee that I never thought or said, that I believed Joseph was his father.

Second Query.—Dost thou mean to be understood, by any thing thou may have said publicly or privately, that thou denies the divinity of Jesus Christ?

Answer.—As respects the divinity of Jesus Christ, I apprehend no minister in the Society of Friends has more often in his public communications asserted the divinity of Jesus Christ the Son of God, than I have, assuring my hearers, that he was fully swallowed up into the divine nature, and complete divinity of his heavenly Father. But I never believed that Jesus Christ, the Son of God, was the *father of himself*, but that he was truly the Son of God, endued with power from on high, by which he was qualified to usher in and introduce the new covenant dispensation, as prophesied long before by Jeremiah the prophet, when all outward mediation should cease, as the law of God was now to be written on the inward table of the heart, and not on tables of stone, or with pen, ink, and paper; after which no man was to say to his neighbour or brother, know the Lord, for all shall know me from the least to the greatest. This is the covenant that I acknowledge, and I acknowledge no other, and this I consider the only real gospel covenant.

Third Query.—Dost thou wish to be understood as denying the authenticity of the Scriptures of truth, or as wishing to undervalue them; or would thou encourage all to the frequent and diligent perusal of them, as being able, under divine illumination, to make wise unto salvation?

Answer.—As respects the Scriptures of truth, I have highly esteemed them from my youth up, have always given them the preference to any other book, and have read them abundantly, more than any other book, and I would recommend all to the serious and diligent perusal of them. And I apprehend I have received as much comfort and instruction from them as any other man. Indeed they have instructed me home to the sure unchangeable foundation—the light within, or spirit of truth, the only gospel foundation, that leads and guides into all truth. and thereby completes man's salvation; which nothing else ever has, or ever can do. But why need I say these things, as all men know that have heard me, that I confirm my doctrine abundantly from their testimony: And I have always endeavoured sincerely to place them in their true place and station, but I never dare exalt them above what they themselves declare; and as no spring can rise higher than its fountain, so likewise the Scriptures can only direct to the fountain from whence they originated—the spirit of truth: as saith the apostle, "The things of God knoweth no man, but the spirit of God;" therefore when the Scriptures have directed and pointed us to this light within, or spirit of truth, there they must stop—it is their ultimatum—the topstone of what they can do. And no other external testimony of men or books can do any more. And Jesus in his last charge to his disciples, in order to prevent them from looking without for instruction, in the things of God, after he had led them up to the highest pinnacle that any outward evidence could effect, certified them, that this light within, or spirit of truth, by which only their salvation could be effected, dwelt with them, and should be in them. And this every Christian knows to be a truth; and there never was a real Christian made by any other power than this spirit of truth; and every thing that can be done by man without it, must fail of effecting his salvation.

Fourth Query.—Dost thou believe there is no accountability beyond the grave, or that there is no state of rewards and punishments after death?

Answer.—This charge, which I hear has been made against me, is altogether such a barefaced and palpable falsehood, that I can hardly believe that any man could be ignorant and wicked enough to fabricate such a story, nor that any man that knew any thing about me could give the least possible credit thereto; as I have spent a great portion of my time in travel and exercise, having travelled thousands and tens of thousands of miles, leaving behind me every tender and sweet enjoyment that this life can afford, for no other cause than to promote truth and righteousness among my friends and fellow creatures, that they might be prepared to die, and enter into that eternal inheritance prepared for the righteous, where the wicked cease from troubling, and the weary are at rest; fully believing that every man will reap the reward of well done good and faithful servant, or receive the sentence, **depart from me ye workers of iniquity, I know you not.**

Fifth Query.—When thou speaks of our coming up to a level with the man Christ Jesus, dost thou mean level in our several capacities—I mean that the one talented servant, perfectly occupying his one talent, is as perfect as the five talented servant perfectly occupying his?

Answer.—To this I need say but little, as thou hast given a correct solution of it. That as God is no respecter of persons, he therefore deals out to all his rational children with an equal hand, as is beautifully set forth by Jesus in the parable of the talents; for had the one talented servant faithfully employed his one talent, and gained another, he would have stood as high in his Lord's favour, as the five talented servant.

Therefore as his beloved son had a much greater work on earth than any other man, so he had a much greater fulness of the spirit than any other man; "For he whom God hath sent, speaketh the words of God: for God giveth not the spirit by measure unto him." John iii. 34. I believe with Peter, when he thus expressed himself, " Jesus of Nazareth, a man approved of God among you by miracles, and wonders, and signs, which God did by him in the midst of you, as ye yourselves also know." Acts ii. 22. And again,

"How God anointed Jesus of Nazareth with the Holy Ghost and with power; who went about doing good, and healing all who were oppressed with the devil: for God was with him." Acts x. 38. This "Holy Ghost and power," I believe is the only Saviour that can cleanse the soul of man from sin, and give him an inheritance among all them which are sanctified.*

Sixth Query.—What relation has the body of Jesus to the Saviour of man? Dost thou believe that the crucifixion of the outward body of Jesus Christ was an atonement for our sins?

Answer.—In reply to the first part of this query I answer, I believe, in unison with our ancient Friends, that it was the outward garment, in which he performed all his mighty works,

---

* John, xvii. 21, 22, 23. 1 John, iii. 1 to 7. Ephe. iv. 11, 12, 13. Rom. viii. 14, 15, 16, 17, 19.

or as Paul hath expressed it, "know ye not that your body is the temple of the Holy Ghost which is in you;" therefore he charged them not to defile those temples. "What is attributed to that body, I acknowledge and give to that body, in its place, according as the Scripture attributeth it, which is through and *because* of that which dwelt and acted in it. But that which sanctified and kept the body pure, (and made all acceptable in him,) was the life, holiness, and righteousness of the spirit. And the same thing that kept his vessel pure, it is the same thing that cleanseth us."*

In reply to the second part of this query, I would remark, that I "see no need of directing men to the type for the antitype, neither to the outward temple, nor yet to Jerusalem, neither to Jesus Christ or his blood, [outwardly;] knowing that neither the righteousness of faith, nor the word of it, doth so direct."† " The new and second covenant is dedicated with the *blood, the life* of Christ Jesus, which is the alone atonement unto God, by which all his people are washed, sanctified, cleansed, and redeemed to God."‡

I may add, it has always been the lot of the Lord's faithful servants, in every age of the world, to be cried out against, and it makes good the saying of the apostle. " All that will live godly in Christ Jesus shall suffer persecution."

I conclude thou hast not given thyself the trouble to read any of my public communications, as taken down by M. T. C. Gould, the stenographer; as in them, all objections are answered, in regard to my belief and doctrine:—Read§ volume 1st, and first communication, and a letter I wrote to a Friend in Chester county, Penn., under date 7th mo. 22d, 1827, in answer to four queries similar to thine, published I believe in the latter part of the fourth volume of the same work.

With love to thy dear wife and children, I remain thy sincere friend.

ELIAS HICKS.

* Isaac Pennington, vol. iii. p. 34.
† Whitehead's Life and Light of Christ, p. 34.
‡ George Fox's Doctrinals, p. 646.
§ A work called " the Quaker," containing sermons, &c.

THE
LAST LETTER

OF

ELIAS HICKS;

WRITTEN TO HUGH JUDGE, OF OHIO.*

Jericho, 2th mo. 14th, 1830.

DEAR HUGH,

Thy very acceptable letter of the 21st ultimo, was duly received and read with interest, tending to excite renewed sympathetic, and mutual fellow-feeling; and brought to my remembrance the cheering salutation of the blessed Jesus, our holy and perfect pattern and example, to his disciples, viz. "Be of good cheer, I have overcome the world." By which he assured his disciples that, by walking in the same pathway of self-denial and the cross which he trod to blessedness, they might also overcome the world; as nothing has ever enabled any rational being, in any age of the world, to overcome the spirit of the world, which lieth in wickedness, but the cross of Christ.

Some may query, what is the cross of Christ? To these I answer, it is the perfect law of God written on the tablet of the heart, and in the heart of every rational creature, in such indelible characters that all the power of mortals cannot erase nor obliterate. Neither is there any power or means given or dispensed to the children of men, but this inward law and light by which the true and saving knowledge of God can be obtained. And by this inward law and light, all will be either justified or condemned, and all be made to know God for themselves, and be left without excuse, agreeably to the prophecy of Jeremiah, and the corroborating testimony of Jesus in his last counsel and command to his disciples, not to depart

---

* This letter was just closed when he was attacked with the paralytic affection which terminated his life, on the 27th of 2d month, 1830.

from Jerusalem until they should receive power from on high; assuring them that they should receive power, when they had received the pouring forth of the spirit upon them, which would qualify them to bear witness of him in Judea, Jerusalem, Samaria and to the uttermost parts of the earth; which was verified in a marvellous manner on the day of Pentecost, when thousands were converted to the Christian faith in one day. By which it is evident, that nothing but this inward light and law, as it is heeded and obeyed, ever did, or ever can make a true and real Christian and child of God. And until the professors of Christianity agree to lay aside all their non-essentials in religion, and rally to this unchangeable foundation and standard of truth, wars and fightings, confusion and error will prevail, and the angelic song cannot be heard in our land, that of "glory to God in the highest and on earth peace and good-will to men." But when all nations are made willing to make this inward law and light, the rule and standard of all their faith and works, then we shall be brought to know and believe alike, that there is but one Lord, one faith, and but one baptism; one God and Father, that is above all, through all, and in all; and then will all those glorious and consoling prophecies, recorded in the Scriptures of truth be fulfilled. Isaiah ii. 4, "He," the Lord, "shall judge among the nations, and rebuke many people; and they shall beat their swords into ploughshares and their spears into pruning hooks: nation shall not lift up sword against nation; neither shall they learn war any more." Isaiah xi. "The wolf also shall dwell with the lamb, and the leopard shall lie down with the kid; and the calf, and the young lion, and the fatling together; and a little child shall lead them. And the cow and the bear shall feed; their young ones shall lie down together; and the lion shall eat straw like the ox. And the sucking child shall play on the hole of the asp, and the weaned child shall put his hand on the cockatrice' den. They shall not hurt nor destroy in all my holy mountain: for the earth," that is our earthly tabernacles, "shall be full of the knowledge of the Lord, as the waters cover the sea."

These scripture testimonies give a true and correct description of the gospel state, and no rational being can be a real Christian and true disciple of Christ, until he comes to know all these things verified in his own experience, as every man and woman has more or less of all those different animal propensities and passions in their nature; and they predominate and bear rule, and are the source and fountain from whence all wars and every evil work proceed, and will continue as long as man remains in his first nature, and is governed by his animal spirit and propensities, which constitute the natural man, which Paul tells us, "receiveth not the things of the spirit of God, for they are foolishness unto him, neither can he know them, because they are spiritually discerned." This corroborates the declaration of Jesus to Nicodemus, that "except a man be born again, he cannot see the kingdom of God;" for "that which is born of the flesh is flesh, and that which is born of the spirit is spirit." Here Jesus assures us, beyond all doubt, that nothing but spirit can either see or enter into the kingdom of God; and this confirms Paul's doctrine, that "as many as are led by the spirit of God are the sons of God," and "joint heirs with Christ." And Jesus assures us, by his declaration to his disciples, John xiv. 16, 17; "If ye love me, keep my commandments; and I will pray the Father and he shall give you another comforter, that he may abide with you for ever, even the spirit of truth, whom the world cannot receive:" that is, men and women in their natural state, who have not given up to be led by this spirit of truth, that leads and guides into all truth; "because they see him not, neither do they know him, but ye know him, for he dwelleth with you, and shall be in you." And as these give up to be wholly led and guided by him, the new birth is brought forth in them and they witness the truth of another testimony of Paul's, even that of being "created anew in Christ Jesus unto good works," which God had foreordained that all his new-born children should walk in them, and thereby show forth by their fruits and good works, that they were truly the children of God, born of his spirit, and taught of him: agreeably to the testimony of the prophet, that "the children of the Lord, are all taught of the Lord, and in righteousness they are established, and great is the peace of his children." And nothing can make them afraid that man can do unto them; as saith the prophet in his appeal to Jehovah, "Thou wilt keep him in perfect peace, whose mind is staid on thee, because he trusteth in thee." Therefore, let every one that loves the truth, for God is truth, "trust in the Lord for ever, for in the Lord Jehovah there is everlasting strength."

I write these things to thee, not as though thou didst not know them, but as a witness to thy experience, as "two are better than one, and a threefold cord is not quickly broken."

I will now draw to a close, with just adding, for thy encouragement, be of good cheer for no new thing has happened to us; for it has ever been the lot of the righteous to pass through many trials and tribulations, in their passage to that glorious, everlasting, peaceful, and happy abode, where all sorrow and sighing come to an end—the value of which is above all price; for when we have given all that we have and can give, and suffered all that we can suffer, it is still infinitely below its real value. And if we are favoured to gain an inheritance in that blissful and peaceful abode, "where the wicked cease from troubling, and the weary are at rest," we must ascribe it all to the unmerited mercy and loving kindness of our Heavenly Father, who remains to be God over all, blessed for ever.

I will now conclude, and in the fulness of brotherly love to thee and thine, in which my family unite, subscribe thy affectionate friend.

ELIAS HICKS.

Please present my love to all my friends, as way opens.

[The three following Letters were not published in any former edition.]

APPENDIX.

TO THE QUARTERLY MEETING OF MEN AND WOMEN FRIENDS, TO BE HELD AT WESTBURY.

Newtown, in Gloucester County, West Jersey, 13th of 1st mo., 1798.

DEAR FRIENDS:

Feeling my mind for some days past drawn towards you in near sympathy and affectionate remembrance, thought I could not do justice to myself or to you without saluting you with a few lines, when convened in the capacity of a Quarterly Meeting, expressive of the near unity, fellow feeling, and regard that has often been witnessed to spread in my heart towards you all since I left you, accompanied with fervent desires that we all may more and more endeavor to dwell deep in the pure spring of divine life, and become established in the one pure faith that works by love, that so the effectual baptism of the one spirit may be witnessed baptizing all into the one body, whereby we may come to drink together in the one spirit, as in this only is the true communion of the body and blood of Christ experienced, even that bread that comes down from Heaven and nourishes the soul up into eternal life, and as each member feels the quickening of this pure life, and abides therein, ability is witnessed (and by no other means) to promote in their varied allotments and stations the cause of truth and righteousness, without envying or grudging one another, and to transact the affairs of the church to the honor of our holy head, and the edification and comfort of His people. May those who stand as delegated shepherds, whether ministers, elders, or overseers, look well to themselves and to the flock over whom they are appointed, that so all may be fed with wholesome food—milk to babes, strong meat to young men, and strengthening cordials to those who are infirm, whether young or old, who through exposure to the fogs and damps that arise from the stagnant waters of this world's glory and friendship, are in danger of being surfeited. And let all those who are called to lead the way ever keep in remembrance that example is more powerful than precept; that through faithfulness and an holy confidence in that arm of power that hath wrought deliverance to all those who sincerely trust in Him, all may come to experience when the Chief Shepherd shall appear a crown of glory that fadeth not away.

May the dearly beloved youth of every description, whether married or in a single state, male or female, be encouraged to trust in the Lord, and more and more to dedicate the flower of their days to His honor and service, seeing he has been graciously pleased in unerring mercy to visit their minds with the glorious day-spring from on high, and is calling them out of darkness into his marvelous light, and fitting and fashioning those who are obediently following in the way of his commandments as vessels of honor in his house, and will make some of them as polished shafts in his quiver as they abide in faithfulness and come up in His holy fear. Therefore, dear young friends, be guarded; keep up a strict watch upon the very wicket of your hearts, that so the delusive and ensnaring pleasures, friendships, and honors of the world rob you not of your chastity nor turn away your affections from the beloved of your souls. Endeavor to keep in view at all times, especially when tempted or allured by the grand deceiver, or the natural propensities of your own creaturely passions—keep in full view, if possible, at those seasons, his self-denying example, the sorrow and suffering of his life, and the bitter agonies of his death, when he yielded up on Calvary's Mount his precious life. I have often thought, did we keep enough before us his holy example and the glorious recompense of reward, it would stain in our view all the glory and honor of this perishing world, and enable us, as one formerly, to account all as dross, that so we might win Christ and be worthy of a name in his house and place at his right hand, where there are rivers of pleasure, and that forevermore. Finally, dear friends, may the love and fellowship of the gospel of peace and salvation increase and prevail amongst you more and more—uniting you together in Him and one to another, who is the head of all principalities and powers, thrones and dominions, and is God over all, blessed in himself, and in his son, Jesus Christ, throughout all ages, world without end. Amen.

From your affectionate friend,

ELIAS HICKS.

Read in the Quarterly Meeting at Westbury, with the partition between men's and women's meeting removed.

TO M———— M————.

Jericho, 8th of 2d mo., 1824.

DEAR FRIEND:

Better late than never. The reason why I have not given a direct answer to thy letter of 7th mo. last has been owing to the want of seeing the right time, and feeling a suitable qualification for it; but having for several days past been led to think of my friends in and about Hudson, and remembering thy kind remembrance above said, I felt an inducement to attempt a reply.

The subject of vocal prayer has very particularly exercised my mind for many years, and the abundant, formal, lifeless communications in that way by the varied sects of professed Christians have been a great burden to my mind, and I likewise believe they are an abomination in the sight of the Lord: hence I have often been engaged to bear a full and public testimony against them. This may account in some measure for my seldom appearing in that way, and from a fear lest the offering might not be sufficiently attended with that life that would exonerate me from my own condemnation. For I consider it to require our minds to be clothed with deep reverence and godly fear to approach and address the majesty of heaven in solemn prayer, nevertheless I believe it may be sometimes consistent with His will and our required duty in the present state of mankind.

For when the dark states of men and women, who, by tradition and an improper education, are settled at ease in sin, the light of truth breaking in upon their minds in the day of God's merciful visitation to their souls, the sight of their deplorable condition strikes the mind with such fear and horror that, like Israel at Mount Sinai, they draw back and are afraid and unwilling to meet with Him in that way any more, which places them in a state that requires a mediator; and, as Moses was appointed a mediator to the whole house of Israel, so I believe, under the gospel dispensation that has no written or external law, nor can have, the states of the people being so various that it is impossible that any literal law can be made to suit all conditions, hence we see the necessity of coming to the new covenant law, that is indited by the spirit of God in every individual, and which is so exactly suited to the state and condition of the individual in whose heart it is indited, the states and condition of the children of men being so varied that it is not likely nor probable that that law is perfectly suited to the state of one man would be exactly fitted to the state of any other man in the world. But as mankind have generally turned away and become dark and blind, hence when, by the renewed visitations of divine love and light, they are brought to see their wretched condition, as above said, they are afraid to come into His presence, yet feel some faint desire after deliverance. Now, on behalf of these, the Lord, I believe, in the present day, as formerly, sees meet in his wisdom and goodness to inspire the hearts of his ministers (as mediators to those low and disconsolate states) with the spirit of prayer and supplication. Not to inform Him of their wants, which he altogether knows, but as a means to prepare the minds of such disconsolate ones with faith and courage, suitably to look up to Him as their only helper, which places them in a condition to receive his blessing with gratitude and thanksgiving. And this, I trust, will be the case while sin abounds in the world; but when men and women become real Christians, wholly led and guided by the spirit of truth or law written in the heart, after the example of Jesus of Nazareth, then all external mediation ceases, for all then are immediately taught of God, as saith the Prophet.

"For the children of the Lord are all taught of the Lord, and in righteousness are they established, and great is the peace of these children."

These have no longer any need to say each to the other, know the Lord, for all shall know him, from the least to the greatest, and these, as to themselves, have no need of reading or studying, however good or useful they may have been, while men and women are groveling along in the way of uncertainty, amidst the mists and fogs of tradition and superstition, seeing, by faithfulness to the dictates of this unwritten law, they are brought through to the clear light of the day, and have no longer need (as respects their spiritual condition) of the light of the sun or moon outwardly, for God has become their everlasting light, and the days of their mourning are ended. And these experience that excellent state described by the Psalmist, viz: "Blessed is the man that walketh not in the counsel of the ungodly, nor standeth in the way of sinners, nor sitteth in the seat of the scornful, but his delight is in the law of the Lord, and in his law doth he meditate both day and night."

And I have long believed that if our ministers who travel up and down to improve the people in their religious concerns, instead of spending so much of their time in recommending the people so much to the letter and the reading of books, however good they may be as such, were more concerned to recommend to them silent retirement and meditation on the new covenant law written in the heart, which only can set free from the law of sin and death, their labors would be more productive, as relates to the people, of real good, and terminate in much more peace and comfort to themselves. And I really fear unless this is the case that we, as a people, will ere long dwindle down into the same state of dead formality as now generally reigns in Christendom among other professors of the Christian name.

In much love to thyself, I subscribe thy affectionate friend,

ELIAS HICKS.

TO SAMUEL EVANS.

Jericho, 1st mo., 24th, 1830.

RESPECTED YOUNG FRIEND:

The manner of my address arises from the knowledge I had of thy worthy father, and the respect due to his character, and altho' thou art to me an entire stranger, yet I willingly cherish a hope that thou, by due attention to the real Quakers' light and law, which is inward and spiritual—thou may arise to the same respectability. But from my general observation on men and things, from youth to old age, I have never become possest of sufficient evidence to enforce a belief that any individual of our society, if he ever was a real Quaker, or friend, has ever added any respectability to his character as such, by the study and practice of the law of our country, or any other, that needs the coercion of war, or the sword, for its support.

And I consider the genuine Quakers' inward law and light, and their outward law and discipline that emanates from it, entirely supercedes all other outward law, as it would never permit any one of its faithful subjects to break any just law of any nation on earth, as the universal law of the real Christian and the real Quaker, both of which are one, consists in passive obedience and non-resistance to all the laws of man, whether just or unjust, and arbitrary, and those whose lives are regulated by this universal law are not afraid to bear their testimony against every unjust law of man, and against all its arbitrary requisitions: neither will they actively comply therewith, although the penalty for refusing should cost them their natural lives, and which penalty has actually been inflicted on many Christians and on some of our friends, in former years, for such refusal.

And, therefore, under these considerations, had I been favored with a number of sons, I should not dare to have encouraged or given my assent to any one of them, to fill the place of a lawyer. Under the full conviction that the calling in the present mode of their proceedure, in our courts of justice, is very injurious to the peace, prosperity, and happiness of every country and government in which they abound, as they encourage litigation, make suits at law more frequent, and prevent the more rational and less expensive and more just way of settling disputes among neighbors, by reference to just and impartial men, by way of arbitration.

For every honest man who desires nothing but the right should take place is very sensible, that when the parties are both honestly disposed, and agree to refer the subject of dispute to two or three, or more, as the case may require, of their judicious neighbors, whose honesty and integrity has been long established, that it is ten-fold more likely that justice will be done between them, than when tried by a jury promiscuously picked up by a sheriff, many of whom may be very ignorant both of law and justice, and who may be easily influenced by the pleading of a cunning lawyer, who is ever ambitious to out-do his opponent, whether right or wrong, to decide directly opposite to truth and justice, and which I believe is often the case when disputes are settled by a jury and lawyers in our courts of law.

Therefore, my advice to thee as a real friend, is to have as little to do with the law in any shape whatever as thou canst possibly avoid, as I do not think it consistent for any member of our society to procure a livelihood for himself and family by practising the law.

And as there are a great variety of honest callings, in each of which every honest, industrious man can procure a sufficiency of this world's goods for his own and family's comfort and which will much less interfere with our religious duty, and conduce more to the general good of society, I would recommend some mechanical branch, which will require but a small beginning, and which manner of life is generally conducive to health, and freer from care, and less burdensome to the mind, than some higher branches of business. Before I close, I will just add, as a token of my sincere regard towards thee, accompanied with a fervent desire for thy advancement in the enjoyment of the best of blessings, a short portion of scripture record, that I consider of so great value as to deserve a place in every mind, in characters that cannot be obliterated by time; they are as follows, viz: " Humility is before honor, and a haughty spirit before a fall ;" this is the motto of my mind. Hear the conclusion of the whole matter, "Fear God and keep his commandments, for this is the whole duty of man."

I will now conclude, and with due respect subscribe thy affectionate friend,

ELIAS HICKS.

CONTENTS.

	PAGE.
Advertisement,	3
Observations on Slavery,	5
Letter to Rufus Clark,	20
" " William Poole,	23
" " J—— N——,	25
" " William Poole,	31
" " " "	40
" " Phebe Willis,	43
" " William Poole,	50
" " William B. Irish,	51
" " William Poole,	58
" " " "	60
" " " "	61
" " Phebe Willis,	63
" " William Poole,	68
" " " "	72
" " " "	79
An Essay on the Birth and Offices of Christ,	81
Letter to William Poole,	86
" " " "	91
" " William Wharton,	96
" " " "	97
" " William Poole,	98
" " Edward Hicks,	101
" " William Poole,	105
" " " "	106
" " " "	109
" " " "	110
" " " "	111
" " " "	112
" " John Merritt,	113
" " William Poole,	116
An Address to Youth,	119
Letter to J. Wilson Moore,	120
" " Nathan Shoemaker,	124
" " William Poole,	129
" " J. Wilson Moore,	131
" " Abraham Lower,	134

		PAGE.
Letter to William Poole,		136
" " Samuel Comfort,		140
" " William Poole,		142
" " Abraham Lower,		146
" " William Poole,		149
" " Samuel Comfort,		155
" " William Poole,		157
" " " "		159
" " " "		161
" " Samuel R. Fisher,		162
" " William Poole,		164
" " Thomas McClintock,		165
" " Moses Brown,		171
" " Samuel Comfort,		176
" " William Poole,		177
" " Abraham Lower,		179
" " William Poole,		181
" " Samuel Comfort,		185
" " William Poole,		187
" " " "		190
" " " "		192
" " Thomas McClintock,		194
" " William Poole,		196
" " Samuel Comfort,		198
" " Isaac T. Hopper,		201
" " Moses Pennock,		202
" " William Poole,		207
" " William Wharton,		208
" " William Poole,		210
" " John C. Sanders,		210
" " Charles Stokes,		215
" " William Poole,		219
" " Benjamin Ferris,		221
" " Elias Wilbur,		222
" " Thomas Leggett, Jr.,		226
" " Hugh Judge,		231

APPENDIX.

Letter to The Quarterly Meeting of Men and Women Friends, held at Westbury,		235
" " M———— M————,		236
" " Samuel Evans,		237

www.ingramcontent.com/pod-product-compliance
Lightning Source LLC
Chambersburg PA
CBHW031751230426
43669CB00007B/577